The Wisdom Factor

Reducing the Control of Bias, Threat, and Fear while Building a Better World

The Wisdom Factor

Reducing the Control of Bias, Threat, and Fear while Building a Better World

Alice Darnell Lattal & Carlos A. Zuluaga

KeyPress Publishing
www.keypresspublishing.com

KeyPress
Publishing

Authors: Alice Darnell Lattal & Carlos A. Zuluaga

The Wisdom Factor – *Reducing the Control of Bias, Threat, and Fear while Building a Better World*

Published by: KeyPress Publishing
Cover design: Jana Burtner
Text design: Jana Burtner
Illustration: Carlos A. Zuluaga
Production Coordinator: Shauna Costello

ISBN-10: 978-0-578-22212-7

Distributed by:
ABA Technologies, Inc.
930 South Harbor City Blvd, Suite 402
Melbourne, FL 32901
(321) 222-6822
www.abatechnologies.com

KeyPress Publishing books are available at a special discount for bulk purchases by corporations, institutions, and other organizations. For more information, please call (321) 222-6822 or email keypress@abatechnologies.com.

"If there is anything the world needs, it is wisdom. Without it, I exaggerate not at all in saying that very soon, there may be no world ..."

–Robert J. Sternberg

Dedication

Alice Darnell Lattal:

Written for my grandchildren—Nicholas, Ella, Alex, Ava, Brendan, Calista, Julia Grace—and the wiser world they and their peers will build. To my children—Matthew, Rachel, Ashley, and their spouses—Jen Maas, Charlie Camp, and Ian St. John—for providing their children the tools of compassion and knowledge. My thanks to Don Hake, Ph.D., for his visionary efforts in the experimental analysis of behavior, exploring the conditions that promote trust, cooperation, and sharing, and who left this world at too young an age. To my brother, Mike Hammer, for always appreciating the richness in diversity and responding with enthusiasm to various ways of living life. And to my lifelong partner, Andy, for his loving support and boundless curiosity. Thanks for this lifetime of discovery.

. . . .

Carlos A. Zuluaga:

I would like to dedicate this book to some of the people that have guided me in this journey called *life*. They have given me examples of wisdom and leadership and inspired me to be a better person each day. To Dr. José A. Martinez-Diaz, Thomas R. Freeman, Antonio Zuluaga, and Frances M. Torres.

> *"Cada persona que pasa por nuestra vida es única. Siempre deja un poco de sí y se lleva un poco de nosotros. Habrá los que se llevarán mucho, pero no habrá de los que no nos dejarán nada. Esta es la prueba evidente de que dos almas no se encuentran por casualidad."*
>
> –Jorge Luis Borges

> *"Every person who comes into our lives is unique. They will always leave a bit of themselves and take a bit of themselves. There will be the ones who will take too much, but there will be none that will not leave something. This is the evident proof that two souls don't find each other by coincidence."*
>
> –Jorge Luis Borges

Acknowledgments

When we began to work together, we had a simple idea about how to write this book, thinking that we had something to say about acting wisely. It has taken approximately 24 months to get from that start to this point. We have had to step back many times to check our understanding. Ours was a *collaboration* in the best sense of that word, each learning new things from one another about behavior and how it relates to the concept of wisdom. It was our mutual pleasure to work and learn together. We discovered that we saw the world and the people in it in much the same way. We did learn that critical elements must be considered when striving to be wise; that becoming wiser is a noble goal, a process of ongoing learning, and a lifelong journey.

Several people helped us in the writing of this book. They include Andy Lattal and Frances M. Torres, who read the book in draft form and made many good suggestions along the way that helped us redirect our efforts and start again. Marcia Cornell edited the first few chapters to help us get started. Gail Snyder edited the first and final draft. A special *thank you* to David B. Baker, Alyce M. Dickinson, Chata Dickson, Patrick C. Friman, Paulie Gavoni, Sigrid Glenn, Steven C. Hayes, William L. Heward, Philip N. Hineline, Jack Marr, Francis Mechner, Terry McSween, Sigurdur Oli Sigurdsson, Shane T. Spiker, Janet S. Twyman, and April Michele Williams. The process and design experts at KeyPress Publications added greatly to the book's professional look and feel, keeping the book on track. Thank you to Jana Burtner for producing a beautiful cover that in itself tells a story about the importance of wisdom in this world. These individuals gave us clear advice about what worked well and what did not, sometimes specifically in sections where we used their work. At times these individuals wrote or talked to us directly to ensure they understood what we were trying to say and that we heard their advice. We listened hard, invited more critique, and in the end are deeply indebted to each of them and others who advised us generally. We thank them all. Whatever mistakes remain, they are ours alone.

Endorsements for
The Wisdom Factor

"It's not enough merely to aspire to be wise; you must create the environments and strengthen the skills that are key to that life task. This book brings a step-by-step, practical approach to acquiring wisdom. Grounded firmly in behavioral science, it never talks down to you, or substitutes aspirations for actions. Instead, it creates a bond of trust between author and reader, and then it delivers. Every page rings true to me. I can highly recommend it."

–**Steven C. Hayes, Ph.D.**
Foundation Professor of Psychology, University of Nevada, Reno
Originator of *Acceptance and Commitment Therapy* and author of
A Liberated Mind

·················

"*The Wisdom Factor* is a wise telling of over a century of psychological science and practice that has grappled with the question of what makes us human. More specifically, it offers an accessible and practical roadmap to make us better humans. In this book, the reader will find valuable tools to chart a course to a greater understanding of ourselves, our environment, and each other."

–**David B. Baker, Ph.D.**
Senior Program Director, Cummings Foundation for Behavioral Health
President, Baker Performance Facilitation
Professor Emeritus of Psychology, The University of Akron

·················

"In essence, Lattal and Zuluaga pose the question: How can I, one person, make a difference for the better in this world? They explore this question through the lens of behavioral science and build their case by addressing some of the biggest societal challenges facing the Western World today. You will come away from reading this book understanding what it means to be a positive change agent and how to act accordingly in tune with your personal values. It will also help you understand why others behave the way they do. That is perhaps equally as important: if we want to build a society in tune with our values, we need to look beyond the walls of our echo chambers. Want a science-based step-by-step approach to make a difference for the better in the world? Ready to look beyond the walls of your echo chamber? Then buy this book."

–Sigurdur Oli Sigurdsson, Ph.D.
Manager of the Quality Board for Higher Education in Iceland

....

"Pragmatic, optimistic, and rich with resources, *The Wisdom Factor* brings together the science of learning and behavior with universal, timeless truths about what it means to be human. Darnell Lattal and Carlos A. Zuluaga do not preach to readers about how we should act; rather, they open the possibility for us each to do what is important to us. They lay out a framework for operating with humility, integrity, and courage. In reading this book we learn that wisdom is not about expertise or information, but it is something that occurs in behavior–wise acting. Wisdom is not some essential or innate feature of an individual. It is a way of being and behaving. This is a beautifully optimistic perspective, because in this view we all have access to wisdom in any moment, regardless of our life circumstances. Developing a robust and reliable repertoire of wise behavior is the work of a lifetime.

The Wisdom Factor is for everyone. Accessible. Universal. Timeless. Instead of a recipe, the reader receives the ingredients that make the work of transformation possible—for our own lives, our families, our workplaces, and indeed, for our world. As soon I finished the book, I picked it up and began again. It will continue to be relevant in new ways as I continue to navigate my way through the challenges and opportunities of life. I'm excited to share this work with my family, friends, and students, and I encourage you to read it as soon as you can!"

–Chata Dickson, Ph.D.
Assistant Director of Research, Autism Curriculum Encyclopedia at the New England Center for Children

"Much has been written about wisdom down through the ages. We've been informed about what it is, what it isn't, who has it, and who doesn't. But very little has been written about how to attain it other than taking many trips around the sun or apprenticing at the feet of a master. This lovely book fills in the gap by explaining how it can be attained simply by turning the knobs and the dials of our own behavior. Furthermore, the many recommendations available herein spring not from the creative imaginations of the authors but from their scrutinous reading and careful distillation of countless studies from behavioral science. Purchasing the book will involve money wisely spent."

–Patrick C. Friman, Ph.D., ABPP
Vice President of Boys Town's Outpatient Behavioral Health Services

·················

"*The Wisdom Factor* is both engaging and useful. Lattal and Zuluaga weave together a tapestry of science and wisdom that points the way to effective interpersonal relationships."

–Sigrid Glenn, Ph.D.
Retired Professor and former Dean of the School of Behavior Analysis, University of North Texas

·················

"This is a sophisticated, scholarly, and indeed wise book about gaining wisdom—individual and collective—through the application of behavior science. As such, it is far, far more than a 'self-help' book. Its scope and depth as well as its science-based approach make the book uniquely valuable."

–M. Jackson Marr, Ph.D.
Professor Emeritus, Department of Psychology, Georgia Institute of Technology, Atlanta, GA

·················

"We all want to act wisely and with kindness, but too often the person who 'shows up' in our actions harms others. Lattal and Zuluaga describe a life-long journey by which each of us can contribute to a better, more just world. A continual process of self-knowledge and learning, the journey involves analyzing the environmental conditions maintaining our current behavior, making our values concrete, changing our environment to support behaviors consistent with our values, observing and measuring if what we do matches our good intentions, and celebrating our accomplishments and progress. If B. F. Skinner and Ben Franklin collaborated on a plan for self-improvement, it might read a lot like *The Wisdom Factor*."

–**William L. Heward, Ed.D., BCBA-D**
Author of *Exceptional Children*, Co-Author of *Applied Behavior Analysis*

·················

"*The Wisdom Factor* is a powerful book. Given the world in which we live, with heightened sensitivity to diversity and inclusion, political divide, a pandemic, and climate control disrupting our environment, each of us can benefit from increasing our wise actions. *The Wisdom Factor* not only gives us the tools with which to do that, but also clearly lays out the scientific foundation on which those tools are based–the foundation that enables us to understand and alter our own behaviors. The book goes beyond self-improvement, however; it also provides ways to help others, most notably our children, become catalysts for a wiser culture and brighter future."

–**Alyce M. Dickinson, Ph.D.**
Retired Professor of Psychology, Western Michigan University

·················

"I loved this book. At a time when our schools are routinely criticized for an exclusive focus on facts and information, Lattal and Zuluaga help fill the void with *The Wisdom Factor*. The book takes the reader on a journey to consider the kind of person they want to be and, in contrast, how they show up in the world in comparison to that ideal. They ask the reader to consider how they behave, and how other people are likely to interpret that behavior, and, importantly, whether that is the person that the reader wants to be. Beyond just reflecting on these topics, the author provides tools from the field of applied behavior analysis and a series of practices for improving behavior and moving toward the reader's ideal person. At a time when so few people reflect on their biases, and too many accept their negative attributes, this book fills an important need. While everyone should read it, I hope this book finds its way into college curricula across the country, as our young people need it.

That said, this book is not just for our young. I had the opportunity to read it as I was entering my retirement. What an awesome time to reflect on the person you want to be. I find this book to be timely in so many ways, and on so many levels. Indeed, I hope everyone will read it and work to apply its wisdom. If you do, it will be a better world."

–Terry McSween, Ph.D.
CEO, Quality Safety Edge, Inc.

·················

"The authors offer a wide-ranging, guided tour through quotations and comments by a large and diverse roster of prominent figures, as well as by dozens of prominent behavioral scientists and psychologists to address such behavior-related concepts as motivation, learning, beliefs, heuristics, compassion, words and language, knowledge, reciprocity, emotions, self-control, experience, collaboration, competency, thinking skills, problem-solving, flexibility, objectivity, values, goals, and of course, wisdom. The authors' behaviorally informed values and ethics glisten throughout their science-based behaviorally informed guidance."

–Francis Mechner, Ph.D.
President, The Mechner Foundation

·················

"The 1st two decades of the 21st century have been marked by multiple acts of terrorism, climate disasters due to a rapidly warming climate, a multi-year global pandemic, and repeated incidents of violence against members of racial/ethnic minority groups. The root causes of all of these difficulties can be boiled down to human behavior. One could be excused for giving in to despair and hopelessness caused by events that seem well beyond our control and too powerful to overcome. Luckily, the authors of The Wisdom Factor present an alternative and, with it, a reason for optimism, which is the wisdom to be gained from understanding ourselves can make the world a better place for all of us.

This could easily be a book of all style and no substance, full of advice, platitudes, and examples of remarkable people to emulate without explanations of how to do so. The key difference between what it could be and what it lies in the strength of the examples and recommended exercises, which coach the reader in the expansion of their understanding of their own (and, ultimately, others') behavior. An incredible amount of information is provided, all of it supported by research and taken from a variety of settings, without being too scholarly or intimidating.

The authors don't shy away from the complexity of behavior but explain those complexities. In doing so, the reader's beliefs are frequently challenged or, more accurately, the reader is frequently invited to challenge their own beliefs. This is the definition of empowerment, and all it requires is a willingness to consider taking a different perspective. This change in perspective is made easier through the explanations in this book and is likely to be life-changing for those who work to adopt it because it shines a light on those parts of our internal experiences we don't understand and reframes them in a way to help us be more flexible in who (or, more importantly, how) we are. Changing perspectives on behavior also releases us from the grip of our past and frees us to move forward with more intention. Following the exercises in this book will give readers the experience needed to carry on in this way for the rest of their lives.

It is a credit to the authors that they present rather advanced conceptual information in such an easy-to-comprehend and useable way. In fact, their advice is so deceptively simple, that the reader may be forgiven for discounting it. Lattal and Zuluaga take abstract principles of behavior and break them down using countless examples. They follow with practices that lead the reader through the work of understanding themselves.

We have not needed a book like this more than we do now. When much of what we see around us seems to be unfolding in a less-than-desirable direction, what else can we do but take ahold of what we can, our own behavior. In fact, we can build the world we want to live in. The work is difficult, but the payoffs are huge, for ourselves and for our fellow humans."

–**April Michele Williams, Ph.D., BCBA-D**
Associate Professor, Rollins College, Winter Park, FL

· · · · · · · · · · · · · · · · ·

"I think we need many efforts to wake and shake people into thinking about and understanding that behavior matters, and that contingencies matter most of all. I love the authors' message that wisdom comes from knowing and understanding the effects of behavior influenced by contingencies. It needs to be in the hands and heads of people whom it can help (everyone!)."

–**Janet S. Twyman, Ph.D., BCBA, LBA-NY**
Chief Learning Scientist, BLAST

· · · · · · · · · · · · · · · · ·

"Perhaps I'm an optimist, but I believe that, in general, most be people share a common wish to do well by themselves and others. With the best intentions, they pursue short and long terms goals while taking care to avoid harm to themselves and others. But even those possessing great enthusiasm and meticulously laid out plans fall short as their intention fails to produce the outcomes they value the most. This is because there is incongruence between what they value and how they behave. Often it is because they fail to recognize the misalignment between ways of living that are truly important to them, the behavior they are engaging in, and the impact of this behavior on who and what they value.

In *The Wisdom Factor*, the authors shine a compassionate behavioral light on this misalignment through the often used, but nebulous concept of wisdom. Like a ball held and slowly turned to examine all sides, the concept of wisdom is looked at from multiple angles through the pragmatic lens of the science of human behavior. Now, behavior science doesn't give people the answer; however, it does provide them with a clear and practical methodology for determining effective solutions. This book maintains this approach in that it doesn't tell you what to do to be wise. Rather, it provides you with compelling real-life examples supported by concrete, actionable steps for determining both what wisdom is for you, and what behaviors are aligned with the outcomes you have determined to be 'wise.'

As the authors remind us in so many words, becoming a wiser person takes effort, but it may not be as difficult as one might think with the right environmental arrangements. If you are trying to be a better version of yourself tomorrow than you were today, you must have a good understanding of where you currently are. To do this, you must 'know thyself.' Wisdom helps you to do just that. It is the crystal-clear mirror we all need to better reflect on ourselves and take the actions required to live a valued life. I give this book two gloves way up!"

    –Dr. Paulie "Gloves" Gavoni
      Wall Street Journal and USA TODAY best-selling author

··················

"In a time where compassion and science are sorely lacking, *The Wisdom Factor* is a welcomed breath of fresh air. The authors have the uncanny ability to directly pinpoint how we currently respond and where we should be going. This book could easily share a shelf with other behavioral scientists who are striving for a shared vision of a better world."

    –Shane Spiker, Ph.D., BCBA
      Director of Training and Dissemination at Positive Behavior
      Supports, Corp.

Table of Contents

Practices by Chapter

Preface

No matter the times or the circumstances that surround us, the principles in this book speak to the human condition throughout history. The principles are timeless, but as Bob Dylan sang, "The times they are a-changing," as they always will be. We hope this book has something to say about the present, and we believe it speaks, as well, to creating a better world in the future.

While finalizing this book in the winter of 2022, major events that emerged into public consciousness in 2020 were still taking place around the world. A global pandemic is continuing to effect all people on Earth in some manner, and a massive social movement initiated a continued focus on institutionalized racism and the mistreatment of our fellow humans within and across nations. War among nations that could absorb the whole world is a possibility. At this moment, we have no idea where this tidal wave ends. Will it end with a whimper, as has been the case with some social and political movements in the past? Or will it result in a declaration of a new world order, bringing long-lasting change to our social fabric?

In 1953, B. F. Skinner wrote: "Man's power appears to have increased out of all proportion to his wisdom. He has never been in a better position to build a healthy, happy, and productive world; yet things have perhaps never seemed so black." As history demonstrates, humankind has had many dark periods, often described as "just human nature." We invite you to use the principles described in this book to reconsider what that phrase, "just human nature," means. We hope every reader comes to understand that in the face of a seemingly overwhelming number of conditions beyond our control, the solution to our largest social problems lies in how we act, each of us. Practices are embedded to help you. We humans do, metaphorically speaking, hold the whole world in our hands. We may have learned that what will be will be, that time and tide wait for no man, or that opportunity has passed us by. Yet, the choices we make every day, and their immediate and longer-term effects, lead us toward or away from solutions that make this world a better place. The task at hand is to learn how to strengthen our skills by acting in ways that lead to better outcomes.

Those outcomes reside in taking better care of one another, not only to coexist but to thrive and prosper.

Consider these 6 action steps when reading this book:

1. Read the titles of each chapter and consider what you think the chapter is about. As you proceed, see if what you expect is what you find and where something new is added. Themes are repeated. You may want to make a list of common themes across chapters.

2. Complete the practice activities as you read each chapter. Think about how you could expand these activities to other areas of your life.

3. Apply the principles described in the book during your day-to-day interactions with others. Identify actions to continue to demonstrate these principles.

4. Reflect on the actions you identify. Assess missed opportunities to practice new insights in new ways.

5. Continue to build behavior-based examples in daily activity that are controlled too much by bias, threat and fear.

6. By the end of the book, consider whether you find yourself better equipped to say and do things that have the potential to increase wiser outcomes.

How We Show Up

Chapter 1:

Behavior and the River of Reciprocity

"No man ever steps in the same river twice, for it's not the same river and he's not the same man."

–Heraclitus

Beginning and Ending with You

The Wisdom Factor is about how each of us shows up in our personal conduct. Do we feel at ease in addressing the conflicts and conditions around us? What helps us become the kind of person we want to be? Becoming who we want to be is a lifelong challenge for many of us.

How are things going for you and for others around you? What is it that you see in the surrounding culture that is good? What needs to change to increase wiser outcomes, to help people have a good chance to accomplish their hopes and dreams? As you read this book, ask yourself, "What do I need to do to behave in ways that increase the likelihood of wiser outcomes—with my family, my friends, my workplace, or the community at large?"

The principles in this book are of no practical value if they do not cause the reader to think about issues that need a little more wisdom. We hope this book gives you two elements that are essential to creating a wiser world. The first: conditions that surround you determine, to a large extent, your words and actions—behavior. That principle of learning needs to be considered and, at times, arranged carefully to produce a wiser world. The second is about how you show up, a question for reflection: "Do your actions today have the immediate and longer-term effects that you want them to have?" The intersection between the conditions that surround you and your actions is where change occurs. We hope this book provides a few practical ideas to increase your very specific effects.

The second component—actions and the effects of actions—is where this book starts: with you. This is a journey of self-knowledge, of inviting others to help you see how well your actions match your words; to learn how to change to have the effect you want; and to learn to see the effects of consequences on our ideals and our immediate actions. Behaving wisely is not a distant or remote goal, nor is it a constant state. While daily actions do not always produce positive effects, your behavior at a given moment is of singular importance. It is these actions in context and at specific times when core values show up, in small or large ways.

Behaving wisely depends on everyday actions that demonstrate your beliefs and how you stand for those beliefs. To do so, the conditions around you, your learning history, how you experience new challenges, all sum to key elements involved in learning to act with greater wisdom. Learning to act with greater wisdom involves not only your words and actions, but how those behaviors affect situations you face immediately and in the future. On any given day, your words and actions may not be wise at all. Wise acting is judged by its effects, not always the effects that you hope for or desire. Being called a wise person can relate to a single act or a series of deeds over time. However, wisdom is not something you have, like the color of your eyes. The label *wisdom* is assigned to observable behavior that advances the values of your unique culture.

A central point to the message in our book is that wise acting is contextual and transitory. Acting wisely involves the effective use of complex behavioral repertoires. Decision-making, problem-solving, self-management, and interpersonal skills help an individual weigh the benefits of one action over another. Actions that are wise to some may not be wise to others. Evaluating wise acting can occur as it is happening or in the future. Assessing the effects of actions involves a variety of value-based statements: wise or foolish, of benefit to a few or to many, a barrier to harmful action immediately or over time.

The *wisdom factor* is defined by how behavior is applied to conditions in the immediate situation and how those actions address the human condition, in immediate outcomes and over time. Values-based actions that affect the good of us all sum to such actions as

1. protecting the rights of one individual in need over the many;
2. protecting the expression of unpopular views;
3. working to resolve issues arising from coercive or abusive relationships;
4. addressing the misuse of power at work or across society; and
5. demonstrating a visible commitment to such values as fairness, trust, self-protection, and care.

Understanding how our behavior is influenced by current conditions and our learning history helps keep personal biases in check. Understanding how easily we may use threat and fear helps us develop greater self-awareness as to our skills or lack thereof in wise acting. We gain little by calling ourselves *wise*. Judging whether our actions are wise can best be done by others when assessing the impact our behavior has on individuals and the larger community. Wisdom is judged by actions that solve problems in ways that benefit us and/or others. Whether the action of the moment turns out to be wise for the individuals involved over time is another issue. Later we return to the question of how to measure such impact.

This book is written to

- develop greater awareness of our own behavior and how it represents what we value.
- share what the science of behavior tells us about choices made and where biases and myths about human behavior blind us to the good we can do;
- illustrate best practices in teaching wise acting to our children and ourselves, a most important topic to influence a wiser world; and
- provide tools that increase individual skills of reflecting on personal beliefs, and words and/or deeds that are disruptive when striving to behave wisely.

Throughout the book, practices are designed for you to explore the conditions that encourage you to act as you do. Sometimes, they are simply reflective; your thoughts and feelings in reviewing how you acted. At other times, the practices benefit you more if you share or do them with others. The concepts presented may help you discuss the supports or impediments to acting with as much wisdom as you might wish in given situations. In part, these practices allow you to better understand the motivations of others' words and actions.

We rarely talk about the effects that our behavior has on others. Rarer yet, do we consider those amorphous and distant outcomes affecting some greater good or bad in our society. It is in those conditions that surround us that our behavior receives the motivational power it needs to move forward. You may say you want to complete tasks on time, run a 5K, learn to draw, or play the piano. You may want to tackle social and cultural issues in your local community. You may want to convey a calmer tone or a more predictable presence around those you love. Being aware of your effects on others and even yourself requires personal insight regarding your words and actions.

PRACTICE 1.1:

What Changes Do I Need to Make to Demonstrate Greater Wisdom?

1. What do you believe would help you demonstrate greater wisdom? Consider your circumstances, skills, emotional behavior, and effects on others.

2. Ask one or two close friends for feedback and/or suggestions. You need not incorporate their advice, but hearing it will give you a start toward seeing yourself and your effect as at least one or two other people might see you.

Perhaps you do not understand the degree of your influence. Your small actions every day are as worthy as actions dedicated to creating, at a grand scale, a wiser, kinder world. The cumulative effects of our individual actions influence how quickly we achieve desired, or, at times, unanticipated outcomes. Our actions, small or large, matter! An ample body of research shows that the conditions around us can be arranged to promote a wider range of choices and influence better decisions. Among many effects, the conditions that surround us have a clear impact on enhancing cooperation, increasing creativity, and in developing patterns of interaction that are judged to be wise (e.g., Hake & Schmid, 1981, 1980; Fantino, 1985; Epstein, 1999; Skinner, 1966; Robbins, 2011; Baltes & Staudinger, 2000).

"It is in those conditions that surround us that our behavior receives the motivational power it needs to move forward."

Today, a very large task awaits us in trying to behave with even a bit more wisdom. A simple reason is that we do what we do because doing so gives us pleasure, keeps us out of trouble, avoids an unpleasant event, gives us a leg up, leads to personal success, avoids threat or fear, or produces affection for reasons we do not always understand. Those kinds of consequence histories can make it harder to change ingrained patterns of behavior, even when they do not match desired effects.

As you read this book, we hope you will come across ideas that help you develop methods to produce a stronger match between your words and actions. Such a match is, in many ways, the definition of *trust*.

Part I: How We Show Up. This section presents areas in which we, as individuals, display different degrees of positive effects through various elements of daily life—our words, how we demonstrate emotions, and how well our actions reflect our positive intentions. It also offers suggestions for how to manage various aspects of our behavior.

"We each face the challenge of matching our words with our actions. Such a match is, in many ways, the definition of trust.*"*

Part II: The Path to Wiser Acting. This section addresses questions about how we learn—the meaning of *knowledge* and how to access it, the importance of science, and an understanding of problem-solving and managing events for the long term. You will learn about the design of 21st-century classrooms that strive to teach children to make wiser choices by providing methods to affect more compassionate and positive outcomes for all of us. Many rules of conduct govern the current educational community, limiting children's potential for rapid advancement. Can some effects, measured often long after individual actions occurred, be traced back to something we might have said and/or done? Can acting in ways we hope are wise, or we know to be harmful, really impact the future we envision? Is there something about the capacity to learn that is capped in some way or can we continue to change and make improvements throughout our lifetime?

Part III: A Vision of a Better World. The final section starts with the idea that context is everything. The structures that surround us, our policies and practices, permissions to act, restrictions about access, or conditions that accelerate learning, create the path to who we can become. Context is how our culture defines in practice who is worthy and who is not. What values do we hold dear and how do those advance or impede others? What do cultures represent as the values that guide the actions of their members? What do you do? To what extent can values become more than platitudes stated with earnestness or added in later to justify how we behave? Are we guided in our daily actions by self-interest, myopically viewed through our own unique lens? This section summarizes elements that scholars through the ages have said are essential to creating a wiser culture. Can we really see our neighbors, if not the world, in a more holistic manner? Taking the lessons we have learned, can we find sufficient reinforcement to act with more deliberation toward designing a wiser world?

Arranging events that contribute to greater wisdom in our community, or our society, is a tall order. Often, the type of behavior that matters most in changing this world is not found in rare deeds and brilliant words, but in everyday actions—awkward, spontaneous, quiet, or unexpected. Again, such change starts with you.

Wanting to do the right thing is a good place to start, but intention isn't enough. The kinds of acts that persist and affect individuals we interact with, helping their journey through life, are the essence of wise acting. Desiring to do things that might stand the test of time versus the things we are often most likely to do, are areas to address. Our past behavior in given situations dictates, to a large extent, our behavior in similar situations. Grand words describing

PRACTICE 1.2:

Values-Laden Conditions that Surround and Influence Me

Keep a list of situations and outcomes that compete with or support core values important to you. You may find many things that seem to demonstrate wise acting, as simple as a person dropping down to eye level to listen and talk with a small child. Someone might comment about a situation involving you, and you think, "That was wise." Listen. Write down words and actions that strike you as wise or not in the moment.

Consider how you show up along the way. This list may include

1. your words and actions in various situations—allowing you to show up in ways you like or regret;

2. your effects on others and their words and actions that you like or do not; conditions that help and hinder getting to outcomes of value;

3. cultural, legal, or political solutions/outcomes that, to you, demonstrate a decided lack of wisdom, affecting your family, your community, or the wider society.

good intent are fine, but they all too often do not influence actions. This disconnect between who we believe ourselves to be when talking about the values we hold dear and our actions can be a great disappointment. Addressing the gap requires us to learn about our behavior and the motivational factors that lead to sustainable change.

You may be interested in discovering the gap between who you perceive yourself to be and how others see you. Finding answers as you learn to see the motivating factors that surround you will help. We will spend some time helping you assess what you respond to in doing what you do, even at times when you want to do something else—a most essential element for any of us is trust. Trust is earned. What has someone done or what have you done to lead to distrust? If you want to begin to act differently, you can begin by assessing your trust meter, ensuring that your words match your actions—sometimes called say/do correspondence. Are there moments, despite best intentions, when you know that you may or may not carry through? We begin with a simple question:

Would you say you are trusted by others? Consider as carefully as you can how others might answer the same question about you. This is a subject we will return to throughout this book. Small changes start mighty rivers of influence.

PRACTICE 1.3:

Trust Meter: Acting as I Promised

1. Would you say you are trusted by others?

2. To what extent do you do what you say you will do?

3. If the answer is "almost always," consider the times you do not do what you say. Why is that?

4. To what extent do you trust others to do what they say?

5. Are there particular people or circumstances when people around you fail to do as they say they will do? Why do you think that is?

Keep a list of situations and outcomes that compete with or support core values important to you in demonstrating critical behaviors. Listen to others. Watch what is happening. Consider the aftermath. What were the effects? Are the effects those you desired? Start jotting down the words and actions that strike you as wise or not in the moment.

Reciprocity

The concept of reciprocity binds us to one another—your behavior affects my behavior; in turn, my behavior affects you. Such actions are not casual, in terms of their potential to help or hinder others. An effect may be very small, almost invisible, or very large. Effects can be potentiated in transmission, strengthening how much particular behavior influences others, even people far removed from the original individuals involved. Everything, from the well-known butterfly effect—the phenomenon whereby a minute, localized change in a complex system can have large effects elsewhere—to the use of slang, which starts in a specific part of a small group to become part of a country's national identity—for example, "woke," "rugrats," "cool," "lit"—are strengthened by how such ideas are passed on. Such new words and behavior patterns materialize at high rates, emerging in unexpected places.

From a pandemic or race relations to new ways of talking and acting, our country's demonstrated commitments change, often in response to competing streams of influence. Those new expectations—ways of acting—may continue to make clear the values you care about, or they may obscure those same values. Many people are satisfied with outcomes in our evolving social fabric that others see as abhorrent. Sorting through your responses to such conditions is a part of every person's dilemma in learning to act with wisdom.

When new behavior occurs, the conditions that prompted it are not always clear. To be sustained, new behavior needs motivational consistency. Full-throttle behavior change requires systems, processes, and structures to keep the desired behavior going in the right direction. The predictable lesson about establishing new behavior patterns in civil rights, women's rights, or any other large-scale social change is that behavior drifts. Desired patterns are difficult to sustain if the conditions surrounding new behavior are left to chance. Remember, we behave as we have learned to behave. Often, our views are more representative of firmly held biases learned long before, about how people ought to behave—inflexible rules supported by the values of our subcultures. Pre-existing barriers, constraints about responding to women or minorities can override our stated intentions. Our committed statements turn to actions far removed from such statements in shockingly quick ways. If the practices, structures, and laws endorsed by the larger society do not change, the conditions immediately surrounding us support old habits. New patterns in search of that ideal future state fade fast, replaced by customary practices.

Those who operate inside a smaller group that worked so hard to embed the changes for civil rights, for example, may become more insistent on making changes. Do something now! To sustain how we aspire to act as a nation, institutional and cultural rules of conduct need to surround and reinforce new values-based actions as fast as possible. Barriers to change, long-held customs are deeply seated. Unseating them requires very deliberate effort. Learning to anticipate and address such impediments to change is part of learning to act with greater wisdom.

Like a river, behavior is always flowing and constantly changing. Some currents lead to calm waters, the way we like it. Some currents in our life lead to white water, turbulence, and wild rides. We may like that as well. Some currents lead to drift. Life events have big and, at times, chaotic effects that dramatically change our path. At times, interactions in life may lead us to believe external forces beyond our control are directing our lives.

"Like a river, behavior is always flowing and constantly changing. Some currents in our life lead to white water, turbulence, and wild rides...
Life events have big and, at times, chaotic effects that dramatically change our path."

Unexpected events like a divorce, the death of a loved one, or the loss of a cherished job can be very difficult. Yet, many people make a significant difference in the world despite having faced great personal challenges. For some, overcoming obstacles is fuel to move ahead. They might see those changes as opportunities to adapt. New policies and practices of law or society do not necessarily dictate their actions. Such individuals show flexibility under difficult situations and engage in behaviors guided by important values. They show these qualities because their experiences have shaped and sustained certain patterns of behavior over time. Some people have "a positive outlook on the future," "overcoming adversity," and full of the "right stuff." Character counts in the sum up of our words and actions, but character does not drive behavior. Behavior defines our character.

An old saying is, "Watch your thoughts; they become your words. Watch your words; they become your actions. Watch your actions; they become your habits. Watch your habits; they become your character. Watch your character; it becomes your destiny." This is a nifty little saying. The saying assigns the start of reaching our destiny to our thoughts that in turn shape our actions, all the way to character. Our immediate actions may shape our thoughts. All in all, this describes a circle of influence, but we need not wait on thoughts to begin moving toward desired outcomes. Our actions shape our thoughts. The conditions that surround us, our histories of learning, our rules and biases, and the experiences we have produce the motivation that shapes our behavior. Actions influence how we turn thoughts into more actions. Moving toward your destiny, the spot you want to reach, requires learning new behavior that takes you to your destiny. The expression might reflect more accurately who we become, if it read, simply, "Watch the conditions that reinforce your actions. They shape your destiny."

In our society, we often talk about people we value as possessing special personal attributes, like *strong character*. Describing others this way leads to the faulty belief that they have the *right stuff, grit, determination* to always act like those we admire. Then, all we have to do is tell such people to "do it," to persist, and show us their capabilities. Approaching people as if a title of strong character is all they need to succeed, reduces our responsibility as a friend, boss, parent, or colleague to arrange conditions to help individuals reach their potential.

Asking a man to fish may not help if there are no fish to catch—or water that can provide a living environment for fish. Asking or expecting a person to overcome poverty may be too large a gap if there are no jobs, education, or transportation. Asking an abused person to forgive and forget is a very big ask. However, having difficulty persisting or forgiving or overcoming poverty has nothing to do with the strength of one's character. Asking a person to speak up may seem like a small ask, but if the person lacks the skills to do so, that can be a very large request. Based on your personal histories and current circumstances, the changes you make may appear easy or very difficult.

The conditions surrounding and shaping actions are where the opportunity to develop "character" resides. We live in an interconnected, reciprocal world. Being influenced by an array of individuals adds richness to the options we face. The methods available to interact with our environment are changing at a rapid pace. It can be difficult for many to adapt to new technologies and ways of acting. Alvin Toffler, the famous futurist, described the changes coming in the 21st century as "Future Shock." And so, today, tossed about on our river raft, uncertain of our journey, bumping into one another by navigational cross-currents, the destination may become a bit murky. Deciding how to navigate can appear an overwhelming challenge. A good first step is to look at ourselves and what we hope to do, measured by current circumstances.

Chapter 2:

Trust Me... No, Really, Trust Me: Matching Intentions to Actions

"If you want to change the world, start with yourself."

–MAHATMA GANDHI

Wise acting is concerned with practical decisions, in context, to maximize beneficial short- and long-term effects on ourselves, others, and our culture. In other words, wise acting is not a philosophical exercise that will transform us. Instead, wise acting is complex, contextual, nuanced, practical, and flexible. *Wise behavior* is defined and determined by its effects. It is helpful to understand the influences on our behavior and how to arrange conditions that promote wiser outcomes. Over time, we can become better at measuring our actual impact on wise acting.

Language allows us to describe an intended future and to envision outcomes we want to see. We can describe goals we would like to accomplish, actions that will get us there, and barriers we might face. In some cases, we might envision skills we would like to master, or events we would like to experience. At times, we might envision how we would like to be perceived, as reflected by our words and actions. And yet, dreaming is not enough. As Thomas Edison wrote, "Vision without execution is hallucination." Committed action is needed to bring that desired future into reality. Understand the influences that tend to strengthen and sustain your efforts, the conditions that stop or redirect your efforts, and the strategies that work and do not work. Consider how the following elements might influence your decision-making and your actions:

- *Response effort*: How much time and effort are needed to achieve a goal? Those things that are within reach are often chosen over things that demand greater time, thought, and care—low-hanging fruit, so to speak.

- *Supply/demand*: Are there multiple, alternative ways to reach a particular goal? If so, those alternatives can promote solutions that circumvent the necessity of desired behavior change. That can make it easier but not necessarily wiser to respond in such ways.

- *Delay*: How long would it take to reach a goal? Immediate consequences have a greater impact than delayed ones, particularly in the beginning, when learning new tasks and skills.

- *Sunk cost*: How much time and effort has been dedicated already toward a goal? The higher the investment, the harder it is to switch direction. Such fallacies of thinking can cost us time when a new approach would, in the end, get us where we want to be.

- *Knowledge overload*: Too much information or too many choices can lead to indecision.

- *Self-reliance*: This includes not asking for help or ideas, having inflexible rules, or not letting others guide us through the maze in front of us. Inflexible rules are problematic. So, developing flexibility to learn when to apply rules is helpful.

Many of these variables influence our choices, which are described in detail by decision theorists and behavioral economists. However, the constant element of influence in our environment is consequences. It is how we are intimately connected with the world around us. Therefore, consequences either increase behavior, sometimes at rapid rates, or keep behavior in place. They can even decrease or eliminate the likelihood of behavior.

The conditions that surround us are a major force in how we show up. We may have experienced the conditions long ago, and yet, they continue to influence us. They are sustained across time by rules about our behavior, perhaps learned at a parent's knee. Consequences have a hold on us in our immediate world, but over time as well, and in varied conditions. Look at the effects of consequences with a cool eye about the impact they have. They provide the secret ingredients of your behavior. Arrange conditions to change their effects to increase the likelihood of acting as you need or wish to act. This is easy to say. And yet, at times—most of the time—it is difficult to do. This kind of examination and redesign of the learning architecture that surrounds, expands, and limits us, is a recurring theme throughout this book. Think of yourself as part of a design team to build the conditions that promote the behavior you want for yourself and others.

"This kind of examination and redesign of the learning architecture that surrounds, expands, and limits us, is a recurring theme throughout this book."

Understanding Our Own Behavior

Have you ever wondered why in the world you did or said something you wish you hadn't? When we do that, most of us look inside ourselves to identify what is wrong with us. There is a faster path to understanding why we speak and act in certain ways. The science of learning reveals that our behavior is constantly adapting to the world we live in. The world is our teacher and that teacher's most powerful tool is *behavioral consequences*. Entering the same conditions will produce the same consequences, maintaining behavior you want as well as what you do not want.

This may sound like bad news, but actually, it is good news. If we have learned to behave as we do now, we can also learn to behave differently. Understanding and making good use of behavioral consequences will help us behave in ways that benefit ourselves and others.

So, what exactly are behavioral consequences? That concept is so important that we need to understand it.

1. When we act, we affect other parts of the world—other people as well as the material and biological environments. For example: Adding water to a drooping potted plant affects its environment.

2. The world usually says *"Back at 'cha,"* by responding in some way to our action. For example, the plant's leaves perk up (or, if we under- or overwater, the plant may die). The world's response to our action is the

consequence of our action and its effects. Such effects influence how likely we are to act that way again. In this example, the plant's perking up makes it more likely we will water a drooping plant.

As you can see from this example, consequences can affect our behavior in two ways. Consequences can make behavior more likely: for example, watering the plant the proper amount. That action is affected by the way in which the plant thrives under our care. Consequences can also make the behavior less likely. If the plant does not thrive under our watch, we may end up saying things like we just don't have a green thumb. That one time may be the end of watering plants. It wasn't fun. The outcome *punishes*, that is, reduces the likelihood of our efforts at plant growing when watering is required. The effects of our actions do matter. Gain practice in how to arrange conditions that help you repeat behaviors that matter.

We might assume praise will "reinforce" behavior because it sounds like it should. We might also assume that yelling will "punish" behavior since it sounds bad. Neither of those statements is necessarily true. One of the difficulties in learning about behavior is that the technical language used is the same as words used to describe things we assume to be "good" (reinforcing) or "bad" (punishing). In fact, right now, we are describing how these two consequences affect the recurrence of behavior. Look at how behavior changes after a consequence is applied—more of it, less of it, or none of it. Behavior that is reinforced will likely increase in frequency. Behavior that is punished often decreases in frequency. However, what we want readers of this book to understand is that by using consequences effectively, you can influence actions you define as good. You can arrange conditions to strengthen or reduce the likelihood of an unwanted behavior occurring again.

A central point is that *punishment* strategies don't increase behavior. They are in almost all cases the wrong approach to eliminating the likelihood of a behavior occurring again. An exception is that if a person is in danger of hurting himself or others, that behavior needs to be stopped! "Punishment" techniques justified as helping people learn new behavior simply do not do that. Learning not to do something is not the same as learning to do something. Punishing others is not an opportunity to build new behavior or better outcomes. Many of us have learned to use coercive strategies of threat and fear (a.k.a., "do it or else"). We use them in many situations because they are highly reinforcing in producing immediate changes—at the cost of often producing long-lasting detrimental effects in our relationships. Sometimes, because we are at the end of our rope, and we believe we have tried everything, we need something done now. Often such threat-and-fear strategies get results quickly. Sometimes we use them because they give us pleasure—or by the compliance they generate, their use is verified. Sometimes, we have been taught to use threat and fear by having experienced it ourselves as children.

Occasionally in life, we do need a bit of a push that the fear of failure produces. An example is turning in an assignment at the last minute. We put it off because the deadline was "far away" and suddenly we burned the night oil to get it done. That pattern shapes the great procrastinators we may all be on occasion. We turn the report in at the last minute, and then, of all things, we get an A. Or we don't. We learn, with perhaps too much confidence, by getting an A, that we have skills to do the work well. Last-minute effort means we have more time to do things we want to do. Successful procrastinators learn that spending time at the last minute is not in fact a particularly important variable. They do it and it works for them.

If you find you use *threat or fear* to get the behavior you want, consider why it might be better for both you and others to change your pattern. If you want to build behavior that lasts, it is reliably more predictable that the use of positive methods creates much more sustainable effects, with decidedly less harm to the relationships between people. Getting that started, however, requires more deliberate effort for someone accustomed to using threats to get results. The cost in time and effort to change can quickly stop us from making the effort to try a more positive approach. After all, "My mother yelled at me a lot and told me I was an idiot just as often and look at me! I turned out just fine. My kids will, too!" or the familiar, "Spare the rod and spoil the child," or "His sloppy work deserves to be addressed in front of the team. That gives everyone a clear idea of what I will tolerate. And it is the only way to get him to focus." Without a clearly understood motivation to change your style of coaching or directing others, these kinds of patterns are very difficult to change. The cycle of immediacy of reinforcement, getting the results you want when you act as you do, is one of the reasons it is so difficult to begin using non-coercive strategies of change.

There is much to learn about the scientific effects of consequences on our behavior. That is a good thing to know, and we will return to science throughout—but this is not a deeply technical book. For now, it's sufficient to know how to determine whether your behavior has just been *reinforced* (strengthened) or *punished* (weakened). Know the effect you have on others around you. Such understanding helps you assess how the environment gives or takes away from sustaining the change you want. Understanding the directional nature of consequences on behavior also helps you assess the strategies you use to influence others. If you yell more than you want, how is that behavior sustained? No doubt you want to change that pattern. This book is about how to change so we end up acting in the way we want to act more often, with positive effects. Understand that these principles are guiding your very personal lifelong learning histories right now. Consequences surround, maintain, reduce, and influence your words and actions. Learn to see consequences as your lifelong guides in helping you act in ways that allow your positive values to shine through.

Until a critical mass of people understands and commits to the deliberate use of positive strategies to influence others, the biggest problem our humanity faces is in the ease of using coercive strategies of control to get what we want. The addictive nature of using threat and fear in advancing individual and group power has wreaked havoc on conditions of peace and goodwill through the ages. Our patterns of using positive or threatening control are well established through our history of learning, the rules we live by, and other elements of development. We all can benefit from a close look at how we show up. That means looking carefully at the role positive and negative consequences played in shaping the person we are today.

"...until a critical mass of people understands and commits to the deliberate use of positive strategies to influence others, the biggest problem our humanity faces is in the ease of using coercive strategies of control to get what we want."

Maintaining Persistence in the Face of Challenges

Aubrey Daniels, head of an international behavioral consulting company, *Aubrey Daniels International* (ADI), transferred an understanding of the science of behavior to businesses across the world. One way he accomplished this was in the design of a tool known as the *PIC/NIC® Analysis*, in which the scientific principles of the effects of consequence on learning were added to a matrix. Consequences operate on behavior across a gradient of timing (*immediate* or *future*), type (*positive* or *negative*), and predictability (*certain* or *uncertain*). To make this analysis understandable, Daniels used *PIC* to indicate *Positive, Immediate*, and *Certain* consequences. When a consequence is *positive, immediate*, and very likely *certain* (PIC), the behavior that occurs is very likely to repeat. For example, doing the dishes for your partner, Luis, who almost always does them, is likely to increase if he notices and appreciates your efforts at or near the time you did them (you receive a PIC). When consequences are *negative*—that is, threatening in some way—*immediate*, and *certain* (NIC), it is predictably less likely that the behavior will occur again any time soon. For example, if, instead of thanking you for doing the dishes, Luis immediately criticizes you for how you put them away, you are less likely to do that again (you are experiencing a NIC). However, you may decide it was just a bad day for Luis, so you try again. If the reaction is still negative about not doing the task right, over time that kind of voluntary behavior on your part is less likely. That second NIC you received, even on the perpetually optimistic and positive you, works well. Your intention was to do something kind, and yet, here you are, given a NIC ... again. Keep in mind that consequences, however intended, positive or negative, are determined by how they are received. In this case, you heard the negative comments in ways that decreased your willingness to do dishes again, not as constructive criticism.

To help us begin to see how learning occurs, the terms *PIC* and *NIC* were created. Both have rapid effects on behavior. Think about times you were delightfully recognized for something you were doing or simply encouraged to keep going. Think as well when something did not go well, and you faced negative, immediate, certain reactions. These elements of type *(positive or negative),* timing *(immediate or future),* and probability *(certain or uncertain)* tell us about the likelihood of accelerating or reducing behavior. How our behavior is affected by consequences is more complex than this tool suggests, even as it takes you through various elements (PFU, PIU, NFC, NIU, etc.). However, it is particularly useful when considering the control that both positive and negative consequences have on predicting how we will behave along a continuum of time and circumstances (Daniels and Lattal, 2020).

When you use NICs to manage interactions with others—finding fault, wanting it done your way, or indicating the work is nowhere near up to standard—it is predictable that learning from you may be very difficult or that you will be avoided as much as possible.

However, think about a time when a teacher or colleague used PICs to encourage small efforts you made, with specificity and sincerity. You may remember loving being in their presence and working hard. People skilled in delivering meaningful PICs are often excellent coaches, encouraging the individual to try again, even if the first time is full of errors. You are lucky to work with someone like that; someone who is clear about the performance that needs to be done but right there by your side, encouraging you every small step toward success. That kind of grounded, mature, and future-directed behavior is the behavior we hope to find in those who influence our lives.

Consider your own history in delivering PICs about performance that is working, and your history with NICs, discouraging, shaming or hostile, even toward those you love. Sometimes people say they use NICs with their children to keep them from doing the wrong thing—for example, to stop a child from crossing the street without noticing an approaching vehicle. Sometimes, we use NICs with our partners or spouses because we are so fed up with their continuing to do actions they have agreed to do differently, at least as we see it. Becoming known as a person who generally approaches the world expecting the best out of people, or expecting the worst, dramatically shapes how you are seen. The initial takeaway right now is to understand that PICs build and NICs remove—skills, confidence, optimism. Training is available in greater detail as well as permission to use the complete tool at Aubrey Daniels International (www.aubreydaniels.com).

Delayed consequences are described, generally, as having less control to initiate and sustain behavior; but, as you will see, that truism may be limited to settings in which one is gaining skills with brand new behavior. Once such new behavior is learned, it can occur in situations where there is a very long delay between recognition (in an overt way) and other consequences. Behavior accelerates to a large extent based on how the environment around it *strengthens* such actions. Behavior occurs regardless of whether immediate rewards or harsh punishers are present, at least to the observer. Our histories shape and maintain actions and often override immediate consequences. We learn the behavior that is correct, and the behavior to perform even when there is little to no recognition. Such patterns can exist often long after we first learned the benefit of a choice made or a rule learned in the distant past (Baum, 2003, 2011, 2013).

Consider how you might use type, timing, and predictability of consequences to arrange the environment to support desired behavior. Many factors enter your perception of *effort*; that is, if behaviors are hard or easy to do. Consequences occurring in the immediate do not fully address how individuals master behaviors that require persistence, but understanding that behavior is affected by the type, timing, and predictability of consequences makes managing their effects easier.

How might you arrange conditions to help you master new patterns of behavior or to eliminate ineffective ones? Your history of learning determines the consequences that you see as positive or negative. Rules of conduct about behavior that is expected of you and patterns of behavior formed by experience operate to strengthen certain actions over time. These conditions surround the choices you make and play a large part in your actions.

Your long history in how you respond to your world means that no one, including you at times, can determine with certainty the elements that maintain your actions. At times, we do not correctly identify why we act as we do. And, as we know all too well, the influences on Jess's behavior may not affect Arlene's. That difference adds to our individual uniqueness. You may continue to do harmful or unhelpful or brilliantly effective things that others want you to stop. You persist. Change involves both immediacy and the longer-term value of repeated experience in shaping your actions. These types of consequences learned over time help to create how you interact with your world.

PRACTICE 2.1:

Identifying the Type, Timing, and Predictability of Consequences on How I Show Up

---

1. Identify your experience in learning a new skill when you were provided with positive, timely, and predictable feedback about the good effort you were making. Identify who, when, how, and what effect that kind of feedback had on you.

2. Identify when you provided positive feedback to someone learning a new behavior. What happened as a result of your effort?

3. Do the same for a time when someone delivered negative feedback about your desire to do something new. Consider the effects on you.

4. Importantly, consider whether you are more likely overall to point out errors rather than recognize effort. Do you know why?

5. Think of someone in your life, right now, who you know would really appreciate your active support as they work to reach a goal. Consider the specific things you could do as they work to get there. Try it.

From the most microscopic living entity to the largest mammal, all operate according to the effects of consequences on their actions. Susan M. Schneider's book *The Science of Consequences: How They Affect Genes, Change the Brain, and Impact Our World (2012)*, offers a good account of these processes. Understanding these processes helps us determine how we show up. Such understanding enables you to consider the forces operating on your current behavior patterns. Hopefully in areas where you keenly desire to change, this kind of information can help you take carefully designed actions to better ensure that desired change occurs.

Let's examine the facts we do know with some degree of certainty about effort and accomplishment. When you want to increase skills, consider Anders Ericsson's advice about structured practice (Ericsson et al., 1993). Golf swings, painting, speaking calmly in front of others—all skills benefit from feedback and practice with a coach who uses clear guidance to keep us from repeating negative patterns from our past. The literature on structured practice provides good tools to consider when deliberately working to increase a desired outcome. We will return to this body of work later.

Gaining control as new learning occurs can require overcoming a lifetime of practices that may still continue, "in spite of ourselves." The accelerants of progressive effort toward desired goals, along with reviewing our accomplishments, help to provide information about restructuring patterns we so wish to amend. Consider your own behavior—the intolerable things you do that you want to stop, that demanding tone you take when talking to waiters, the funny laugh you always emit during awkward moments even though others tell you to stop, or your most annoying pattern of going to bed at midnight and getting up at 4:45 a.m., despite how tired you are. How might you plan new ways of acting to end the things you do not like about your behavior and start the behavior you want—plus get a good night's sleep?

What We Do with the Conditions Around Us

Despite challenges, some people will persist, doing something again and again until they master it. They have learned over time that the pursuit itself is reinforcing. That may indeed be you. The activity may not have been reinforcing at all in the beginning—playing the piano, giving a speech, taking long walks every day, speaking in understanding tones to someone you disagree with, and so on. And yet, you persisted. You got better at whatever you were working to do. Over time, it became more enjoyable to play the piano or give a speech.

Our histories of learning make rewards and punishments unique to each of us. Behavior can continue through thick and thin for long periods of time—days, weeks, months, and years—in conditions that may appear to others to be very "punishing." The behavior is being maintained by the *reinforcing* conditions surrounding it. However, to make that a true statement, it must include our histories of learning and events in our distant past. That includes the impact of our constant traveling companion, *experience*, moving along beside us through life events. Public heroes like Gandhi, Nelson Mandela, or Marie

Curie persisted for decades through seemingly very difficult events. It appears that the reinforcing properties of moving closer to outcomes that reflected their core values, learned through actions, and maintained by their histories of learning, kept them going.

Even if the source of reinforcement is invisible to us, we only need to ask, "Does the behavior persist?" If so, reinforcement is occurring in some form. Self-talk, that invisible pattern repeated in our heads, can be a source of reinforcement, not necessarily of enjoyment. A private rule of conduct learned long ago about how we treat one another often continues in words and deeds that move us closer to desired outcomes, despite pain or extreme challenges. So-called "punishment" may simply sustain us in persisting. *Doing the right thing* can be a sufficient mantra for us to persist, seemingly against all odds, a rule of personal conduct that overrides the immediacy of circumstances that might look to others as putting oneself in the path of extreme harm. Remember that the effects of consequences are defined by the actions of the performer, not by anyone else. It is most likely not the italicized phrase, *do the right thing*, but years spent learning the meaning of that phrase to you. Such meaning may be influenced by your parents, those you love, your faith, and even negative experiences across living conditions.

Behavior, aligned with our values and goals, has a greater likelihood of producing frequent conditions in which to experience the power of reinforcement. The reinforcer may come from you saying, "One more day along my route to the desired outcome." No doubt you have had experiences with maintaining behavior after others think you would (or should) surely give up. To sustain so many things of value in this life, we need to surround ourselves with environments that strengthen behaviors we want to do, in the ways we want to do them. That extra strengthening can sustain us when acting on something far removed from the immediacy of everyday encouragement (Baum, 2003).

"To sustain so many things of value in this life, we need to surround ourselves with environments that strengthen behaviors we want to do, in the ways we want to do them."

Doing the Right Thing: Rules and Experiences

Rule-governed behavior means that the person learns indirectly, without direct contact with consequences. That is, a person does not need to experience the consequences directly but learns by reading or hearing from others or by watching the consequences unfold. A person does not have to touch a hot stove ever to learn the rule not to touch the stove, for example.

The expansion of learning through rules has had a large impact in the development of cultures. To illustrate this, we learn science through rules. Scientific knowledge builds on the contributions of others. Thus, the saying, attributed to Isaac Newton, "If I have seen further, it is by standing on the shoulders of giants." Each of us doesn't have to start from scratch and wait for our behavior to be shaped by direct consequences. Skills build on one another, allowing the direct application of research designs, using available and established tools of scientific inquiry. This applies similarly with history. We do not experience events that occurred before we were born, but we are told about those events. We can learn from the histories of people or cultures preceding us. When we learn to drive a vehicle, we are told the sequence of steps, how to follow road rules and conventions, how to avoid running out of gas, how to avoid accidents, without having to learn this through step-by-step, first-hand experience. Rule-governed behavior plays a very large part in supporting doing the right thing as you have been taught.

The *Oxford Dictionary* defines a *rule* as "an explicitly understood principle governing conduct within a particular activity or sphere." Rules teach us how to behave within a unique culture. Such rules of conduct are often obvious across a culture. A country like the United States or Japan may have very clearly understood rules of conduct their citizens are expected to follow. However, those general rules of conduct may seem odd to the other country's citizens. They can take on different expressions in particular parts of their countries, leading to rankings and worth determined by the part of the country a particular person is from. For example, behavioral expectations in Shelly, Idaho, may require, at times, major differences in behavioral expectations in New York City. Correct conduct in Nara, Japan, may be different in several important ways than expected conduct in Osaka. The Texan in Midland might say, "You ain't from these parts, are you?" to a fellow American from New Jersey. It could be the dialect or the deed or the look that is different. Reverse this example. A Texan in New Jersey might be seen as very different, based on dress or accent, and possibly because of the New Jersey native's biases about Texans' beliefs or how Texans; act, sight unseen. Rules about proper conduct across many dimensions are expressed in beliefs and hardened into unexamined but tightly held biases. Classic stereotypes are built surrounded by the cultural biases in which we spend our days.

Differences in local customs are sometimes of little meaning in terms of how you are treated. However, they can imply in subtle ways who is worthwhile. Such rules hold sway over many of us for most of our lives. They color how we evaluate the richness of diversity, or the degree of threat we see as disrupting our values. Such biases about the value and dignity of others are hard to change.

You are often subject to the rules you learned early in life about how to treat people and yourself. Society expects rules of conduct to be followed by "well-taught" human beings. When is it okay to speak? When is it okay to challenge someone in authority? Our religious teachings provide rules for how we are to treat one another. Rules are at times a barrier to evaluating, let alone doing the right thing. Sometimes the rule itself becomes more important than its effects on others.

Often a rule is learned as an absolute creed; violating the rule is often understood as leading to bad things for the rule violator. For most of us, the absolute nature of a rule learned early in life changes with experience, allowing helpful deviation. A simple rule might be, "Never cross the street on a red light." You did not do that even once when growing up back home in Connecticut. If out in Wyoming, however, facing a red light and no cars in sight from any direction for miles, you cross that street and suffer no consequences of note— unless it is in a town where a patrol car awaits, ready to roar out from behind the Hires Root Beer Float Shoppe sign on the corner to issue you a ticket … hypothetically speaking.

Some religious codes of conduct are clearly taught in a manner that you know, if you violate them, you will regret that act long into the future. You may be told you will not enter the Kingdom of Heaven, a decidedly good place to go, one that you want to enter someday. Religious codes can offer opportunities as well to enjoy the best of this life in ways that you find celebratory, with no threat or fear. Religion may offer full-on love and forgiveness. Striving to follow the rules in such settings can be inspiring and keep you going.

Gang membership can depend on rule-following as well. While the gang may have many rules that are abhorrent and depend on threat and fear to maintain, a gang offers a strong sense of belonging and protection as a member of the group. Sometimes those initial rules of doing harm to perceived enemies or strangers to gain entry to the gang become part of one's sense of pride in protecting the gang's territory. In doing such deeds, the person is demonstrating behavior steeped in loyalty and heroic actions, as defined by their subculture.

Should the reader ask, "Oh, are you saying their concept of good and good deeds should be accepted, no matter their consequence?" No. The important point is how actions are often justified as the right thing to do even when they have no redeeming value. Remember, in 9th grade, you, or a person just like you, wanted friends, so you joined a "we hate fat kids" clique? If you think about it carefully, most of us have at times behaved in ways that exclude others or indicate that our side is the best side. This may sometimes be harmless (cheering for your school team) but can be very harmful at other times (the "we hate" clubs).

Many rules of conduct are followed by the guarantee of safety as a member of a certain community. Such rules offer a continuation of a way of life valuable to its members. At times, a diverse society like ours requires examining the rules of our unique communities. When deciding to violate deeply held social norms about differences, a superordinate code of conduct helps in guiding our interactions with people who are different than we are. If only we each had the presence of Jiminy Cricket on our shoulder. Jiminy, representing that voice of conscience, sees us all as part of a common humanity, of equal value, and guided by inclusion. How in the world do we get to the place where that cricket, metaphorically, is influencing our actions if all we have operated under are different kinds of rules about who is worthy? For many of us, Jiminy/conscience is of little influence. As we will describe, many cultures are taking on the effort to better ensure that new generations demonstrate behavior that shows up as respectful and empathetic toward others. Hopefully, through examples and practice, new generations are experiencing in real time a shared benefit in treating one another well.

Barriers exist to behaving differently than expected. Particularly, acting outside the immediate biases of family and community raises real challenges for each of us when faced with difficult choices. At times stepping up to protect someone requires acting in ways that are not easily tolerated by those we care about. Little motivational fuel to do the right thing exists in such circumstances. Beginning to see beyond the limits of our myopic points of view can help. Education can help. Living with people who are different from ourselves can help to increase understanding about the common humanity we share. Work on those things that help you visualize how you want to be in this world. Practice. Not all such events of standing for things you value will end badly and often, not nearly as badly as anticipated. Use examples of personal heroes to guide you. Learn how to help someone else in small ways that lead to good outcomes to strengthen your responses in more difficult moments. What are the outer limits of your tolerance? Are you worried that you will disappoint your family? New, untried behavior does occur, beginning in small ways around small issues. Practice in those conditions. Courageous behavior in the smallest of ways helps to build a culture in which diverse people feel safer and valued. Take the small steps to wiser acting.

Rules arise from practices that have worked. Establishing a new pattern of behavior according to a new set of rules, through trial and error, also creates a model by which behavior can begin. Learning a rule may not provide answers for how to address all situations. Addressing changing conditions requires becoming alert to seeing the limitations or costs in following particular rules. Most likely, we know that the rules we learned in kindergarten have value in some situations, and sometimes not at all. Explore how the rules you follow support or impede behavior in your life that supports the values you cherish.

Other events beyond rules, guide and maintain actions. Skills learned by direct experience are called *contingency-shaped* skills. They are not rule-driven *per se*. Remember, rules are learned without having direct experience with consequences and they are often very efficient in getting good things going, like how we treat one another in public. Taking rule-driven behavior into a contingency-shaped context often calls into question how a rule might tell us to act;

PRACTICE 2.2:

Examining Cherished Rules of Conduct

Rules of conduct can be hard to 1) evaluate objectively, and 2) change. Do you have rules about how you and other people should act?

1. List the top rules of conduct that guide your behavior.

2. Can you list any rules that you followed once but no longer? Do you remember where you first learned the rule?

3. Think of a time when someone followed different rules than you in the same situation. How did the person talk and act? What would have been different or better if he and you had followed the same rules?

4. From your experience, write down how rules build valuable character, patterns of what you or others do that you define as good.

5. Be direct with yourself. Do the rules of conduct you grew up with make for kinder, better people? Do they make for harsher, more judgmental people? When and why or why not?

Be aware of how you judge those who violate rules of conduct. Consider if certain rules you use to judge right or wrong conduct limit your vision about how to behave wisely.

---

rather, we look to actions supported by our experiences. Assessing the utility of following the rule versus the demand characteristics of the conditions in which we find ourselves is a large part of acting with greater wisdom. At times, rules are seen as principles or values about how to live our lives. They may add up to how we believe good people should act. Unless we have learned somewhere along the way that when faced with new information, violating the rule is okay, a gap and related feelings of shame or embarrassment can occur. Some of us still remember when we did something our parents told us was wrong, and the terror associated with them finding out about our behavior. Teen years hold many such violations. You may now see those violations as unimportant, or, even today, view those actions as a low moment in your life. Violating rules is the stuff of many a great novel (or a life) of regret for many and, hopefully, redemption: *"It is a far, far better thing that I do than I have ever done."* The characters in Charles Dickens' *A Tale of Two Cities*, 1859, were in constant pursuit of the right things to do while the landscape was redefining, for various characters, the right thing to do.

Rule-governed behavior is considerably more efficient than contingency-shaped behavior in establishing initial behavior. Rule-governed behavior helps us interact with strangers, start a new craft, and be comfortable using our problem-solving skills in new settings. Rules add the potential of predictability to our actions. However, requirements across settings change quickly. Reliance on rules requires that the stated or implied consequences of following the rules are consistent enough to address a multitude of problems. Rules need to be flexible enough that innovative practices find reinforcement, resulting in the discovery of new solutions. Rules may also contain exceptions that tell people, "Break this rule when needed."

How parents and teenagers negotiate rules can be very instructive to teaching when rules are valuable and necessary throughout life and when breaking them is the first thing a young adult wants to do. When a young person goes off to college or moves out of the parents' home, there can be a sudden release from "home" rules about personal conduct. A release from rules includes when to get up, how late to stay out, who to run around with, when to do homework, and deciding to go to class or not. Sometimes rules are imposed in ways that make independent decision-making a very scary thing. When the possibility of punishment is removed on the first night at college on our own, we, perhaps with some trepidation or wild abandon, begin to disregard rules our parents took years to teach us. "Party animal" at college is not the image most parents want for their child; but "ah, freedom" to experiment may be much more immediately reinforcing.

Rules of conduct can also be learned through positive strategies when parents give greater degrees of freedom in clear ways. By the time we go to college, they may have allowed us to experiment with some freedom. That kind of graduated rule setting may build respect for why the rule existed, as well as learning experiences from doing things differently.

Rules that lead to a sense of well-being often stay in place. Rules remain that are first imposed by parents, or churches, or governing bodies. The laws of the country, state, and city most likely are followed by most of us. Our own moral code often imposes a set of rules to follow across conditions. Some people do that well. At times most of us understand it is wiser to modify our actions according to the events happening in the environment around us.

Contingency-shaped behavior allows us to adapt to nuances. This is illustrated in the difference in performance observed in a skill learned through practice (the precise behavior of an experienced practitioner) versus learned only through theory (the rough performance of a person fresh out of school). Therefore, competent performance demands frequent practice. Such behavior helps us elaborate on rules defined as essential to being a good person. *Contingency-shaped behavior* enables us to adapt in spontaneous ways to conditions around us. Yet, mental echoes of rules that limit choice and make little sense, may stay with us, justifying our behavior patterns. These "mental echoes" can still produce guilt when violated, long after the utility embedded in the rule has disappeared. Rules, however, support actions we do because of highly reinforced beliefs in a variety of settings, leading on occasion, to unintended actions.

In 1963, in Tuscaloosa, Alabama, Vivian Malone, an African American woman, entered the University of Alabama, violating many racially defined rules of conduct, written into law, imposed by the state, and embraced by most of its white citizens. Her act was one of singular courage. Arriving in her economics class, she took a seat in an empty row. The professor then announced as others were entering, "Where you are sitting is where you will stay throughout this semester. None of you are to move from the seat you have chosen." No one sat in her row.

At the end of the first class, a white girl, Addy Hammer, unintentionally walked beside Vivian out of the classroom. Addy quickly knew, in retelling this story to a few trusted friends, that those simple steps had affected her in significant ways. They both faced a group of shouting white boys making gestures and saying terrible things. By walking at Vivian's side, even unintentionally, the white girl was violating rules of conduct deeply held in the Deep South of the 1960s. Self-described as "shy," Addy did not want the kind of attention she was receiving. Nevertheless, during that first encounter, it became clear that, accidentally initiated or not, she could not let Vivian walk down that long hall alone. They ended up talking a bit as they discussed class assignments, but they never exchanged names nor met up after class. The white boys never failed to line up and shout on both sides of the hall until the semester ended. Over time, Addy began to think she was invisible, not really a target of their intended effect. That conveyed to her the depth of blindness surrounding deeply entrenched racial bias, believing whiteness was protecting her even as she violated deep-seated, "proper" codes of conduct.

For Addy, the hall walk was unexpectedly terrifying. In violating a rule of the society of which she was a part and that surrounded her, Addy instead followed a rule she had practiced for much of her young life, essentially to "be nice to those in need." She knew that this brave woman, Vivian Malone, was doing something that would change Alabama, universities, America, and hopefully, those white boys, for the better. Addy said later that once she took those first steps, she could do nothing else. She did keep thinking, every day, that her actions could lead to real jeopardy for herself. However, experience was becoming a profound teacher, reinforcing her breaking of one social norm and acting on another.

Never facing extreme consequences except to have words used and gestures made that were shocking to this young woman, most likely helped to keep her behavior going. She did receive sideways smiles and brief eye contact from Vivian. She continued to walk with Vivian, every day. Addy's behavior, initiated, no doubt, by a coincidental exit from class, was simultaneously maintained in part by her companion's shy smile and exemplary hallway walking style—head held high. Her behavior was maintained by reinforcement at many levels, but perhaps most succinctly by beginning to understand that, in a very small way, she was a part of honoring a greater good that Vivian represented to her.

Perspective

The perspective or vantage point we have about how we respond to conditions around us are based on our unique experiences, related to such conditions as gender and race. These uniquely shaped responses help us identify real threats or misunderstandings. When acting wisely, this notion is key to knowing how and when to act. For example, women walking at night alone are very often much more alert to the environment around them than are men. They may see a threat where a man would see only a little peace and quiet, even as another individual walks close by.

Dr. Chata Dickson, principal researcher at the New England Center for Children, reminded us of the importance of how perspective can both broaden and limit our attention, based on our histories and the lessons from our environment in responding to conditions that surround us. She said, "Individuals, whose day job is teaching young children, go on a picnic with friends in the park. They are ever vigilant to those preschoolers jumping up and off teeter-totters. At any moment one is bound to fall, be injured. They see that potential in ways their friends do not." Differences in looks, sexual orientation, age, or skin color open very different ways of interpreting conditions around us when responding in situations that at times require anticipating more than is occurring at the moment. Understanding the different ways we may see the same set of circumstances can help in how to respond to many situations we face. Sometimes perspectives, sensitivities, and alertness to threat allows us to act with much greater wisdom. Dr. Dickson also shared that her mentor, Maria Ruiz, Ph.D., has written about the invisible contingencies, those discriminatory cultural practices, unidentified by most but important in how women, in particular, show up to others in many parts of our culture and in ways that diminish their importance (undermine their power). As Ruiz (1998) observes, "Whether an individual interprets a cultural practice as offensive, oppressive, or objectionable has everything to do with the effects of those practices on the person's behavior."

Certainly, rules can be applied to novel situations when learning a new skill. Rules are not, in themselves, sacred. The clash with beliefs behind the rules may become obvious as we interact with experiences beyond rule-governed patterns. As odd as it may sound, rules we hold may lead us to do as the rule says, in much more forceful ways even when our experiences teach us better ways to act. When treated with extreme care and goodwill by someone who is part of a group we have been taught to hate, we may immediately discount the care we receive as an exception, too small to ignore the rule that we hate that group. Unexamined, the rule controls our behavior. Engaging more with the person means giving up a lot more than just a "dumb" rule. Violating the rule could lead to losses of much significance—the loss of inclusion and more.

At times, as with strong moral codes of conduct, experiences expand our definition of doing the right thing, well beyond a stated rule. As we have learned in various wars, saying, "I was following orders, but they were against my personal code" is not enough to be forgiven by the larger society. However, for soldiers, they may face the firing squad if they don't follow orders. They may be there against their will—as in previous U.S. wars and the draft. Unjust orders occur and are, on occasion, disobeyed. As a person learns to weigh many sources of information, experience often replaces absolute patterns of behavior by encouraging going beyond the teachings of a particular rule.

Just how much we ask of other people and hold them accountable for their deeds is, at some level in any society, a soul-searching activity. Nevertheless, the complexity of such an analysis competes, some would argue, with the good of the whole, even in cases of swift justice. Holding individuals accountable for their deeds is a bedrock foundation of our society. Our society has sometimes held people accountable for actions that were beyond their control. Understanding behavior does not necessarily lead to perfect or fair or unbiased outcomes from all sides, even when it is obvious how the conditions that surround people limit their choices. Sometimes biases about a person and circumstances are all important, limiting sentences or even a guilty verdict.

Much has been written about how the justice system finds one person (often white) forgivable and another (often a minority) not, for essentially the same crime. It does no good to assume that wrong guides one side and right the other. Looking at evidence related to bias is something our society not only allows but often encourages. Describing the effects of rulings across people is one thing. Labeling the character of the judge or the jury is another. It can be so tempting. We do it with legal decisions we don't like, and we do it about people whose actions we don't like.

In courts of law, rules matter. How rules are applied matters. Conditions that surround and reinforce choice matter, both those surrounding the judge and the judged. Justice is often passed down through centuries of case law and how our society views fairness and equality. Being aware of the conditions that surround the person who violates the law does not mean that such acts will be forgiven. Many circumstances influence how a judge or jury render a verdict. Many factors influence how we see the outcomes of individual deeds and where responsibility lies. The biases and values of the judge that show up in written and spoken behavior is also on trial in many ways when we look at how our justice system acts in the name of *justice*.

Where You Want to Show Up

Since context matters in wise acting, consider how you want to show up in various life domains, such as family, friendships, professional work, community service, recreation, and health. You may have other areas to add as well. The conditions that surround you in these domains can be quite different—and you may show up very differently in each venue as well. Take some time to think about how you want to show up versus how you do show up. Ask others how they perceive you in those areas—you might be unaware of the effects some of your actions have on others.

Focus on behaviors you want across domains in need of work. For example, you might want to be more "adventurous" when going on vacation with your family. However, being "adventurous" might not be something you want to display when promoting safety in the workplace. These ways of acting might even change priorities within a domain. As situations change, some ways of acting are better than others. Let's say, one of your family members shows signs of being distressed and afraid when asked to go whitewater rafting during your planned vacation. At that moment, "adventurous" might need to take a back seat to "caring" and "flexible." The table below illustrates some possible life domains and examples of how one might want to show up in each situation.

Life domains

	FAMILY	FRIENDSHIP	PROFESSIONAL	RECREATION	HEALTH
How to show up	· Caring · Forgiving · Kind	· Authentic · Honest · Intimate	· Assertive · Contributing · Persistent	· Adventurous · Flexible · Open-minded	· Accepting · Fit · Mindful

Example of showing up across life domains

The examples presented on the table, as stated *values,* need to be translated into actions visible by others. This doesn't suggest acting in a way with the goal of being perceived as "good" by others. Rather, the goal is acting in a way that reflects those *values* that are important to you so that you can "do good." The focus is on achieving congruence between your words and actions that are consistent with the effects you want. Others respond based on how you interact with them and how it affects them. However, do not assume that means they or you will show up as you want. Behaving under a variety of circumstances is an adventure. To go on this adventure, bring a sense of humor to get through the unexpected during our most well-intended interactions with others.

"Behaving under a variety of circumstances is an adventure. To go on this adventure, bring a sense of humor to get through the unexpected during our most well-intended interactions with others."

PRACTICE 2.3:

Actions Across Daily Domains

1. Look at the list of domains on the previous page.

2. Select the one most important to you to address. Know you can add others as you go.

3. This is not an exhaustive list. Substitute as you wish.

4. Some domains need immediate attention, even if not as important to you. Think about the values attached. Where might it be helpful to demonstrate open-mindedness? What does that look like? Notice when you engage in those types of behavior (or when you don't).

At the end of the day, reflect on your actions, and how other people responded to your actions. Such reflection by you may be very difficult to translate into pinpointed actions. Identify instances when you wanted to show a new or different pattern but did not. Collecting examples and non-examples helps. The table on the next page is one method for collecting such data, a notation list that you carry around. Jot down examples/non-examples of when it is easy for you to show a new pattern of responding, and when not so easy. Hopefully this kind of assessment alerts you to specific barriers standing in your way. Consider possible alternatives to demonstrate how you want to behave to produce better outcomes. Remember these are attributes or labels representing the words you want to say and the actions you want to take, attributes that get assigned to you. You can broaden this practice by using a matrix like the one on the following page if you find value in it.

PRACTICE 2.4:

Introducing How to Address Uncomfortable Situations

Look for clues in your self-talk as to what beliefs or rules lead you to do and say things you wish you did not: "Those people might make fun, walk away, dismiss me, demean me, ignore me," etc. Consider your history with rules about good conduct, for example, "Polite girls never interrupt, don't make other people uncomfortable, don't disagree with authority, and support others before themselves." Perhaps you have a good view about the world around you and trust it to treat you fairly. If you find it does not, are you prepared to put such treatment in perspective? Such unexpected treatment can be hard. Practice what to say and do, whenever faced with challenges in finding your voice. Rehearse with a friend. Rehearse again. Strive to match the words you use with the words you want to use, taking small steps one day at a time.

1. Envision the effect you want to achieve at the end of uncomfortable moments.

2. Prepare through speaking out loud with friends.

3. Practice calm and clear words, relaxing the tone and pace, representing how you want to show up in situations that make you uncomfortable.

4. Contrast your words in friendly conditions to your words in less-friendly conditions.

5. Examine the effect those conditions have on the ways you act.

Think about barriers that compete with the ways you want to behave. Which conditions make it harder to act in the manner you want? Barriers can include your interactions with others, but also private events, like difficult feelings or thoughts. Adding those disruptors to your notes list helps you anticipate and even remove some of those barriers or prepare alternative routes to get to the other side. Often, congruence between your words and actions is especially

FAMILY DOMAIN:

Caring, Forgiveness, Kindness—Customize to your family/your values; select up to 3; several may show up across activities.

How I Show Up	When	Values Conveyed	Barriers, including feelings and thoughts	Self-Management Plan
1. Impatient with children	After dinner	I don't care; they are a nuisance; they have to pay attention to my rules—maybe I seem harsh and unforgiving. Violates my rule for what a good dad does.	Fatigue: I don't plan for quiet time with the children or other times; it's easy to let my partner do the work in the evening with the kids. I disrespect them as people with needs. They wear me out.	Reserve 1 hour after dinner; plan ahead; let kids know. If I'm too tired on occasion, I'll do bedtime. I'll explain and be more friendly; tell them I appreciate them in specific ways. My partner and I set up a system of mutual support to reduce feeling burdened. **VALUES this might demonstrate:** Caring; kindness; keeping my word; showing respect to my children; letting them know I am human, but in a kind way.
2.				
3.				

Friendship Domain:

Authenticity, Honesty, Intimacy—Customized to your concerns: friendliness; interest in others, dependability

How I Show Up	When	Values Conveyed	Barriers, including feelings and thoughts	Self-Management Plan
Pretty good except when that new neighbor Sam horns in, then I'm unfriendly; disinterested; a bit angry	Only with Sam and only after he joins the group	Dismissive Don't care Superficial Possessive	He is more popular; I used to be the one people wanted to hang out with. Don't even know him Never spend any time Judging and unfriendly, even hostile in words and deeds. Never laugh at his jokes (they are funny, but I don't laugh)	Invite him out for breakfast just the two of us; ask him about himself and his family; find a common core to build on; promise to follow up. **VALUES:** interest in others; beginnings of compassion; a person to count on; open-minded

important when situations make that congruence difficult. To illustrate this point, behaving in a way that shows "assertiveness" could be difficult when another person might act in a manner that you perceive as threatening. Fear, born of prior moments when you did speak up, can show up in your current setting—long after the earlier source is no longer present—but acting in an assertive way could be especially important at that moment. Luckily, learning to be appropriately assertive can be done while learning to handle various degrees of emotional behavior at the same time.

How you approach uncomfortable situations may set you up to do and say things you really do not like about yourself. The best takeaway from a chapter like this is to be alert to the match between the actions you hope to take and the actions you, in fact, do take. When is it easier or harder to behave as you want to behave? Examine the conditions that influence your behavior. Begin to think of very specific behavior patterns that you want to exhibit. Consider your biases, at your core, about who is and who is not of value. What principled values do you want others to see in accomplishing the daily tasks of life? The next chapter provides suggestions that may help you design and accomplish specific goals.

Chapter 3:

Motivation Outside In: The Sources of Self-Change

"Ultimately, knowing what drives us puts us in the driver's seat."

–Susan M. Schneider

When we desire to set up a self-management system—a method by which to collect both objective and subjective data on how to be more of who we want to be—a question looms: How do we find the proper motivation to get going, to begin to do things differently, and to make progress on any plan of self-improvement? In preparing to handle difficult situations, some aspects about how we are hoping to approach an event in fresh ways is already in motion. We are already responding, and not in new ways. Good intentions aside, here we are again behaving as we have always behaved. Perhaps we already feel a bit of fatigue about making the change. Surrounded by our history of learning and conditions of the moment, responding as we have in the past may be all we know to do. We certainly want to reduce the noise or chatter of our internal debate (our thoughts and feelings) about the requirements for changing our approach. Let's begin by identifying the motivational source for changing behavior.

Motivation lies in the context around you, rather than taking place *inside out*. At the start of any personal, self-change program, the very biggest threat to our good plans is the effects of negative consequences. Begin with the unequivocal idea that you want to change, to act differently, and to handle known barriers to change, including your thoughts and emotions, in new ways. Don't doubt that you *want* to change. Take the burden off your shoulders. Don't tell yourself that if you fail at a task you intend to do, it is because you really don't want to succeed. We are so often taught that if we want something bad enough, we can do it. Stop! Begin with the simple declaration that you *want* to change. Start there. Blame and shame have no role to play in learning something new. Having been at that beginning point many times in life, we all know how much we wanted to change. Occasionally change seemed to happen without much forethought. Nevertheless, wanting to change was not enough, as sincere as it was. So, how do we reduce the likelihood that our past failures, current routines, assumptions, and feelings don't dominate and/or undermine our beginning?

The important point in looking *outside in* is that you are not limited by other people's assessment of your character, your race, or your immediate past or current actions. These qualities may feel like the only thing members of your family or friends see when assessing your capacity to change. If you can start to manage yourself from the outside in, nothing is predetermined as to your potential, beyond certain limits of your physical self. Your control lies in the conditions that surround you and how you have learned to implement new activity through the rules you follow and experiences you embrace.

> *"Generations have misunderstood the freedom that comes from identifying external sources of motivation. Those conditions build patterns of behavior mastered to habit-strength over a week or a lifetime, seemingly automatic and spontaneous."*

Generations have misunderstood the freedom that comes from identifying external sources of motivation. Those conditions build patterns of behavior mastered to habit-strength over a week or a lifetime, seemingly automatic and spontaneous. Think about the behaviors that helped you learn a new skill that you do with ease today. Note the things that you remember. Recognize that you have made many changes in behavior successfully in the past. You are not where you were as a young child just learning to read, which is a complex set of skills, even if it felt very simple.

Whatever you mastered in situations leading to new skill mastery in the past provides you a good set of principles to apply in new conditions. Such moments may also have taught you behaviors to avoid if you want to be successful.

What helped us get to step one when we think of our enjoyment in learning new things? Again, if the first step in your plan has not yet happened, it is not because of a flaw in you, something about you that makes change difficult. The words you say about yourself and your potential, the words others may say, can be real barriers, but those are still learned behaviors. Change lies in how the conditions that surround us, certain words, rules, learning opportunities, and experiences, have influenced us across a lifetime. Those conditions can be arranged to motivate and spark sustainable actions needed to achieve desired outcomes in the present.

Goals are achieved by *pinpointing* desired outcomes at the start and acting in a manner that moves you closer to those outcomes over time. *Pinpointing* refers to describing the outcome you want to achieve in specific, observable terms, *what, by when, where,* and *with whom,* or *under what conditions.* Pinpointing clearly understood steps in setting goals helps you live the life that you want along the way.

Indeed, if you are to get to your goals with as much ease as possible, arrange conditions for success. However, please grab that initial motivation, that *eager to start* feeling. Make sure you do not set up too many "rules" for yourself before you can begin, whatever it might be. If it is exercising more, all you need to know is if you are fit enough to start. However, you might spend a lot of time buying the right shoes, clothes, and equipment before starting. Can't find that special shoe? The clothes look too baggy. That band is not the right tightness. "Geez, it is already Tuesday and I promised myself I would start on Sunday. Ah well, I'll start next week." What if you don't want to stop exercising to talk to your neighbors? Start early or late but do start. Put on earphones; that reduces spontaneous talking. You can begin to exercise. "Start" by rolling out of bed and walking. You have started; step one … literally. Then you can begin to properly prepare with additional things to help you reach your goal. You probably know to lay out (on the night before) the clothes you are going to wear on the morning walk. If fitness is the goal, starting to move more does not require a lot of equipment or the perfect shoes or the proper clothes.

Many goals in life are defeated by pondering how to start properly such as writing that novel. Oh. You say you need to read more novels before you start? Is meeting more people your goal? You need a proper haircut (or weight loss which is why you wanted to exercise in the first place)?

Then, some goals overlap in the moment, each goal important to you. Let the discounting and shifting priorities begin. Achieve the "be a better teammate" goal by finishing work often needed by others. Today you are working on something the team needs by 4 p.m. to finish a very important presentation needed by 5 p.m. in the Office of the President. He will use it to make an important pitch to the Board of Governors in the early morning.

Oh, I just got invited by that person I have long wanted to meet outside of work, to go to the park, a short walk from the office. It is 2:15. I'll only go for 30 minutes. I promised my part of the report to the team by 4 p.m. I have about an hour and a half left to do it. I do want to make better friends, my personal goal—and walk, my exercise goal. The work will be just a little bit late. So, what if it is? I want to say yes! The walk took 45 minutes. I turned in the report 40 minutes late. A value was missing in a calculation I made in the report. I recalculated the number. The report would not print as needed. New tables are needed. And the rest is fate. I delivered the report at 5:30 to a very angry team that did not get to leave or finish on time. The president went home, frustrated. The presentation was delayed but delivered. Like Scarlett O'Hara, "After all tomorrow is another day..." and that walk was so good.

Choices we make always have effects. Join the endless slippery slopes of commitments and opportunities: motivation strong, motivation weak, promises made but not kept. Sometimes that walk in the park is worth it and you know you will make the work up—but sometimes that is the last straw for others. How do we address such competing contingencies? How do we prioritize and how do the conditions around us help us do something less desired? Isn't it, after all, consequences that drive our behavior? In the last example, a simple modification would resolve the conflict, "Love to! Let's do it at 4:30" would work. That outcome requires us to use our good problem-solving skills. We have such skills but sometimes we store them well out of sight. After all, who wants to interrupt the enthusiasm of the moment by pausing to think?

These examples are not complex. Alternatives often exist. However, caught in the motivational moment, we do make small choices. Later, we may say to ourselves, "Next time, I'll say, 'Let's do it at 4:30.'" Small decisions that meet one goal can damage a more important one; in this case, the *"way we want to show up"* goal.

New behavior is often hard to start, but once it begins, small successes accelerate the pace of change. Patience in delay while gaining skill and discovering how well you work through the hurdles experienced, can be reinforcing in and of themselves. First, understand those lessons in pinpointing why and what you want to accomplish and by when, to ensure you have the motivational fuel to get to your goals. One might call this "readiness activity to get you started." These activities may not yet be sufficient to create a behavior action plan or other systematic processes of change but are necessary to ensure you have a clear idea of your goals.

Specific practices outlined in this chapter and in later chapters will provide tools to help you prepare before engaging in situations where you are anxious or uneasy. Emotional behavior very often does interrupt our words and actions. If you want to become clearer, more direct, and less emotional in certain situations, the words you use are important. We will provide specific tools to address emotional behavior and word use, as well as simple designs to help you start something new.

However, right now, remember that to get to any goals, deliberately enter environments where such behavior finds encouragement to keep on going. Don't go over to Uncle Joe's to start something new when the first thing out of his mouth might be, "What? You again, trying to make yourself better? Hah. Ain't going to happen." If Uncle Joe is a person whose expressed confidence in you matters, or even if it doesn't, don't put yourself in such a situation. Once again, a point repeated: motivation lies in our surroundings. Motivation is found from an innate quality we have or do not have, but from the world in which we live. Those sources can be understood as coming from God, things that make you happy, or the motivation that comes from your persistence in accomplishing a difficult task. They can also come from your very rich history of how you respond to varied\challenges.

PRACTICE 3.1:

When I Persisted and Learned a New Skill

1. Describe a time when you persisted to engage in new learning.

2. What was different about that time as compared to other times when you did not persist?

3. What role, if anything, did the threat of failure limit the possibilities you could envision about your skills in mastering a new area of learning?

New patterns in building a behavioral repertoire are always possible. Consider the barriers as opportunities, conditions deliberately arranged. Your words and actions should be carefully arranged as well. Take a moment to read about how one man deliberately arranged conditions to persist in achieving his goal.

An Exemplary Role Model in Striving to Live a Good Life

Learning the right thing to do and then doing it is not always easy. If that were not the case, most of us would be exhibiting wise actions all the time. In the real world, circumstances are often complex, and competing events influence our behavior. Like many of us, Benjamin Franklin found this to be the case. He wanted to become a "moral" person but realized it was more challenging than he thought. Old habits, "inclinations," temptations—all contributed to failure to achieve his goal. To succeed, he developed a simple, yet effective, system of self-management.

He began listing the virtues or values that he believed would lead to a moral life—general ways of acting we will describe in chapter 13. For each virtue, he described the actions needed to demonstrate them:

BEN FRANKLIN'S LIST OF LIFE VIRTUES

1. Temperance	Eat not to dullness; drink not to elevation.
2. Silence	Speak not but what may benefit others or yourself: avoid trifling conversation.
3. Order	Let all your things have their places; let each part of your business have its time.
4. Resolution	Resolve to perform what you ought; perform without fail what you resolve.
5. Frugality	Make no expense but to do good to others or yourself; i.e., waste nothing.
6. Industry	Lose no time; be always employed in something useful; cut off all unnecessary actions.
7. Sincerity	Use no hurtful deceit; think innocently and justly; and, if you speak, speak accordingly.
8. Justice	Wrong none by doing injuries or omitting the benefits that are your duty.
9. Moderation	Avoid extremes; forbear resenting injuries so much as you think they deserve.
10. Cleanliness	Tolerate no uncleanliness in body, clothes, or habitation.
11. Tranquility	Be not disturbed at trifles, or at accidents common or unavoidable.
12. Chastity	Rarely use venery but for health or offspring; never to dullness, weakness, or the injury of your own or another's peace or reputation.
13. Humility	Imitate Jesus and Socrates.

He used this list to focus on one virtue at a time. To measure his improvements, he drew a table in a notebook to mark the frequency in which he showed those virtues. This table provided him with a visual representation of his progress.

On the horizontal axis, Franklin wrote the initials for the seven days of the week (i.e., S., M., T., etc.). On the vertical axis, the initials for his 13 virtues leading to a moral life (i.e., T., S., O., etc.). He then used a simple tick mark to ensure he had done the actions that could be done as events allowed.

	S.	M.	T.	W.	T.	F.	S.
T.							
S.	•	•		•		•	
O.	• •	•	•		•	•	• •
R.			•			•	
F.		•			•		
I.			•				
S.							
J.							
M.							
C.							
T.							
C.							
H.							

This table was used by Benjamin Franklin to keep track of whether or not his 13 virtues were accomplished each day.

In addition, Benjamin Franklin used a diary to schedule important activities throughout the day. This way, he made sure he allocated his time and used it in the best way possible. He even scheduled time to reflect on his goals for the day and on whether he had accomplished them. While more complete examples exist of his journal, consider this as a start. Remember his request, stated earlier, that you ask yourself the good you can do in this life today.

Although this system of self-management didn't allow Benjamin Franklin to arrive at "moral perfection" as was his stated goal, the system did help him address so many important issues of the day. Along the way, he became one of the most influential people in American history. He was a prolific inventor, writer, and traveler, founded many civic organizations, and was one of the Founding Fathers of the United States of America. In his own words, "… tho' I never arrived at the perfection I had been so ambitious of obtaining, but fell far short of it, yet I was, by the endeavor, a better and happier man than I otherwise should have been if I had not attempted it."

Doctor Franklin (several universities granted him honorary doctorates) was a flawed human being, just like the rest of us are at various times. He may have been simply wanting others to applaud him as a good man in striving to reach perfection, but in fact, not really doing much about his 13 virtues. He may not have pursued these virtues at all in making daily choices. Since we cannot know his intention, we can look at his effects. He left us quite a journal. We each may learn something from the goals he strived to achieve. Whether he was doing these activities for show or not, judging his intentions is irrelevant. He spent time identifying a complex path that he determined would help him achieve a moral life. He left us an extensive design that we can use to seek our own perfection or just to make our days better.

Franklin's system contains many of the elements of a behavior-change plan. The content was based on his view of the behaviors that make for a moral person. How we summarize the actions of others, attributing to the person qualities of good or bad, vain or naïve, reflects how soon we move from objectivity to judgment. When someone we know states a goal he wants to achieve, particularly based on how we have already come to see that person, his statement might set off a litany of judgements about intention, foolhardiness, deceitfulness, braggadocio, and other labels. We do it, oh so easily. This move to interpret ill to the motives of others seeking to demonstrate valued-added behavior in their lives is one of the biggest barriers for many who need a fair shot at change. To guide others toward successful self-change, we need to understand how to ensure that new behavior-change plans have an opportunity to succeed, without frontloading the plan with our own cynicism.

Finding the Motivational Fuel to Start New Behavior

Nadia Goodman, social media editor at TED, offers a good strategy to identify outcomes you want to accomplish. She suggests asking, "Why do you want that?" three times, requiring tiered answers. You may need up to five or more times to get to the core of actions you want to take in terms of a value proposition. See the following example:

Q: *"Why do you want to schedule a meeting with your boss?"*

A: *"To advocate for a co-worker who has been working hard on a project."*

Q: "Why do you want to advocate for that co-worker?"

A: "So that he can get recognition for the excellent work he is doing."

Q: "Why do you want him to get recognition for his work?"

A: "Because I value a work culture that promotes cooperation, fairness, and excellence."

In a real-life example close to this narrative, Alex advocated for a coworker, Ian, to Julia, the manager. Julia ran an efficient office, but work was done in cubicles and little interaction took place outside the groups that at times worked on projects together. After Alex's advocacy, Julia did begin to look at that hard-working employee, Ian, in different ways. Alex, in advocating for another in a desire to be part of a culture of cooperation without criticizing Julia, helped her look at the culture more closely. Julia may begin to see more clearly how she could warm up the office culture, to overtly recognize the efforts of individuals and the team. She did not start immediately identifying the good work various teams were doing, but she expressed public gratitude to Alex for telling her about Ian's good work and she encouraged others to do the same. Significant change can quickly happen in a culture where people are encouraged to speak up, and the manager is prepared to keep that door open. Ripple effects often occur when a person, like Alex, expresses appreciation regarding the actions of another to the person in charge. The perceived rules in a workplace often create untrue beliefs about actions that can and cannot be taken.

Creating a work or family culture where individual effort is celebrated in ways that produce greater cooperation and goodwill might not happen overnight. In this example, Julie's kind but quiet approach had established a pattern of "Keep your heads down, do your work, and no real need to talk about things you see that could make things better. It's just a job after all."

When Julie shared her delight in Alex's behavior, a ripple effect started. For example, Ava, Brendan, and Matthew worked together in an efficient way. They enjoyed each other and Brendan was the guy who kept the mood mellow and humorous. They rarely talked about each other's work, but they were glad they were assigned to their group in tracking and monitoring sales data, delivery schedules, and client satisfaction. Ava was a wiz at data analytics. Matt remained steady and got work done in very efficient, errorless ways. At the end of the day, they could go home without dragging work with them. Ashley, the newest employee who was to be assigned to their group, had not known how to ask for help. Everyone seemed so efficient, and she often felt lost.

Ella was Julia's office assistant. Julia relied on Ella to keep her informed in terms of deliverables and general issues of office management. Ella was seen as advocating for improvements and was well liked. She began to tell Julia things she could do to make improvements, not only in how people received feedback but in her own performance. Julia found that disconcerting. She worried she was not effective. Ella, however, along with Calista and Nicholas, the most outgoing members of the team, understood how all this new feedback could hamper Julia's confidence, even though she was viewed as kind and fair. They worked to tell Julia good news as they saw her change.

Two people who had long advocated cross-training and a method to share skills across groups when needed, wanted to get a process designed to do just that. Julia had worried that it was unnecessary and distracting from the work that needed to be done. Frances and Charlie worked with Ella to get a process designed to easily share work in ways that allowed for improvements in the results and presented it for Julia's approval. She liked it. The morale improved dramatically! Ashley was the first to ask for help under the new plan.

Arjen, the Regional Director, arrived for a regular quarterly visit. He was stunned by the change in energy and output. These small changes that acknowledged each person's contributions, grounded in values the team could understand, made the office stand out. Small changes, sharing how they wanted to work in new ways, similar to the "why" questions suggested by Nadia Goodman, let the good ideas of the team shape the output. Such discussion led to a much better sense of belonging and enjoyment across the office.

Throughout this chapter are practices to help you prepare to take the actions you want to take. Consider these as steps to gain a better idea of what you and those around you may need to do differently.

Getting Real about Showing Up

Now back to the earlier example about how to choose among competing priorities: going for a walk versus delivering a report on time. Such real-life choices may not seem of much importance. Here the consequences were highly visible, and you might think that taking that walk was an unwise thing to do. Neither choice is so important, you think, to affect how you might score on something as grand as a core value. However, they do affect something bigger than the immediate accomplishment of either—the value assigned to "how you show up." In seeking to act more wisely, that kind of concern is of utmost importance. It gets back to trust, to doing the right thing in the right way. You are more likely to choose an action you do in the immediate moment if you understand

PRACTICE 3.2:

Asking Why

Conduct your own why analysis when establishing goals in such areas as your family, workplace, or as an individual. In each area, ask yourself "why" until you can identify the value that will be demonstrated, in a small or large way.

Evaluate your actions in making choices among the opportunities that surround you in meeting one goal over another.

How might your actions now affect longer-term goals and the values you want to demonstrate? Specifically consider how your actions could have an effect on your immediate surroundings or through potential ripple effects across your social setting, even potentially across the larger culture?

its link to fundamental, value-driven benefits for the longer term. You are increasing your skill in assessing the future. We will delve into values in Chapter 13. You may be, as with many of us, unclear about your paramount values. Make values a part of your words and actions but first work to fully identify your values.

Receptivity to Your Values: Mindfulness

In consideration of how we want to show up, a method exists that can help. It is called *mindfulness* and helps us attend calmly and with focus to the conditions around us and how we respond. A definition frequently cited is, "*Mindfulness* is awareness that arises through paying attention, on purpose, in the present moment, and non-judgmentally." (Jon Kabat-Zinn, Ph.D., Center for Mindfulness, UMASS). Many people engage in practices designed to increase a focus on the present through such activities as yoga and meditation. Stress-reduction techniques include useful strategies to relax into the moment and carry that relaxed approach into addressing the most urgent of situations. Smartwatches will alert us that it is time to breathe deeply and slowly. Apps play mood music to help us be calm, to prepare for sleep. It is often hard to listen in the moment—so much to do. If you are to act with greater wisdom, getting your own emotional behavior under control requires doing things for yourself that help to ease the pressures that surround you. In developing a method to be kind and non-judgmental about others, be kind to yourself as well. Allow yourself to gain greater understanding about your values, how you really want to show up in this world. Adopting mindfulness techniques can be of real benefit. Here are three ways mindfulness can benefit you:

- Cultivating awareness about your surroundings and learning to respond calmly

- Attending to what is occurring in the present moment (simply observing thoughts, feelings, sensations as they arise; listening to understand)

- Increasing an approach to others that is non-judgmental, curious, and kind

Defining *Success*

You may see a disconnect between arranging the conditions for success and how to achieve success in general. Unable to achieve your definition of *personal success*, you may assume success is beyond you. The examples we use are often about people who have grown up in extremely difficult circumstances. In changing the conditions that surrounded them, they arranged to be surrounded by varying kinds of support. Good intentions do not always have good effects. We can, however, look at our effects, especially through the eyes of others, and gather clues that might help us better understand the changes that we need to make.

The beginning steps to change are difficult for many of us. Peer review, strangers measuring us against goals we do not achieve, an unfair comment at work, a family that uses abusive words, or worse—those are the stuff of late-night, coulda/shoulda/oughta internal narratives.

Another way to gain a better perspective on our actions is to visualize the results of achieving your desired end goals. Seeking to achieve a values-based outcome provides an incentive to keep going.

Our words and actions matter well beyond ourselves. However, our words may not totally reflect our true aspirations. For many of us, it is the statement that provides us inspiration. Often, we have no idea how such descriptions are reflected in our individual lives. That is worth taking the time to consider. One of our colleagues has written on her byline at the bottom of every email: "The noblest question in the world is, 'What good may I do in it?'" (Ben Franklin). If you, like she, ask, "What good may I do?" and you love the thought but cannot identify the good you do, then take the time to consider the behavior that approximates that aspirational statement: small things, maybe; good enough to begin; a fine thing to aspire toward. You might do many things to determine the values that matter to you including visualizing/imagining the possible effects of acting on your values.

Find a picture representing your values. Perhaps words spoken in the past may be a good trigger to put up on your wall. The "I have a dream" speech by Martin Luther King has shaped a whole generation to pursue goals with positive social impact as their guide. A phrase you put at the bottom of your email may express how you want to be measured for the impact you have. *Practice 3.2* provides a visual way to examine why the action you want to take matters in striving to achieve the impact you want.

To make values concrete, come up with symbols that represent them—involving your senses (something you can see, hear, touch, smell, and/or feel).

Making such values public puts a different kind of accountability on you. Perhaps such statements can serve as a part of getting to your "why I want to change" proposition. You can do concrete things to turn vision into action that counts.

PRACTICE 3.3:

Making Values Concrete

A VALUE I wish to demonstrate:	Physical: Touch or feel (a tree trunk; the wind)	Visual: Images or objects	Olfactory/ Auditory: Words, sounds, smells	Spatial: Symbolic spaces

Here are some suggestions to help others understand your aspirations:

1. Record a family meeting. Share the contributions you hope to make. Ask the behaviors the family members want to do, large or small, to extend both individuals' and the family's positive impact.

2. Ask someone to write you a letter about their hopes for you to do better at meeting life's greater needs.

3. Write a letter to another, a visual representation of the type of relationships you would like to build. Post them or record them for others to understand the effect you want to have.

4. Set up conditions where you frequently get in contact with people who support your efforts to do so in a values-driven way while striving to meet your goals.

5. Discuss your aspirations as you go. Aspire, please.

Making a Commitment

Making a stated declaration of your intentions helps you get to end goals. Incremental behavior changes in one area may create concurrent behavioral changes—some planned, and some that come from others, unanticipated and unplanned. Choosing specific behaviors you want to start doing helps. If outcomes give you a destination, behavior—both your words and deeds—gives you a path to get there. Work to create a behavioral repertoire to help increase consistency in a variety of settings. Remember, however, that whether you keep on or off-track boils down to consequences. It is not enough to have strongly felt intent to get us to end goals. You need environmental anchors you can rely on as well. Clearly stated commitment, how you behave across diverse conditions, and sharing with others, helps.

Rather than changing too many things at a time, focus on a few important ones. One to three target responses will do. Focus your effort on something easy to change. Practice and observe where such patterns are easier; then extend your reach to different settings or people that make it harder to do. Later, you may want to focus your effort where the biggest potential for improvement exists. Sometimes, asking others can provide good clues about the areas of performance improvement on which to focus.

When making the commitment to engage in behavior that brings you closer to your values, Patrick Smith and colleagues (2019) describe the following components: (a) Value, (b) Specific context, (c) Action, (d) Deadline, (e) System of feedback. During COVID-19, you and your children may have been together almost every minute of the day. Later, you may have noticed a reduction in the amount of time you spend with your children if, as we certainly hope, COVID-19 no longer requires quarantining. That reduction in time may be affecting them. You might write, "I value being a caring parent (the value). I've been very busy. I am not sure they know how much I care. So, when my children ask me to spend time with them after work (context), I will not simply say I'm too busy but rather, dedicate set-aside time to listen, talk, and play with them as a group (action). I will find 10 minutes to spend individually with each of my three children as well (action). I will do this for at least three weeks and at least four times a week (timeline, deadline). I will discuss the effect my behavior has on my children and significant others (feedback system). Do they, outside of my prompting, describe my behavior as showing that I care as they, at their particular age, might express it?"

You may find it is not the total time *per se*, but the quality of your words and actions that matters. Individual time may be more important than group time, even if it comes up as about the same amount of time. Make a "habit" of recognizing and valuing your children for the unique people they are. It may turn into something you truly enjoy. Do not assume you must always be this kind of parent, always attending in 30-minute timeframes. Of course, you do what you can do, giving more and in varied ways, but to get started, give yourself some initial targets. Children quickly learn how a smile, a nod of approval, a hug signifies your loving belief in them when you are busy. But actively give your attention to them. Do it deliberately. Make a commitment to be "there," to be present. Listen to them and consider how you respond. Dr. Scott Geller has been saying for 40 years or more, that we all can gain by demonstrating, in visible ways, that we actively care for the wellbeing of others (Geller, 1991, 1995, 2014).

The reinforcing properties of such a commitment can be compelling and sustaining. Strategies to increase your children's comfort with you at home may extend to how you set up time at work for individuals you supervise, or with friends. If a desired goal for you is to increase the number of people who invite you out for coffee, consider making a commitment. Make small changes to see if you get, as a desired byproduct, that kind of outcome.

Having an individual goal that adds value to your life does not, as some might say, diminish the purity of your motivation to make a difference in others' lives. We can add great value in many ways to one another, and nothing about that diminishes the value in spending time with others to get others to spend time with us. We are trapped too often in that kind of logic—*if something is of benefit to me, I am doing it to benefit me. Therefore, I am not really doing this for them, but for me.* Again, stop that kind of thinking! If you gain through good deeds or if you do the good deed without the gain, good for you in either case. If you do not get invited out for coffee after a good deed, and that is the outcome you want, try something else. How about inviting her out to coffee? Reciprocity often starts from one act to another.

Another consideration when making a commitment to action is considering barriers to your progress. This might include uncomfortable thoughts, feelings, and sensations. Barriers might include policy and process rules of conduct. Barriers might include things that leaders assert are necessary for you to do to get ahead at work, but you see it differently.

How good are you at taking on challenges not supported by others to better achieve goals more consistent with your values? In the words of Randy Pausch: "The brick walls are there for a reason. The brick walls are not there to keep us out. The brick walls show us how badly we want something. The brick walls are there to stop the people who don't want it badly enough. They're there to stop the other people." If you do not know who Randy Pausch is, it is well worth the effort to look him up. Wanting something badly enough may not remove the brick walls in life. Not giving up is Randy Pausch's point. The brick walls right in front of you that thwart progress may require alternatives to reach the end goal, by addressing your issues in different ways. But, as Randy would say, not by giving up. Again, giving up in this book is a motivational question, not a question of character.

When called upon to speak in public about a topic that could help your community, what do you need to do to help you give the speech, particularly if you are uncomfortable when speaking out loud to a group? What about confronting a verbally abusive person at the risk of being verbally attacked? Would a good coach help? Practicing out loud? Receiving feedback from a friend about what you say? Approaching novel as well as abusive situations is not easy.

If speaking the truth with care and clarity when you know others disagree is hard, that may be a fine place to begin your preparation. Experiment by practicing new words on a gradient from friendly folk to less friendly folk, all of whom will help you by how they react. Their reactions help refine the ways you make your points, with greater clarity over time. Learn how and when to back away. Not all battles must be fought in an afternoon. Small steps forward can make these tough barriers easier. Real threats to life or limb are times to retreat. No question. It is important to evaluate shifting conditions that put you in jeopardy and to make the wise decision to walk away. Remember, you have nothing to prove at any given moment. Your commitment will remain. *Indeed, Scarlet, tomorrow is another day.* Later, more tools are introduced in more detail to help you handle threatening conditions. Right now, consider, once again, how you show up.

Stop, Start, and Continue

Stop, Start, and Continue, a simple but rich tool, is useful anywhere you interact with another person. The authors, having used it in various settings, different countries around the world, believe it is one of the quickest ways to get in touch with how our actions affect others. Three questions are all that is required and a safe way for others to give you feedback. It is a practice you repeat. Start with you. Then ask others. Then compare. Know that no matter how much we want people to see us as we intend, the proof of the pudding is in how *they* see us. They may be wrong, and you may continue to do things your way, but consider the feedback they give you.

Perceptions about who we are can begin with a single action. While the interpretation may be wrong, it may contain a great deal of information. Don't ignore the one bit of feedback that is different from the feedback others give you. Remember the little boy in Hans Christian Andersen's tale, *The Emperor's New Clothes*, surrounded by many fawning adults? He was the only one to say, loudly into the crowd, that the emperor was wearing no clothes! There may be more to learn from the outlier who states the truth about your behavior, perhaps more than you want to know. You may know someone who says, "I don't need to change how I talk to my staff. Only one person complained about how off-putting and irrelevant my stories are. Everyone else laughs, praises me for my energy and my great stories that make excellent points." Consider, Emperor, if they are saying these words because of your insistence that your examples are excellent or because of their histories that complementing the boss is the best and safest track. The real pearl of wisdom may reside in that one criticizing comment. Look at the extremes carefully. Do not embrace them nor dismiss them out of hand.

Pick who you want to target in this practice. Your family? Your workplace? Your neighbors? You don't need to know who gave the feedback. We all may want to know when doing this, mostly to justify how seriously to take the feedback. You *do not* need to know who made each comment. No Spanish Inquisition should take place after this practice, please.

Set up a way to make this exercise as confidential as possible. Sending responses to a trusted person can help. It is truly a good experience for your team or family to hear about your willingness to work on yourself. Invite them to help you act in ways that matter to them.

After reading these results, your feelings may be a bit raw, but consider how much you gain knowing how your intentions do or do not match your actions. What if you find you are spot on, a beautiful match? Congratulations. That is rarely the case, so don't worry. All the mismatch means is you are part of humankind, intending one thing, but all too often being perceived as doing something else. We are all works in progress and have potential for improvement.

Stop, Start and Continue, done across many settings, is an eye-opening exercise. Try it. Commit to showing up differently. You will soon get in touch with how conditions that surround you affect your words and actions. Ask your colleagues for their help—to let you know when you do those behaviors you are committing to do. Understand that asking others to provide their perception may not be the "truth" about your behavior, but it may tell you how others see you.

Perception does become reality. Unfair, certainly, when you deliberately try to treat people better, and yet, no one sees it that way. Unfair, but that is the nature of how most of us evaluate behavior—how it affects us, not solely by how the behavior was "intended." In fact, the great gap between intention and effect is the place where we often need help. We are often quick to read intentions. In fact, accuracy in how we interpret the actions of other people and their intentions allows us to respond quickly. We have learned to read intentions to understand a range of actions. However, reading too much into our beliefs about another person's intentions often keeps us stuck in the muck of judging and labeling others.

PRACTICE 3.4:

Stop, Start, and Continue (SSC)

Being with you.

1. What behavior do I need to stop doing?

2. What behaviors do I need to start doing?

3. What behaviors do I need to keep doing?

4. Complete your responses before you ask others. Do not share them before others send their responses.

5. Now ask your family/or selected others, the same three questions.

6. Compare and contrast what you hear.

7. Read the feedback and compare it to your answers about yourself.

8. Thank all for their feedback. Let them know you appreciate this opportunity to examine your effect on others.

9. Make a public (to the group) commitment to address at least two areas. Start with no more than three. Ask them to tell you when they see you doing those behaviors you are committing to do.

10. Remember their perspective is not necessarily about "truth" but it is their reality. Leave them feeling good about your willingness to address a couple of things.

Back in the River of Reciprocity

In designing a self-management plan, you must not simply "to thine own self be true," but see yourself as you impact others, no matter how well you believe you show up. That part of your behavior needs to be managed most carefully. To become a more effective leader in his workplace, Sam, a manager on an oil rig, asked direct reports for feedback on behaviors he could change or needed to start doing. He also wanted to know the behaviors that he did well. He said he would report on everything he learned from the feedback.

Outgoing and full of goodwill as he saw it, the feedback was a "harsh" surprise. Believing as he did that a promise was a promise, he kept his word about acting on their feedback. Without his public commitment to act on the feedback, he might not have worked on identified areas for improvement. He might easily have stopped. After all, he was the boss. Although it was difficult to hear some of the comments, he listened and took action to achieve his goal. He told his crew how he heard their feedback in general, and specifically, talked about three things he would begin right away. He asked them to tell him when he made noticeable changes. He modeled desired behaviors in ways that were important to his colleagues. Small changes he made led others to report that they then saw him much more consistently as how he wanted to be seen.

It took time. He had critical pinpoints to stop, start, and continue: Stop telling individuals in the group what they did wrong compared to what someone else did right. Stop insisting that you have more knowledge and thus know how everything must be done. Stop speaking over other people's comments. Stop threatening overtime if we can't get a problem fixed on time. Start listening before speaking. Start acknowledging good ideas even when not perfect. Speak in a level tone. Continue to treat us with humor and sincere and positive comments about our performance that you like when you meet with us individually. Continue being the persistent and dedicated person you are. Continue to inspire us to do good work.

This feedback told him that in certain conditions, early morning problem-solving meetings, he showed up differently than in individual conversations. That taught him he had the skills. Sometimes he felt he had to show up as the boss. He could still listen better, but he needed to let them know why he could not do everything they suggested and not because he thought he was smarter. He learned that in his desire to help people understand how to do tasks correctly, he could seem harsh and judgmental. It helped him stop some actions and start new behavior.

Measuring Progress

Measuring progress plays a critical role in self-management. With the help of technology, this process has become easier. Portable ways to collect data are available that can help you with consistency such as

1. making marks on a piece of paper or on your cell phone,

2. using tally counters, and

3. counting beads every time you engage in the desired behavior.

These are all simple, portable, and inexpensive ways to measure your behavior. Apps, activity trackers, smartwatches, other people keeping track of a particular target you have set—all can be used to measure daily activities. You are only limited by your imagination.

Immediately measuring progress toward goals helps achieve accurate records of your behavior. Moreover, measuring your behavior can increase your awareness of its occurrence. This "awareness" can lead to changes in behavior that seem to automatically occur. For example, if my goal is to increase my contributions to a group discussion, I can mark each time I participate. Each mark brings my attention to the occurrence of this desired behavior and how close I am to my goal. You might even track how you act when experiencing certain private events. For example, how many times did you feel "upset" in a situation, and yet, you acted in a productive way? By quantifying your progress, you can compare it to your goals. Are you getting closer? Do you need to adjust the steps you are taking?

Here's an example of some targets along with their goals per week. You can use a similar form to keep track of your own progress. Enter your progress for each day of the week on your tally sheet. Compare the totals per week to see if they meet your goal:

SAMPLE BEHAVIOR TRACKING FORM

Targets	Sun	Mon	Tues	Wed	Thu	Fri	Sat	Total	Goal
Number of pages read	0	25	10	30	0	22	5	92	100
Minutes invested in talking to and playing with children after work	N/A	30	30	15	27	30	N/A	132	150
Minutes practicing mindfulness	10	10	10	10	10	10	10	70	70

The most effective way to make a change visible to you and others is to graph it. Graphing your progress keeps you going because graphing allows you to see how your behavior improves every day. Looking at numbers written on a piece of paper is not the same as seeing them graphed. Visual inspection of data reveals interesting patterns of behavior, showing whether a behavior is stable or variable. It can show whether behaviors are increasing, decreasing, or maintaining over time.

Graphing your progress is important for two reasons:

1. Graphing helps you see the progress you have made.
2. Graphing shows you if you are headed in the right direction.

Having a visual representation of progress helps you what is notice behavior that is or is not working. You can then troubleshoot issues right away. Keeping in close touch with your data leads to more effective strategies to reach your goals. Several other things you can add to track your progress include documenting the conditions that surround you that make it more or less likely to make progress, as in tracking *when, where, what, and who* statements when tracking your success. To keep it simple and better ensure that you will do it, note the exceptions—interruptions or other conditions that clearly keep you from making progress.

Finally, seeing you are getting closer to reaching goals is, in itself, rewarding. Once any change happens, that pattern is more likely to continue. Seeing progress and seeing how you got there is often highly reinforcing. It helps if you talk out loud about how you made the achievement. Discussing the effort along the way creates a preliminary template to consider in other conditions. Noting the behaviors that helped, and the barriers and workarounds are useful to hear. Remember, downward trends make it less likely your behavior will continue. Make one change at a time to see if you can reverse the downward trends. Keeping data is a very worthwhile activity in managing self-change.

Here's an example of a simple graph displaying the total number of minutes practicing a new skill and the progress toward a goal.

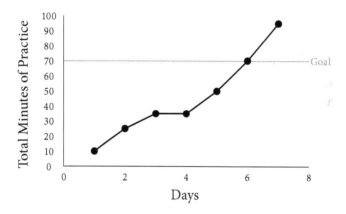

Remember we asked you in Chapter 1 to consider, not only if you get to the outcomes you want but how you will measure their impact. Consider using the strategies described to help you measure both the long-term as well as the short-term effects on various stakeholders. Stopping the bully in the schoolyard may protect the younger child during recess. However, the younger child may still be beaten up on the way home. The short-term good may have set up a bad outcome, but it may also set up a model for how to continue to challenge and redirect bullying behavior over the longer term. Keeping our eye on our short-term effects and looking to evaluate longer-term good is part of the Wisdom Factor. Refining and expanding positive effects over time is a highly desired outcome for us all.

Arranging Conditions to Promote Desired Change

Making the right choices is an important aspect of self-management. Arrange conditions that promote behaviors leading to valuable consequences and bring you closer to your goals.

Make your goals public. Share them with others. Build a support group. Get the people you know to provide positive, immediate consequences when they see you engaging in the desired behavior. You may have a central belief that you want to strive toward your whole life—the rights of minorities or those with different sexual orientations; the free expression of unpopular opinion by tackling the censorship around you; the dignity of all. You may have a much less-noble goal of service, closer to home. You may want to show up differently in the lives of a couple of elderly neighbors who could use help setting out the trash each Wednesday and bringing in their mail. You may not be a Gandhi or a Martin Luther King; rather, you may have certain core values that you want to demonstrate and begin to adopt an analytic approach to removing roadblocks.

Even though consequences are extremely important, self-management consists of arranging antecedents, an outline of your intended actions, at the beginning, before consequences strengthen the likelihood of repeated unwanted actions. Antecedents include rules of conduct or expectations that come before we act. This is when arranging conditions for your success as you begin to act comes actively into play.

Also, look at behaviors that are working for others. Who are those people that display the behaviors you want to display? They can provide you with a model of the needed conditions for success. First, to get behavior going, the conditions to arrange are in the environment you find yourself in as you set out to walk a mile, play the piano, confront a boss, help your neighbors, or complete a task. Copy the strategies your role models use. They can help you prepare for your journey. Sometimes it isn't necessary to re-invent the wheel when

PRACTICE 3.5:

Find the Behaviors That are Working

1. Look at when and where you tend to engage in the desired behaviors.

2. In which situations do you show wiser actions, as you assess yourself? It is not the absence of skills necessarily, but how those skills show up.

3. Determine the circumstances and conditions that must be present for you to speak and act as you want, keeping the longer-term good of others as well as yourself in mind.

4. Replicate aspects of those conditions to begin to increase your ease in promoting desired behaviors.

the key to success is in front of you. Once you begin, consider other aspects of your role models' behavior: calm, clear, steady, friendly, funny, serious? Consider the conditions and what will keep you going (motivational aspects of playing that piano or confronting the boss).

Changing behavior doesn't happen overnight. Change demands planning, effort, consistency, and time. To succeed, attend to data about progress toward goals and targets, ways to measure progress, strategies to change your environment, and methods to embed support in the processes, systems, or people around you. We are confident, if you take these steps and do these things, you will start seeing meaningful changes in your life. If you add a value proposition to the achievements you are working toward, you are taking a bigger step toward wise

acting. For example, how will it benefit you and others? Nevertheless, the best of intentions will fail if the conditions that surround you, including your prior history and current contingencies, do not reinforce new patterns of behavior. Whatever we accomplish has to some degree to do with the contingencies that support us in moving forward, toward the goal.

Adopt a Shaping Strategy to New Learning

If you are seeking to manage yourself and others better, keep these truisms in mind: Forgive error. Help to recalibrate. Celebrate the effort that guided the response, instead of waiting for perfect outcomes. Applaud small steps in the right direction. Understand that behavior can change, particularly with your clarity and help. Start celebrating new learning in all its forms. Include the evaluation of errors as an opportunity to learn. Errors tell you about behavior, but it does not tell you about the dignity or worth of a person. Errors are about learning. Begin to reinforce small steps toward new ways of acting. Ben Franklin said, "Carve mistakes in sand." Start building actions you value through trial and error, demonstrating, when possible, both hopeful and joyful engagement.

If only we could take it on ourselves to create mutually reinforcing conditions where people need not fear failure. Rather, each finds delight in learning, even in errors, noting potential progress toward the goal. Dr. Franklin also said, "Carve success in stone." To move toward that kind of reinforcing acceptance in the here and now, we need to consider how spoken words support or impede objective understanding of human behavior, including concepts like failure, error, or mistakes that somehow end up defining a person's worth.

Chapter 4:

Like a Mighty Wind:
The Power of Our Words

*"Words are singularly the most powerful force
available to humanity. We can choose to use this
force constructively with words of encouragement, or
destructively using words of despair. Words have energy
and power with the ability to help, to heal, to hinder, to
hurt, to harm, to humiliate and to humble."*

–Yehuda Berg

*"Words—so innocent and powerless as they are, as
standing in a dictionary, how potent for good and evil
they become in the hands of one who knows how to
combine them."*

–Nathanial Hawthorne

A large part of our reality is affected and expressed through words. From the moment we are born, we hear the people around us making specific sound patterns. Those sounds become familiar, and we recognize them by making physical movements in their direction or in their presence. Quickly, we associate those sounds with the world around us. Through these associations, words start to have a motivational effect on us. We emit vocal approximations that will shape our language over time. Babbling gradually transforms into clear words and phrases. The language we are exposed to as infants will, in most cases, become the language we develop as we grow up.

Language facilitates the development of knowledge. Language includes rules, stories, and the unexpected in our process of making decisions. Heuristics, close-enough problem-solving based on facts and stories, can make the words we use advance learning. *Use* is not defined as only written or spoken language. We are referring to any form people use to communicate with each other. The deaf, mute, and inarticulate humans among us can be among the most knowledgeable and wise. The words we say to ourselves, those loud internal sounds only we each can hear, influence us. Seeking that elusive definition of *behaving wisely,* of necessity, leads us to consider the words we use.

One characteristic that differentiates us from other species is our use of words, spoken or written, to set goals, among other things—a very deliberate part of demonstrating intentions, a role words play in anticipating and expressing expectations. We look forward to reading a book from end to end, playing the piano, organizing a conference, learning a language, planting a garden, getting out of an abusive situation, raising children to be curious. Words tell us our aspirational options, the factors that govern our interactions with others, and how the context that surrounds us supports or impedes the words we choose. Words, words, words—a most important resource. In the process of seeking to act more wisely, understand how the controlling properties of words help or hinder that outcome.

Language as an Expression of Knowing

As humans, we share similar experiences. We often go through similar stages in life. We make friends, experience heartbreaks, graduate, may marry and/or have children, live alone, suffer the loss of loved ones, have enough food or too little, or experience illness and limited physical capacity. Our different experiences illuminate our individual lives. Living life to the fullest involves experiencing varied, and at times, challenging feelings. Language can help us learn to identify what we experience, often participating in other people's lives as they share advice, stories, or writings. This common stage helps us prepare for the future. We begin to learn how to act when faced with new circumstances.

Hearing, watching, and reading how to prepare for parenthood, retirement, or growing older, give people options to draw from. We access words in many forms to help us prepare for various physiological experiences. Words regulate and modify our reactions to barriers and opportunities that may otherwise be overwhelming. This socially acquired knowledge is available to us, thanks to language—often called *knowledge by description*. We learn how to act when faced with unexpected physiological effects, in part through the words and actions of others. We learn to apply lessons gained through observation; but at times, our interpretation of our observations can distract or misdirect us.

Language expands learning from immediate contingencies to remote ones. Storytelling makes the transmission of learning, and accumulation of experiences, across people, groups, and generations possible. Through words, we can access events experienced by others but not directly available to us. People describe thoughts, memories, and feelings, accessing immediate experiences in one condition or in different places and times long ago. A rich vocabulary allows us to learn from people that came before us as they went through similar experiences. Mentors, teachers, parents, friends, novelists—all can teach us better ways of doing things. Reading books about the way others address issues often helps us. How wonderful to learn from the successes and mistakes of others, not just through our own trial and error!

Words, and their meaning, are a most important method of matching the stated desire about what you want to do and the actions you end up doing (Hineline, 2021, personal communication). Words offer a snapshot summary of how others come to "know" who you are. We learn how to know about our world writ large or small, through language. Science, history, and art are transmitted through books and discussion. Language transforms knowledge into an accumulation of personal, group, and cultural experiences. It accelerates (or hinders) progress. It conveys meaning and power. Learn as many words as you can in the language you speak.

Words to a large degree maintain much of our behavior, with strong elements of persistent reinforcement. Just consider how many of us love to talk!

Philip N. Hineline, professor of psychology, Temple University, wrote about the important role of narratives, storytelling, and fables in how we acquire a vast repertoire of verbal behavior—the words we hear, the words we say, the behavior we observe, and the behavior we attempt to model (Hineline, 2018).

While Dr. Hineline's article is directed toward a specific science-based interest in the meaning of words, it applies to all of us in understanding the power of words and their effects. He writes "...narrative and storytelling... are ubiquitous human activities, and they are important to understand" in how they influence our behavior. He also states, "Stories are prominent in essays on social issues, fund-raising appeals and political speeches, and they are the bedrock of theater. Foundational narratives are at the roots of major religions and of conflicts between them, and narrative has been proposed as an organizing basis for psychological well-being as well as a source of empathetic reaction. The ongoing process of reading or hearing a good story entails interlocking relations between establishing stimuli and their related, differentiated reinforcing consequences, with a story's coherence providing a key to its reinforcing effects." We should consider ways in which a behavioral understanding of narrative can serve both us and our surrounding culture. We read or observe the storyteller; we model after those individuals in stories or narration, sometimes to act as they act.

Words are central to how people behave. Behavior responds to words; in turn, words we speak, and words spoken to us reinforce new patterns of behavior or words reduce and eliminate behavior. Words influence actions through their own reinforcing or punishing properties. Learning from our history to understand how the novel we read in high school still influences our actions today, is not about reaching into the far-distant past. The story and its descriptive power is present, here with us. Tomorrow our history of today will move forward with us, becoming who we are, tomorrow. Seeing behavior in that manner helps to make the value of our learning histories important in achieving outcomes, addressing errors, and repeating successes, surrounded by conditions in the environment today that accelerate or impede desired effects. Ronnie Detrich (2018) said, "If we are to reach different audiences it is important to identify the specific cultural values and norms influencing them." Seeing words as powerful antecedents and consequences greatly influences how individuals with different histories show up. They can become our most immediate and useful tools for learning to be more empathetic or, better yet, *compassionate* as we define it in this book, and can lead to a reduction in bias, threat, and fear contained in different worldviews that words contain. Words may still be full of views we dread, but how they control and influence us in acting as we do is a good thing to understand. This book is about learning new ways to respond.

In reading the following example, consider how words sent powerful signals that changed circumstances and the lives of those who expressed words, reaching well beyond the speaker's intentions. This story still influences many of us today.

Words Across the Years

Ziauddin Yousafzai, as a child, understood the importance of words for envisioning a future of opportunity. He listened as his father gave speeches to crowds, and he was mesmerized by the effect on others. Ziauddin understood the power of language to influence the way people view the world. Ultimately, he opened his own school in Swat Valley, Pakistan, and taught young people to think critically and test information. He hoped this education would help his students become less susceptible to manipulation: a positive belief that would show up in the actions of his first-born child.

When his first child was born, a girl, Ziauddin looked at his family tree and noticed all registered names were male. In his country, Pakistan, women were not recognized in that way. This bothered him. Immediately, he grabbed a pen and wrote his daughter's name, Malala, on the family tree. He was determined to give her an education and expand her future opportunities in society. He wanted to teach her that words influence change. Words can change the way people look at differences—in this case, females in a culture that for generations valued males as dominant, wiser, and more "able" than females. Malala Yousafzai was raised in an environment rich with expressed words, where ideas were exchanged and thinking encouraged. She learned to love books and school. She started dreaming of becoming a doctor and a speaker, like her father. All this changed the day the Taliban came into town.

The Taliban viewed critical thinking and new ideas by women as a threat, or as they would say, going against the religious order. So, they limited access to information and banned education for all women. To enforce this ban, they threatened to kill any person that disobeyed their mandate. Yet, Ziauddin and Malala continued to fight for women's right to education. They became activists in their community and spoke publicly against the Taliban.

On October 9, 2012, Malala Yousafzai was shot while traveling back from school. She survived the attack and made a full recovery, becoming more resolute to her mission after this incident. She moved to England and extended her advocacy to other countries. Malala saw education as a key element in "eradicating extremism and ending poverty." In her 2013 UN speech, she declared: "... let us wage a glorious struggle against illiteracy, poverty, and terrorism; let us pick up our books and our pens; they are the most powerful weapons. One child, one teacher, one book, and one pen can change the world. Education is the only solution." She was awarded the Nobel Peace Prize in 2014. In our definition of *wisdom,* she personifies addressing specific problems for the immediate good that surrounds her and shaping the long-term good of the whole.

Malala Yousafzai, like her father, saw first-hand the good and bad side of words. Words—written or spoken—expand ideas and create greater flexibility. At other times, words narrow people's point of view and create prejudices. Words set up terrifying rules and consequences about disobeying the commands of others. She saw the ways in which the environment that limited tolerance for certain groups, especially women in her case, made new actions risky. But at a young age, Malala took action to offer education opportunities to women in her community because such actions were maintained at a high rate of persistent reinforcement, most likely by those closest to her.

Clearly, Malala Yousafzai is a person influenced by her value-rich history and the loving endorsement of her family. Her words affect the greater good for other people as well as herself. Malala acts according to highly reinforced rules of conduct, including one rule that taught her to persist even when the odds were greatly against her. Those kinds of rules, reinforced in many overt and subtle ways, can lead us all to wiser action. Behavior must be anchored to good values that protect and advance the human condition. Although Malala faced, and may still face, great danger, she spreads a message of justice and equality for women around the world. She understands the power of words, as does her father; their actions led to wise outcomes for measurable and noble purposes.

Interpreting Meaning

The stories people tell us, and the stories we tell ourselves, influence our perceptions and reactions. Words increase or lessen certainty, cause us to stop moving toward goals, or add fuel to continuing the effort. Interpreting the meaning of behavior in given situations and applying that interpretation to other situations, easily begins a process of misinterpreting reality. Interpretation moves to attribution of cause: Why did that crazy, powerful, wonderful, regrettable action occur? Our skills in this regard are shaped by our learning histories and how we respond to people or circumstances. Our subjective interpretations of why something happened often are far removed from the actual cause of the behavior. Judging actions as to intent is influenced by our certainty about how well we read behavior—that crystal-gazing skill easily added to our collective sense about our own good judgment.

One example is how quickly labels, the summary descriptions of behavior, limit how we see one another. Let's illustrate this. Assume we have never met John, a new employee at our company, but we have heard rumors that he is a "selfish person who takes advantage of people." One day, John walks into our department and introduces himself. Even though we have no personal experience with John, we might hesitate to work with him because of the descriptions associated with his name. Now, imagine those rumors are not accurate. They don't describe John's actions but slant it to fit summary descriptions of his perceived intentions. Nevertheless, instead of reacting to him based on his behavior, we react to the labels we and others have so readily attached to him.

We put a lot of trust in our friend, Daisy, who told us about John who "would not help her with a small request and she really needed his help." In fact, according to Daisy, her assignment was dependent on it. We only know that he did not help, and her interpretation of his tone or the value she associated with his "unwillingness to help." According to Daisy, "He did not care." She is certain about it. She describes him as a selfish person. Her assessment is rarely wrong about people. In fact, our friend is very careful to avoid describing people in negative ways. We solidify our wrong assumption when John is asked to stay late and help the team file a last-minute report before it can be sent to corporate. When asked to do so, John says he must go to his son's soccer game; that he made a commitment to do so.

This is interpreted with little data and the usual compassion offered to others who put parenting above work life, as, *"Yeah, a commitment not to help the team."* People start to label John and the label sticks, earned or not. Before too long, people don't want John on their team; not because they have seen anything wrong in his workplace behavior, but because they have heard that "he is not a team player; he really doesn't care." These verbal descriptions stated as the true cause of why people behave as they do are how prejudices are learned and spread.

Labels, good or bad, are called *errors of attribution*. If this well-honed skill of ascribing worth to another's very being were used less often, so many of the deepest wounds that separate the rich diversity of our humankind could begin to mend. Ascribing the person as the source of the thing we don't like, gets passed on to broader characteristics of worth: "Nah, you cannot count on John. He wouldn't stay to help even when everyone else was up against a deadline and needed him. He made up an excuse involving his child for good measure. He knew we would never stop him if it was about his kid." A bias is born. Multiply that by biases about race, gender, religious association, age, ethnicity, and so on. A very big source for blinders and harsh treatment resides in unexamined assumptions about the value and worth of other humans, trapped inside this simple little thing called a "label." Labels are embraced with gusto by the cultures in which we reside. Look for labels in the paper, on the news, in books, among your friends. We will ask you to look at the labels you use very soon.

> *"A very big source for blinders and harsh treatment resides in unexamined assumptions about the value and worth of other humans, trapped inside this simple little thing called a 'label'."*

Certain stereotypes are transmitted early through verbal interactions within members of a group. If we are extremely lucky, we look at behavior objectively to deal with the person's actual behavior; however, dollars to donuts, we all have used labels. Often justified as a commonly understood shorthand to explain or describe characteristics, we often end up seeing others in ways that are harmful.

Language can help us objectively respond to events by putting aside labels about another. Look at the actual behavior you see. Look at its effects. Take care that words don't limit your interpretations. With words, we can become blind to the very reality in front of us. As we will discuss, someone of influence can tell us the sky is gray when we know it is blue ... and we begin to see gray. A person can say Kaya's laughter is fake and we, previously thinking it was quite spontaneous and fun, begin to see it as forced and manipulative; a dangerous slope we so easily begin to slide down once on the *interpretation-of-behavior* bandwagon. After all, why not interpret meaning? We are not fools. We can see, can't we? Well, maybe, but sometimes through a glass darkly.

What We Say About Ourselves

Language gives us the capacity to develop a private, inner dialogue; the thoughts or private events in our heads about ourselves, and how we think we appear to others. Be sure, as with any labels, that you check these self-reinforcing beliefs by measuring them against the events taking place around you. If one is not careful, inner dialogues can compete with those dreary, everyday, external events. The labels you apply to yourself can be as destructive as labels applied to others, even good labels, if they limit your potential to see and act in new ways. For example, the self-label of "Always Ready to Help Others" can keep you taking on tasks you do not want to do because you don't want to disappoint someone else. After all, that label is at least one good thing people say about you. Think about it. How much time do you spend engaged in an inner dialogue of wanting to act differently but see yourself as locked into certain patterns each day? How much time do you spend noodling over what is right and what is wrong with the way others see you? How much time do you spend reinforcing your own beliefs about how things should be?

We learn to assign a word to describe physiological reactions called *emotions*, guided by the context in which they are experienced. The physiological responses to two emotions, love and hate, for example, might feel the same; and yet, the context in which they occur makes a difference in whether we label them as one emotion versus another. We might feel that same rapid heartbeat and sweaty forehead while looking at a person we care about as we do while looking at our enemy. We might ascribe to one event, the word *love* and to the other *hate*. If, because of the effects of consequences in other settings, we do not identify the things we love—or hate—correctly, this mislabeling can create a large gap between the words and actions we really want to say and do in given settings. Mislabeling is the source of large barriers to emotional health. This mislabeling—as well as over-assigning meaning to our emotions—is one of the biggest disconnects between feeling congruent with who we are and being at odds with ourselves or others. So many issues arise out of behaving in ways that are based in whole or part on misinterpreting meaning and related feelings.

At times, you might report being controlled by your emotions. It seems more likely that you are controlled by how you talk to yourself about an experience. The words related to your feelings—depressed, excited, joyful, angry—attached to your responses in the moment, take on a life of their own. You are controlled to a large degree by the very words you use to describe your situation. Choice is blocked. Physical activity may be blocked. Words you use to explain your emotions sound weak and ill-defined, off topic, or full of sadness, fear, and dread. Dreaming may be composed of words and visions that are formed in part by our awake hours, a source of uneasiness. Fatigue may be a constant condition. You do indeed feel trapped!

The more you engage in internal debate that discounts your value, cementing your arguments about how the world around you is treating you, the more isolated you can become. You may want to prepare; rehearse how you will point out just how wrong "they" are. Taking time to rehearse before reentering aversive situations can be a very good practice. However, those impassioned but unheard speeches in your head done ever so privately may engage you in the wrong kind of rehearsal. Blaming, shaming, or belittling can create an internal dialogue dominated by anger or sadness about the injustice of it all. Feeling alone and isolated can take control over how you live your life, the words you say, and the actions you take. Reality may appear to mimic your view. There are no people around to support you, as you see it. Sometimes that internal, verbal control impedes your very first steps toward change.

Your privately held, loud, internal verbal debate can grow way beyond the actual event when you first tried to speak up on an issue. Here you are after that meeting, words coming at you in such painful ways, leading to now. You sit alone in your bedroom, wrapped in a soft blanket, dog at your feet, a bowl of chicken soup for your soul balanced on your lap, by yourself, talking loudly with wildly expressive hands to help you make your points, engaging in what you see as elegant, righteous self-talk. *If only I could have said that!!* Hooray! However, all of those actions will not get you back in the room ready to go. First, let's look at the events you are reacting to, the words that were said.

When in Doubt, Rule it Out

It can be extremely difficult to get out of one's head. Look at those private events, the words, and emotional expressions you attach to the world around you. Use the same kind of objectivity to look at yourself. This inner dialogue—the powerful role we assign to our own thoughts and feelings—increases our certainty about people and ourselves. Often a string of words details consequences that have happened or might happen, that are either good or not so good. Often, they are about past events not occurring as intended, or events yet to be. Words can quickly blind you to reality. In any case, we all need a way to become more objective about assigning intention to the words and actions of others, including ourselves. Take a step back and review any event containing troubling elements that interfered with you saying or doing as you wanted.

A tip out of clinical interviewing: always seek contrary evidence. If you keep hearing or thinking one detail about the way you show up, review a time you did things better or differently. How did you accomplish a good outcome? Describe those success elements specifically: The crowd is my friend; I have done this before and they didn't judge me if I got my words wrong; even if they do, I do get through it; I have a good level of expertise; I am comfortable with confrontation" and so on. Start to build the list of barriers in other conditions and reframe them as simply small steps of new behavior to begin. Work on, for example, making simple statements of fact in the presence of bullies. Move toward more declarative statements, reflecting your opinion, as you build skill in managing physiological reactions that cloud your perspective. In later chapters, we will continue to describe how to demonstrate the behavior you want, even when under aversive conditions.

Making Self-Talk Visible

Instead of events around us forcing our internal talk and physiology to escalate, words can help us get in touch with such events in a more effective manner by using a "running commentary." This is a strategy of talking out loud, in a problem-solving sense, a strategy that can help us all restructure our views of events. What is *really* happening? Russ Harris, in his book, *The Happiness Trap: How to Stop Struggling and Start Living: A Guide to ACT*, describes using factual descriptions to get in touch with our environment and our reactions to it. Rather than being distracted with inner dialogues like: "*What might happen if I don't get a promotion? I wonder how my wife will feel?*" "*Why did they all look at me when I suggested we take a different approach? What are they thinking? They hate me and hope I quit.*" These inner statements are about anticipating events in the future, events that might not take place. They reflect your history with decision-making and problem-solving. You may need a new way of seeing and anticipating outcomes. Your running commentaries about the past keep you reliving moments long gone. Words may reflect how you have addressed injustice as it might have happened to you. Words possess power! They can either enhance or inhibit wise acting. They can quiet fear and reduce anxiety or greatly increase a loud symphony of dread.

A supervisor at a manufacturing plant where Darnell worked, when asked how long he had held his stated strong, negative feelings toward his manager, answered, "11 years and ... let's see ... 215 days. They started ever since he told me, in front of my crew, I should wear a paper sack over my head for the dumb mistake I made on the shop floor. I'll never forgive him." That kind of highly self-reinforced hatred bubbling in one's head is difficult to change. His inner dialogue most likely repeated this insult in some form every time he saw the manager. His crew may have well reinforced his hostile perceptions, or in subtle ways, increased his embarrassment, or they may have dismissed immediately the manager's words or had forgotten the incident entirely.

One's internal dialogue keeps many things going, impeding objectively seeing how events around us or people are currently treating us. Our internal dialogue can also keep anger going, long after it does not matter what that boss or someone else said to us, limiting our skill in moving past the control that individual has on us. Even when their overt behavior changes to our advantage, we all too often discount it. "That bozo could never change. He's faking it. The real him is a stupid, mean son-of-a-gun." To replace that dialogue means to see behavior in the current condition separate from its near-past or distant history. It requires building a new narrative about the current condition to respond appropriately to that condition.

In the "woke" work cultures of today, we would like to think that such behavior by a manager to an employee would not be allowed; but in fact, there are many such examples. People abuse, berate, and shame others with tone, words, looks, and social isolation at home, in school, at work, in our communities, and wherever humans interact.

Words used to describe emotions are rich elements of our verbal community. When expressed, they provide meaning for others as well as for us. We relate to how others feel through words like *happy, sad, scared, hopeful, hurt, ashamed,* or *joyful*. While we cannot know exactly how others experience a particular emotional event, we can certainly use our own experience to understand others' emotions and come to better understand our own. Emotions and the special conditions of the words used will be explored more fully in Chapter 6.

Sticks and Stones and Self-Management

To get to our own wiser acting in the face of egregious behavior, we need to move beyond a personalized sense of wrongdoing inflicted on us by others. If their words make them forever less valuable to us as people, we are repeating with our words the hurt they may have done with theirs, intentionally or not. Somehow, the words used make them, and the people who said them, way too important to our well-being. You could ask lots of "why" questions, maybe going down a level or two beyond the three *whys* Nadia Goodman used in her practices. Internal words are a most powerful and immediate source of self-management "planning." Changing their power over us requires developing a more objective view of why people do what they do. Speaking that new view out loud can help to reinforce new ways to self-talk. Learning to see human behavior objectively is one of the most critical change-management tools at our disposal. *Isn't it interesting that my boss gets right in my face and yells to make her point? A long history of learning how to get her way must have gone into that* (say that to yourself of course.) Be sure to talk very quietly and directly when responding to her, with a smile and great eye contact.

An objective commentary running through our head and focused on the present can keep us in contact with the now, not our history or the anticipated, much dreaded, maybe never, future occasion. One train of thought might be, "My boss asked how things are going and I haven't finished this important component needed in the project. My values are to be honest; so, I should tell her I am behind, even though this makes me anxious." In this example, our inner dialogue helps us address conflicting emotions regarding communicating with others, our actions, values, and feelings. This can help us remain in the present and react to it in the best way possible.

The rules we live by— "I don't let my team down; I deliver on my promises; I never express self-doubt"—sometimes take extensive control over our internal narrative, our self-talk. This keeps us from building new ways to act and/or develop new rules. We may act in wiser ways but for labeling ourselves as imperfect, not measuring up, or other ways we tend to criticize ourselves.

Of course, words are not neutral. They encompass many elements of how we see our world and, often, are overlaid by difficult emotional content. Words often create our emotions. Words direct us toward expressions of hope or despair. They in turn increase our physiological response in given situations. Understanding how you respond to conditions, in anticipation of outcomes is essential to gaining more control over the situations in which you find yourself. Words pull you into or can help you exit such situations—ideally with greater clarity and a sense of calm.

Useful self-management strategies, discussed in Chapter 3, require learning to behave in ways that demonstrate to others your beliefs of good and right in this world. Emotional patterns and how we express them can make us blind to events happening in the moment. Often, we cannot remain present, in the sense that the actions we want to take are overcome by our physical reactions. Such moments make it impossible to explore the possibility of new ways to respond. We might as well be literally blind.

Choosing Words Carefully: Should, Ought, & Must

Words rule how we evaluate the events that happen to us and around us. The hermit in the desert who wanders for years may not have spoken a word but showed through his actions his objection to an aspect of society. Other people then describe in words his wandering, and their view of its effect. Was wandering in the desert a good or proper thing to do in the first place? Using one of our most destructive words, *should,* we might say, "One should not leave society and our duties to others behind, just to prove a point."

A deep well of judging words addresses those who live like hermits or refuse to move to the back of the bus or insist on a helmet before going into the mine or stand up in loud ways for the rights of another in a public setting. Acting wisely in such circumstances is affected not only by the words spoken in such moments, but how the words are said. Never fear. Judgmental words about how we need to behave are always on the ready. Listen carefully. They may pour out of your mouth, with unintentional harm to strangers, colleagues, and family members. Remember, in such cases, to err is human ... to learn to forgive yourself, quite divine.

What does it mean to be good, fair, honest, kind, accountable, upright, a family member, a gang member of a band of thieves or a gang member of lifelong friends, a member of our religious community but not of another, or a member of our team inside a larger division of a company? What does it mean to those individuals in those groups? "Thou *should/ought/must* ... " all such expressions reflect how not to disappoint others. You may be rigid about following these three verbal commandments we are about to describe in some detail. Following *should, ought,* and *must* may help you be the kind of honorable person you wish to be. And yet, they can blind you to the impact such rules can have on your good intentions. From a wisdom perspective, these words, and their controlling properties, need clear exploration.

The first word, *should,* is used to convey obligation, duty, or correctness. It is typically used when describing behavior that, if continued, will lead to criticizing someone's actions. "You should do it this way, or ..." At times, we apply *should* to ourselves, feeling bad about a rule we *should* have followed.

The second word, *ought,* is used to express the advisability of doing something necessary to achieve the desired outcome. The word *ought* addresses a sometimes-unstated potential consequence that, if not done, implies negative things will happen. *Ought* is about predictable and expected duty: pay your debts; take care of your health; arrive on time; say, "thank you." Add "or else ..." to each of these phrases and you get the predictive quality of an "ought to" or "should do." *Ought* is a clarifying term about duty, a suggestion. On the other hand, *should* is a directive term about obligations, the actions you need to do to meet your duty.

Must, the final word in this trio of judgmental words, may impede our looking at behavior. Ruled under such a word, we may not see behavior as selected by current contingencies and histories of reinforcement. *Must* is defined as an imperative of duty, an essential element of a person's day—and often of a person's persona. It is used in reference to duty or when commanded or requested to do something: "You must stop!" "You must read that book." *Must* is also about being compelled by physical necessity, such as "one must eat to live" or be required by immediate or future need or purpose: "We must hurry to get to the meeting on time." It can be a much more definitive term as well, as to be compelled by social considerations or required by law, custom, or moral conscience as in "You must obey the rules;" or "You must do this to show your faith."

Must terms also convey a need for politeness or consideration of others as in "If you are ready to leave for the meeting, you must wait for me, so I won't arrive later than you." It can be descriptive of an unreasonably demanding characteristic of the person, as in "Why must you argue about everything?" *Must* may be logically inferred in "It must be time to do what you promised months ago." In other words, "*What must be, will be*"—a requirement of fate.

These three words guide us when facing choices that could lead to problems if we don't take a moment to analyze what a *should*, *ought*, or *must* statement tells us about how "good" people act. These three words sometimes destroy objectivity even when doing things in a perfectly fine way. While many lessons can be taken away from a book on wise acting, none is more important than seeing yourself as capable of mastering the environmental triggers of daily life. This requires addressing difficult situations in a calm and thoughtful manner; recognizing that a *should*, *ought*, or *must* rule sets up how you respond, dictated by your history of learning. Once anyone moves away from a history of responding to commands in the moment to evaluating them against principles established over a lifetime, we have a greater opportunity to increase our control about choices we make. Such a process becomes reinforcing in itself. This kind of analysis is part of showing up as we want to show up. How we approach our world is determined by years of learning about how to do what we do. Nevertheless, our behavior right now does not necessarily dictate how we will act or speak, even later today. Self-management skills, for example, can change. Even understanding the origins of our *should*, *ought*, and *must* words begin to change their controlling properties. Again, words are tools. Learn to use them wisely as well as stop using words that lead you to do and say things you surely wish you had not.

Following is practice for incorporating mindfulness into assessment. It's not necessarily a comprehensive exercise for doing so, but it's a beginning.

Practice 4.1:

Becoming Mindful About the Words I Use

- Write down when you use or hear the words should, ought and must over a five-day period.

- Write down when, how, why, to whom, and the effect of those words.

- Put a plus where the words in various settings worked and a minus where they did not.

Provide your own quick assessment as to when these various command words worked and when they did not. Were there any reactions beyond the simple statements? Consider the tone and context of the words said by you and to you.

Telling the Truth

When it comes to overwhelming emotional events or regret or pain about something we have done or others have done to us, there are, often, no more healing words than the truth. "I saw what you did, and it was wrong." Those words can be the most freeing of words. Tell your truth back to my truth—something I most likely already know if you are kind enough to provide me specific feedback. Knowing you can rely on someone else to provide feedback about your words and actions can be a great comfort, even as it may be difficult to hear. That feedback can lead to much relief just from hearing another's clear descriptions of the messages your behavior conveys, not feedback used as a weapon but as a tool for change—and hope.

It can be very wise to say, "Your actions (or words) were wrong. But it is done. Our friendship is still alive and well." If your friend asks you if you can understand why she behaved as she did, and you cannot, be honest. Tell her your truth, "I understand you regret your behavior. I can see you are experiencing deep sorrow, and you see it as devastating for you. So now, we are here; together, right now. You are still my friend. I won't desert you as you work to move forward … as we move forward. You did the wrong thing. You can make things better with your actions now and in the future." If your friend says, "Please, please! Haven't you ever done anything you regret?" you might respond, "Of course I have, and I know how terrible that feels."

Remember, you can help a person stay stuck or you can move a person forward by your words and actions. The wiser path is to get to solid ground, away from the sticking points of old. Sometimes rules of conduct that seem to indicate a particular response, may get in the way of the words and actions you want to take in given situations. The rule may dictate your response, while you want so much to attend to the actual behavior in front of you.

To illustrate this point, you might describe a way of acting that predicts generally how you are seen by others. Let's say you state that you are "empathetic." A lot of "how to" books are available about the types of behavior that could be described as acting with "empathy." Expressing certain words is often seen as demonstrating this wonderful human quality of empathy, understanding the perspective of another person. Behaving empathetically can be learned. Indicating you are empathetic indicates you ascribe to an expected set of rules of conduct. Whether or not you are, in fact, empathetic is not easily assessed. However, making the commitment does indicate you understand that such behavior is highly valued and takes its place alongside other rules of conduct that some see as essential to being a part of humanity.

Many people will say that empathetic patterns are innate, a higher order of understanding, a deeper human connection to one another. They may say that such qualities reside inside the person and cannot be imposed by externally demonstrated patterns of behavior. That is not true. Empathetic behavior is learned. As soon as you begin to believe that you have "*It*"—empathy or other valued qualities, arising from your innate self, like wisdom, unaffected by new learning and experience—you are headed down another slippery slope pertaining to assumptions you make about those special traits that are unique to you.

Importantly, sticking to a script to be sympathetic or empathetic does not mean your actions are in a person's best interest, or are done with *compassion*—the next word to examine in terms of how we act when wanting to help others.

Compassion

Among words that are often intended to tell us how a good person acts—*empathetic, sympathetic*—the most behavior-based word in this trilogy is *compassion*. Entering the English language in the 1500s and adding new meaning over time, *compassion* means not just reflecting feelings (empathetic words) or experiencing a similar loss (sympathy) but *acting* to resolve another's suffering. "The component of action is what separates compassion from empathy, sympathy, pity, concern, condolence, sensitivity, tenderness, commiseration or any other compassion synonyms." (Webster's).

Compassion contains two elements: 1) an understanding of another's pain, emotion, or actual experience as if it were our own, or, as part of the human condition and 2) actions taken to mitigate that pain. Timing, circumstances, and your good judgment come into play in taking actions. To support a person through loss with empathy and sympathetic responses is a very appropriate thing to do. Other patterns of behavior lead a person to experience outcomes that are harmful to them and the patterns of behavior that got them there are unhelpful. Sometimes people interpret mitigating the pain as withholding the truth from another about their situation. Sometimes that is operating from great care, first assessing if you believe they can't handle the truth in the initial moments of loss, but it might not be the behavior they need over time. "For goodness sakes, I know Marianna and she cannot handle the truth. She gets nervous and tries to stop the conversation. Better to lie a little than take away her justification for why she acted as she did." The circumstances and context you find yourself in often influence how to act appropriately. Responding warmly and with empathy is kind, and at times very necessary to help a person move from great loss and pain to a time where healing may occur. None of us are here to judge and no book can tell you exactly the words to say or the actions to take in every circumstance. Many times, however, we fail to help even when we want to show our support.

These kinds of responses show diplomacy, timing, and sensitivity to the person and the situation, but they may not demonstrate *compassion* as we have defined it. In every group, someone has said, "Sammy cannot handle the truth. Don't do that to him. Please be more compassionate." Pick a friend described as fragile or someone who shows anger, fear, or denial, or someone who drinks too much and blames it on hard times. Do we tell the truth as we see it to such a fragile human being? After all, we don't walk in their shoes. Providing another with compassionate clarity is important in our journey to help one another. However, figuring out how to provide compassionate clarity may be very difficult.

Deceitful actions on our part, large or small, justified "for compassion's sake" may keep someone from reaching his full potential. Such is the full-throttle protectionism we might do for our own sake. We want our friend to think of us as "true blue," a person by his side through thick and thin. We want to feel we are not harming him by being too honest. But just how do you then offer your friend a bridge? In many difficult, emotionally laden events, a person may have no idea why she acted as she did. Rather, reinforce, to the degree you can, more adaptive behavior patterns without interpreting the causes. Stay objective. Practice alternative ways of responding in the presence of difficult situations.

Learn to speak the truth with compassion in a manner that helps another person rather than adding distress. Provide clear advice about behaviors you see that work well or those that might hinder the results your friend wants to accomplish. Consider time and place—and take small steps as needed. Most people do not see themselves as lying when they offer a compassionate response, such as, "You did the right thing." It is not because we are deliberate liars. Rather, we often learn we are kinder if we don't disrupt or distort another's point of view. As Eric Utne, writer and founder of the *Utne Reader,* said, however, we "might do that out of compassion, to protect her ... she could never handle it, but that clearly comes more from cowardice than compassion."

How do you tell another person the truth about their effects on others without sounding like a pompous jerk? Let's consider words used to justify how we try to help others move forward when they appear "weak and unable to handle this world." Words like *tenderness, patience,* and *kindness* are good words, often valuable to consider in our words and actions. Just make sure that you don't justify your words as being tender, kind, and patient when, in fact, telling the truth would be more helpful, as well as more tender, kind, and patient. The temptation to mask the truth with words we consider as caring is a very big part of why acting wisely is often difficult. We know the words to say, and yet we don't say them because of barriers such as fearing we are treating someone unkindly.

Regrets on the Way to Wiser Speaking

Why are regrets so terrible to handle? The worst of times can be spent deeply mired in our own regret. Regret comes from a vast separation of who you hold yourself to be, your true moral compass—as you have learned to read it—and the things you do. As Steven C. Hayes, psychologist, and author, put it: "You hurt where you care, and you care where you hurt." Very often great regret comes very specifically from what we say. When you break away from your core belief system through regrettable behavior, you might change how you assess the worth of your whole life.

None of this is trivial. All of it is difficult. You might feel better when someone is compassionate, sympathetic, and empathetic. Yet, when someone states that your past behavior is done and does not define who you are today—you may feel a bit better. That may add up to the real definition of *compassion*. This approach may not produce great emotional calm, but it may, step-by-step, allow you to move forward. Experiencing your own pain is not the point, but it may add clarity about regretted behaviors. Having regret is a good thing. Regret highlights a gap between who you want to be and how you behaved. Regret alerts us that we are basically not doing the right thing. Getting caught can add shame. A loss of status with those whom you care about is crippling for many. If your actions were too destructive to you and others, and you cannot move on at the pace you want, seek help from someone trained in helping you get to real behavioral change and a place of self-forgiveness. The following practice may provide initial ideas about how you can move forward.

PRACTICE 4.2:

Compassion Starts with Me

If you are a person who has used threat and fear to control others, you may experience regret, but you also may truly need to change. This practice is a first step toward reducing your use of coercive strategies.

1. Hold a figurative mirror up to yourself as if you are looking at yourself objectively. Be honest with yourself. Start there. Understand the motivations behind your regretted behavior.

2. Treat yourself with care and truth. Look squarely at your behavior.

3. Do not forget that your actions were wrong, vile, unsympathetic, deceitful, or so harmful that others will live with the effects much longer than you might have wished. Remember that you let people down.

4. At this stage, define the actions you must take to increase positive effects. Try a first step in a situation where you usually respond with aggressive words or acts.

5. You may need more structure to ensure you encounter enough reinforcement to continue. Additional practices in Chapter 6 may help.

Words as Central to How We Show Up

Remember, we are mostly known by the words we speak on a day-to-day basis. Words are a tool we have—the most important one in how we show up. Wise acting is, at heart, about how we use words—written and spoken—and how we match our words with actions. Consider how much you use words to command and control, shape, guide, and advance ideas. Consider how your use of words keeps you acting in certain predictable ways. Your words are sources for others to "see" or experience your values and if your actions are true to your words. Always keep in mind that the words you hear and speak may reinforce outcomes you don't want.

Words influence our actions in unexpected ways. Words shape how a person thinks, learns, and talks in familiar and unfamiliar situations (e.g., Robbins, Whorl, Sidman, Goldiamond, Wixted). Words have an active life of their own, affecting the ease by which we show up. Our words are influenced by the confluence of competing, non-linear intersections of prior experiences and current conditions. No matter how crazy it sounds, our words can be analyzed in terms of logic to advance individual behavior.

If we learn to listen to our speech patterns as they define contingencies that reinforce our actions, we begin to understand how to arrange conditions to help ourselves or others speak with greater acuity and impact. In doing so, we may change how we see ourselves as capable of behaving. Our histories of learning can trap us in huge, internal emotional turmoil. We assume we are trapped in this turmoil and we cannot change the internal narrative. The good news is that we can learn how to calm the turmoil and understand how we are operating in the world that surrounds us and gain more control of how we show up.

PRACTICE 4.3:

Tracking the Effects of Words

Track conversations you have during a two-week period in varied settings: home, work, friends, miscellaneous events. Consider how you respond to and use words. Keep a journal of your experience with words. Note the emotions your private thoughts and feelings trigger as you experience words. Note the context, who you were with, and the conversations that went well and those that did not. The six questions below are suggested to help you collect information about your experience with words, either said by you or to you.

1. Under what circumstances do words flow most easily?

2. When do specific words impede your level of enjoyment?

3. When do you stop listening to the words of others?

4. When in awkward or difficult verbal exchanges, what conditions help or hinder your ease?

5. What triggers emotional reactions, good and bad.

6. Examine how your words affect others, considering tone, pace, and choice of words. How do those speech patterns by others affect you?

Once you have identified when you use certain words and their effects on others, write them down on a small pad you carry. Right before the condition repeats, if planned, read your notes to remind you of the words to use or avoid. Pay attention to the differences those words make, if any. If the situation is un-planned, it will require more discipline, but can be done.

As for words others say that can trigger a reaction from you, practice saying those words when you are alone, so they start losing effect. Repeat the words once a second for at least thirty seconds (Hayes, 2019). For example, if hearing someone call you "loser" upsets you, practice repeating "loser, loser, loser" so you habituate to its sound. Hearing a word repeated over and over reduces its jolt, its meaning—moving from incredibly embarrassing to *just a word*, "Not me, not about who or what I can be. Just a word." Repeating the word helps reduce how labels used by others or ourselves may set up controlling conditions for us all. Notice if emotional reactions decrease over time. We will describe additional strategies to manage emotional behavior in Chapter 6.

Words Connect Us in Good and Bad Ways

"Sticks and stones can break my bones but words"—well, in fact, they do hurt almost all of us. Yet, hurting and controlling are two different things. Self-management helps us understand how to act objectively, hearing and responding to current situations—a needed skill if actions we take are to ever reflect wisdom. Words are part of that self-management equation. Managing the emotional whirlwind that often accompanies our experiences is equally important to "see clearly" again.

Each day is a new day, a "Groundhog Day," designed for each of us to strive to get it right, full of potential. Is the kind of friend or colleague or counselor you want in your life someone who sees you as capable of behaving better than you have? As difficult as squarely facing oneself may be, being advised to be less than you can be or want to be because of something you did, can often feel like getting stuck in one's own muck. Listen to the undertone in the words expressed by others. Listen to your undertone. Watch that the company you keep does not, through their words alone, quiet or define you in ways you know are not at all who the "potential you" can be. Watch out for that stifling effect you might have on others. Watch out for that reinforcing high that might come from getting your way by being a bully. Words can reinforce being stuck in quicksand or climbing upward, moving ahead.

Chapter 5:

From Labels to Liberty: Seeing Behavior Clearly

"The most important and most difficult thing that you can change is your fixed false beliefs."

–Debasish Mridha

Examining our deeply held beliefs is an important and difficult thing to do. Beliefs grow out of perceptions and opinions based on experiences that cement beliefs we see as true. Belief is how we make sense of our observations and experiences, explaining how we behave in certain environments or how we engage with other people. Belief is not a thing that exists. We name our actions as coming from our beliefs. The statement we make about our belief is one way to summarize our aspirations. Such statements remind us of how we want to show up. Belief statements help us navigate this world and include many "truths," including our views on fundamental character, government systems, the worth of the human in front of us, or the truth of information we receive. Rules of conduct may provide the *how to* of how we behave, but belief born of experience provides the color commentary.

Beliefs have carried us through many of life's more difficult moments. Unfortunately, many people seem compelled to undermine or falsify any belief that is contradictory to their own. Rarely do we question whether information is true if it confirms our beliefs. If it threatens an already established belief, we tend to ignore it. We don't question or explore those kinds of beliefs. Our certainty about the absolute correctness of our belief keeps us from seeing the world in new or different ways at times. If something happens that competes with our belief, it is often relegated to "noise," "nonsense," or "stupidity."

Knowing what you believe is very important. Many of us cannot fully describe our beliefs. At times this is because belief forms in the moment. A belief might even morph as we describe it, or sometimes takes final form, as a creed or words to live by. However, for large parts of our lives we operate without necessarily stating the guiding principles or beliefs we embrace. We impose our beliefs on others on occasion. We seek out those who believe as we do, potentially creating a "bubble" and the impression that most people agree with our point of view. All of that can be a way to navigate through life. Articulating the beliefs you stand for is a good skill in living a congruent life, responding to changing conditions.

From Belief to Bias

Beliefs are often attributed to experiences that are confirmed in actions we take and can be modified by "evidence." While a very thin line exists at times between bias and belief, *biases* are defined as inclinations, feelings, or opinions we develop regarding right and truthfulness that are often unresponsive to facts. Biases are often inconsistent with our stated beliefs. They are not easily changed through logic or reason. In courts of law, individuals are often asked if they can set aside their beliefs about a person or event to evaluate the evidence in an impartial way. Such a request tries to eliminate bias. Much is written about the differences between beliefs and biases. For purposes of this discussion, *belief*, unexamined, and *bias* are very similar words. In Chapter 11 we will pursue the dangers of how we justify our actions when untethered to evidence.

Biases gain strength through beliefs we hold about "truth." Giving up a bias involves questioning many aspects of characteristics we like about ourselves. Little can shake our notions about people, the news, or how the world operates. We can interpret events even if they factually contradict our biases to fit our own spin or narrative. Biases are elastic, transforming reality to fit our beliefs. Our biases are not easily permeable. Lots of different events are confirmed, not by the facts, but by our biased interpretation—even when others see something very different. Biases are often rock hard and do not change with "visible" data. Our biases are our verbal shelter that at times protects us from assessing our effects. After all, when the unexpected occurs, it was because someone else didn't behave according to our version of right. Biases are endless circles of justifying our truths about this world. Our behavior justified by stated beliefs can become actions based on our unique biases that remain stubbornly unresponsive to evidence.

Justifying a belief can be based on many things, but if we are never required to measure the worth of our beliefs, we may never know how else we could positively impact our world. Bias grows as methods, including words and actions, are designed to get to outcomes, sometimes quicker than as originally conceived. Many groups talk about the need for speed, that the ends really do justify the means that will help so many, thus validating their beliefs. Biases about who is valuable on the road to a better world is a concept that can overtake many types of groups. A community can start with inclusive ideals and end up keeping out the "riff raff" where only a few, with a certain history, remain valuable. Whole societies have been built and are being built, by thriving on "righteous bias." After all, we have a mission to accomplish. This way is better!

Believing that we are better than others justifies so many harmful actions. Look at examples in which a group blindly follows a leader's commands, without considering the impact. Many of us do these things because we are certain of the action's value, core to our beliefs. It is at this juncture, however, when our conduct clashes with the behavior appropriate in the moment and, certainly, for the longer-term, greater good. All too often we don't examine alternative ways to behave—ways that may not hurt others along the way. The way our bias is expressed often is highly reinforced by those around us, keeping the chatter alive and well.

When our actions are called into question by others, we often attribute our actions to our beliefs. Such attribution adds a layer of certainty as to why we do or don't follow certain rules, or why we see people or events as we do. We will talk more about that when we get to values and foundational beliefs about worth and dignity that surround our concept of good and bad actions.

A strong belief system is important in many ways. Knowing how we should act based on such a system is an intricate process. Consequences happen continuously and sometimes change a previously well-defined path of action.

Our conduct based on belief provides certainty and speeds us along in many good ways. However, beliefs can add a barrier to needed change. Beliefs can lead us down a one-way street, into a tunnel, or up a mountain. They can lead to undesired destinations, blind us to alternative routes, or expand our horizons.

Belief systems provide the rules. And rules end up governing our world, for good or not so good. Learn to candidly evaluate yours. Do so, not just by your words, but by your actions and the effects of your actions. Sorting through your own behavior, perhaps you can remember when a belief you held for a long time changed. Can you remember why? Do you have an example of when your certainty about your beliefs impacted your actions in ways you failed to examine? Did you in the end think you had done the right thing? Who was hurt along the way? In completing this practice, please remember that beliefs don't cause you to act. You act based on the lessons you have learned or are learning, and we all at times justify our behavior by how well it fits into our belief system.

PRACTICE 5.1:

Measuring the Impact of My Beliefs

1. Write down up to 10 beliefs you consider to be defining for how you wish to show up in this world.

2. Do you see evidence in outcomes that your beliefs show up through good effects on yourself and those around you?

3. Where do you see evidence for your beliefs showing up in the actions of others, near to you or in the world at large?

4. Specify the circumstances that help you act with ease on your beliefs?

5. When looking back, can you identify a situation when you did not act according to your beliefs? Can you identify the barriers to such action and how you could act to respond differently in the future?

6. Can you identify any beliefs you held that changed and the reasons why?

7. Can you remember when you did something based on a belief that you doubted, even as you did it? What caused the doubt?

Use your answers to explore how belief shows up in your behavior.

Many kinds of beliefs are described as truth. We hold many beliefs about the worth and dignity of others. We hold some beliefs because we see a characteristic we love in someone or something. Assigning meaning to experiences that come from deeply held biases wrapped in noble belief can diminish seeing the world as it is. Learning to see people for their abilities is not easy when you are biased about the potential of others. Anything that stands between each of us seeing things as they really are, requires work. Becoming more objective is a key skill in behaving wisely. Objectivity is blocked by beliefs that distort our view—including situations when emotional behavior might play a big role.

Using a filter that teaches you to look at the details surrounding events, is a step toward seeing your effects more clearly. If you find you are applying labels like "stubborn," "a jerk," "insensitive," "mean," "industrious," "giving," think about why you do that. Hey, you know why. It is right there in how *they* behave. Since this very robust labeling activity is done everywhere in the world, take a minute to explore how it works for you or against you.

Humans act in varied ways depending on circumstance and lifelong learning. Awkward or unfamiliar or inappropriate behavior does not mean that such actions are caused by a flaw of the person or of biology, solidifying a belief that people like "that" can't be expected to be more than selfish or worthless. As obvious as this may seem, it is an important concept and so hard for all of us to apply.

Sometimes people may appear incapable of learning. Why would we label the totality of a person's potential, rather than simply describing their behavior? We, most likely, don't mean any harm using labels. We may see them as accurate summaries of how people act. However, labels do limit potential in so many ways. Labeling others and not giving them the opportunity to change, can end careers, eliminate inclusion, and block opportunities for living a good life.

Ugly labels are applied to groups of people we dislike, describing them in ways that make them appear unworthy of kindness or respect—even of basic human dignity. We know you may never use such words nor think of people in stereotypical ways; but if you do, consider how you developed those stereotypes. Nothing is more important than addressing the actions we should take to create a wiser world by addressing our own racial, ethnic, gender, class, or other biases. Labels distort the way we see an individual's behavior, justifying at times harmful, even terrifying actions toward those labeled as of lesser worth—even when just standing around the water cooler.

PRACTICE 5.2:

Assigning Labels

1. Write down the names of five people you know.

2. List the words you use to describe them?

   a. Labels to describe people include compassionate, friendly, capable, intelligent, smart, generous, giving, and successful.

   b. Labels can also include words such as ugly, stupid, unpleasant, competitive, weak, fat, loser, hopeless, selfish, unworthy, poor.

3. Why do you use the shorthand labels you do for each of these five people?

4. How do they talk and behave and in what circumstances do they earn that label?

5. Do you ever see them as capable and quite different from the label, perhaps outside of work? In their own homes?

6. Do you think your use of labels limits them, even if positive? How?

7. Finally, think of times you have been labeled by others in ways that you did not like. Why? How did those labels affect you?

Learn to see people objectively, subject to the conditions that have surrounded them. Describing their words or behavior leads to the label of "lazy" or "shiftless" or "friendly," and so on. See them as learning beings with diverse biological and cultural differences, interacting using the behaviors they have been taught, with the *capability to learn* from and teach one another.

Do you want to encourage some behaviors? Watch small changes or observe when people behave in positive ways. Be generous and specific in reinforcing the behaviors you like. If they care about your opinion of them, you may see more of the behavior you like.

Has someone in your life seen you as having unlimited potential? When have others behaved toward you as if you cannot change? Such faith or lack thereof makes all the difference in either creating or limiting how you approach your opportunities for growth. Perhaps those ways are to your advantage—"the brightest person," "the most giving human being,"—but often they may limit your capacity—"cannot do things well," "fumbles when facing conflict," "has a chip on her shoulder," and so on.

Labels are summary statements of behavior; and sometimes, not even behavior you or anyone else demonstrates. Bias leads us to assume we know a person "just by looking at them." Superstitions, like interpreting the meaning of someone standing with folded arms, leads armchair psychologists to label the person as guarded or lacking confidence, or emotionally withdrawn. A smile on a face may lead to interpretations of happy to be here, full of contempt, "fake" agreement, manipulation. Smiling may indicate to others a lack of trustworthiness. Why are people seen as they are? Why do we do that?

These kinds of labels come from our learning history, the pride, perhaps false pride, in knowing how to read people. The lessons a person has learned about the meaning of behavior may be far removed from reality. Clear biases about other people or situations may form long before an individual even encounters such a person or situation. If you tend to take pride in your skill in reading people, revisit that. Be sure to check your understanding. Observe in real time. If you wish to help, be direct about behavior that might not be clear or raises a question.

And as trite as this might sound, give yourself a break. Stop using your thoughts or words to judge mistakes or unsettling new customs harshly. Learn first to describe behavior objectively, not subjectively. Then look as well to the conditions that maintain the behaviors you observe. In fact, sometimes it is best to start with the conditions rather than the behavior. Change the setting. You need not engage in behaviors that are leading down a bad path. Reset, restart. You might have a positive impact in many ways. The break we want you to give yourself and others is beginning to see behavior as it is, for how it came to be from a history of learning. Begin to look at how to shape better outcomes; that is, support the behavior you like, ignore the behavior you don't, and celebrate the potential in front of you. This is a much better way to see and work with people than always through the tangle of judgments about the value of the person, his capability, his values, and his intentions.

Good things happen when individuals understand that someone believes in their unlimited potential as compared to a judgment that conveys little to no confidence. In practical terms, look at a person you have labeled. Start with observing the occurrences that surround the individual's particular words or actions. Pinpoint the words and deeds that lead you to your labels of that person. Think of ways to move away from labels by observing specific patterns of behavior and conditions that seem to affect, even encourage, that behavior. Doing so will help you identify behaviors and conditions that may need to change or just to understand another person's behavior.

Beginning to See Clearly: Objectivity

If you had a science course, you may have learned about this concept of objectivity already—"Just the facts, Ma'am," as Jack Webb, famous 20th-century TV detective would say. We will discuss this more in a later chapter related to science and knowledge. A lack of objectivity and the quickness with which beliefs and biases color our world frequently leads to misinterpretations about the behavior of others.

In philosophy, objectivity is the concept of truth independent of subjectivity. In contrast, bias is defined by how one interprets one's perception, emotions, or imagination. In practice, an objective assessment is based on evidence or facts. Assessing behavior is often subject to whether two observers reliably describe the same actions, including new conditions where the behavior is repeated. Two or more people agreeing that the words reported, or the actions taken measure the same result is important. Reliability alone may not tell us much about how valid the results are in producing specific effects—and it does not tell us if those actions or effects will occur again. It may provide us some degree of certainty that the actions will occur again.

While you do not have exact measures every time you work to be objective, and none of us leave our biases completely at the door, work at seeing behavior as it occurs. Remember, to literally describe the behavior you see. These are steps toward objectivity that many who read this book know well; and yet, even among the best of us, this concept fades when we only see the behavior we believe we see or want to see. It is so easy for us to see what we want to see. When bias, emotion, and intention enter your observation of behavior, you step into subjectivity. Most of the time people move quickly from observing a person's behavior to putting such behavior into a framework that they expect to see but often when observed by another, do not see what they report at all, considering only its subjective meaning. When working to keep bias out of the equation, stay fixed on descriptive "reality"—those actions apparent, visible to others. A simple method to increase objectivity can help: Specific (describe precise actions we can see or hear—what the person says and does—in a manner where other can see the same behavior); Clear (describe important features of behavior—e.g., how often it occurs, for how long, how quickly, how fast, etc.); Contextual (under what conditions those actions occur).

Once there, you need not pile on biases about whether the behavior you see is worthy or unworthy, good, or bad; but rather, simply, that it is. Behavior just *is* at any given moment in time. Once you master objectivity as a strategy of observation, you begin to shift through the conditions that maintain behavior. You see the ways in which you and others have affected outcomes by how you respond. Again, the rather unglamorous and objective truth of learning from behavior is not in your interpretation about a person's behavior, but in describing the behavior you see and hear as it occurs. From this, you then start to build meaning. You begin to evaluate whether such behavior is good or bad for others. Be alert to bias in how you assign meaning. Once you add a non-objective element beyond the behavior that two or more people observe and agree upon, you are moving into interpretations that are, more often than not, unhelpful.

Keeping Biases in Check

Tools exist to help you sort through bias. Often biases are not of particular importance beyond an expression of a preference for one thing over another. However, biases become more difficult when they justify harsh treatment of other people, from small slights in the workplace to social policies about fundamental worth—an unwise outcome for all.

We learn to assess a real threat or harm heading our way. Sometimes reactions stem from deeply ingrained beliefs, but in fact, generate no danger to us or others. Rules we follow may tell us that winning is a sign that "On the final game between the Seahawks and the Badgers high school championship, God was on our side," a most scary notion for all those young, God-fearing kids who lost the football game. Rules of conduct might tell us that wrongs we experience must be righted. "No one talks to me that way!" "I cannot stand his smirk; it makes me sick. I'd like to knock his block off." The anger we may feel in the moment often dissipates. Sometimes however, we do act on such thoughts. Being blocked about how you should react leads to high degrees of frustration. Depending on your personal history, you might "laugh it off" or continue a narrative about how you have been wronged, often feeding a bias you have about the person who wronged you. That person becomes part of a larger group of people who have to have their way, who are liars, who need lessons about who they are. That dialogue is dangerous and wrong but so easy to begin, with no easy ending.

Assessing When to Respond

Acting wisely is often associated with individuals reacting to situations and the conditions around them with a degree of calm and composure. They do not say and do things that are not good for the long run. Emotional control is considered an asset in such situations. Emotional reactivity—yelling, crying, or throwing things—is often seen as "impulsive" and if done too often, manipulative, tiresome, or dangerous. Too much emotional reactivity gets in the way of wise acting. Labels such as "impulsive" and "manipulative" resulting from such behaviors may even keep us from helping a good friend develop alternative responses.

You may already consider contrary information applied to both values-based and long-term thinking about the right thing to do. Many right things to do may apply in a given instance. We know many wise acting folks exist, alert to the damage inherent in their former biases. The world needs that kind of self-assessment when seeking to act with greater wisdom.

Chapter 6:

Cool as a Cucumber
or Hot as a Pepper:
Emotional Behavior

"A man to be greatly good must imagine intensely and comprehensively; he must put himself in the place of another and of many others; the pains and pleasures of his species must be his own."

–Percy Bysshe Shelley (18th-century British poet)

As living beings, we experience a wide range of emotions. We laugh, cry, and yell. Most likely, we have thrown a tantrum or two in our childhood or our adulthood. At some point, we experience the loss of a loved one or go through a divorce. We feel intense anger or fall deeply in love. We watch a movie, attend a concert, prepare for a party, or hear the rustling of leaves, transporting us to another time and place. In an instant, we find ourselves outside the immediate, remembering in detail an event from our youth. These are a small sample of the richness with which events in life, tinged with physiology, profoundly reflect our human connection. At the core of that word, *emotion*, are some of the most satisfying moments in life … and, at times, the most difficult challenges in living the life we want to live.

When people are in situations that demand immediate, mutually respectful, or longer-term solutions, wise acting concerning emotional behavior must also enter through that same door. We need to understand this thing called *emotion* to (1) deal with it appropriately, and (2) move beyond the power of the words we use to express our feelings. Emotional events alert us to elements of life that matter, elements that are important to address. They shape our sensitivities and make us wiser about the meaning of being human. It is difficult, even demeaning, to ask someone to put emotions aside. In many situations involving others' needs and rights, we learn how to address feelings in ways that identify reactions that work or do not work, behaviors we like or do not like, and the wants and needs of each party. Emotional behavior alerts us to danger in situations where words and deeds escalate and cause harm. How we manage our emotional life is often at the heart of acting wisely.

Identifying Emotions as a Valuable Part of Our Behavioral Repertoire

The brain transmits physiological responses—flight or fight, for example. The brain and behavior are always interacting. Physiology occurs every day of our lives: heart rate, pulse, breathing, sweating, chills, upset stomachs, blushing. A common debate continues about which comes first: (a) the brain alerting our physiology, sending a signal to our limbs, or (b) our interaction with the world around us sending an alert to the brain. Regardless, people may get the same signal from the same event, but their emotional reactions often differ.

Learning to cry or wiggle wildly when uncomfortable, or coo when feeling comfortable and content as an infant, are common to us all. Our first words allow us to put those cries or coos into action to express our needs and wants. We also make sound, point, and look. Such actions connect the tears or coos with the desired outcome.

At times, physiology provides excellent signals, keeping us safe from harm or alerting us to experiences of great delight. They often set us up for success. They allow us to understand our wants and where sources of satisfaction exist. Yet, when we use the word *emotions*, they are more than physiological responses *per se*. They are not the same as an increase in heart rate or pupil dilation. Rather, they are defined in how we apply verbal descriptions about our feelings to the situations around us linked to varied physiology. As a simple example, your heart beats fast and your palms sweat when in the presence of someone you love. You call the related feeling, the emotion of "love." Just then, a person you hate walks up. You feel your heart beats faster and your palms sweat. You call that feeling by the emotional word "hate."

Whether events and related emotions we associate with them are easily managed or directly threatening, depends on how "meaning" has been attached to such events and the actions taken to avoid, embrace, or escape from their "emotional" conditions. When a big gap exists in how we expect or even simply hope that our friends, family, or workplace treat us, our first reactions may be "Why me?" For some of us, that statement may often be accompanied by "I deserve it." It may be that we have been taught that good people will be treated fairly. If we perceive ourselves as treated unfairly, we may say, "Well then, we are simply not good people." Sometimes individuals think of themselves as having sinned in a manner that cannot be forgiven, with little they do to reduce the shame. Their private thoughts about themselves or even stated out loud to others, produce intense physiological responses. With such a bias about themselves, they quickly misread situations. Every interaction becomes very personal; it's all about them. Individuals punished or bullied in the schoolyard often feel high rates of humiliation and embarrassment. Even at a tender age, the shame of those moments leads to feelings of worthlessness. People who have been bullied may carry their reaction to such situations into adulthood. We are often surprised by how strongly and easily the emotional reactions, first experienced years ago in that distant schoolyard, return when current events trigger similar feelings.

Emotions Are Not Causes of Behavior

It is important to refrain from assuming that emotions drive behavior. Since we feel so strongly at times, that common-sense awareness of the strength of our feelings leads us easily to conclude that our emotions are in control. Emotions are demonstrated through complex reactions to events. Something unexpected elicits a feeling of "fear." Often characterized by a combination of such responses as increased heart rate, pupil dilation, and corticosteroids released into the bloodstream, our body signals a readiness to escape. As labels, words that provide a way to describe our feelings are only that—descriptions. Those labels are often helpful for knowing how to operate in the environment in useful and predictable ways. They provide context to our behavior, telling others how to respond to us as well.

Our behavior comes first. Words explain how we see the causes of our behavior. Saying we are sad gives the impression that "sadness" is driving our behavior. Conversely, contact with people or things we value leads to words expressing feelings of "joy," "happiness," or "confidence." Our behavior is not driven by "sadness" or "happiness," but by conditions in which we find ourselves, ones we might say are buried in feelings of sadness—or happiness. *Sadness* is a descriptive word, spoken or unspoken, that may follow quite logically the sudden removal of the presence of someone we love, or the lack of kind words, or of being ignored. Such events diminish the ways in which our world works to keep us secure: equated with conditions of sadness, the loss of love or status. We may use the word *happiness* to describe finding a sense of purpose, a generalized sense of contentment, or the development of a new relationship.

When we experience events that generate extremes of emotional behavior, we often want to stop interacting. Emotional behavior is equated with crying, a sense of anxiety and dread, and many variations, including withdrawing. Such feelings are uncomfortable. Such discomfort might generalize to any occasion when emotional behavior of any kind occurs. Perhaps maintaining physiological and behavioral control is an absolute for an individual. Anything less leads to a general state of anxiety. Even expressing unusual happiness may need to be carefully managed so as not to *lose control.*

A principle to hang on to when learning how to manage emotional behavior is that our behaviors change how we feel, not the other way around. It may seem more logical to think that we must wait on our emotional life to improve. But research indicates clearly that actions and the words we use have a profound effect on our emotional control. For example, scheduling activities, role-playing situations, self-management strategies, learning problem-solving skills, engaging in physical activity, and other actions lead to contacting contingencies that compete with losing control—that person-environment interplay. You *have the capability to* develop skills to master what you do in emotional situations.

Behavioral Activation (BA) and *Acceptance and Commitment Therapy (ACT)* offer practical and immediately applicable workshops, books, demonstrated effects, direct and clear advice, and respectful coaching and guidance in this area. The death of a loved one may generate feelings that manifest in patterns we attach to sadness throughout our lives, sometimes coming at us through a word or a smell or a forgotten event, long ago. That sense of loss does not mean we are out of control but that we are experiencing the void of a portion of our world that gave us meaning, that sanctioned who we were. Intense emotional behavior is often expressed disruptively, interrupting living a meaningful life.

Asking ourselves why we feel as we do starts to teach us valuable lessons about the important people and events in our lives. With the loss of a very close friend, colleague, or family member, we identify the void we feel. We might experience anger when witnessing an injustice, which indicates it is important for us to see change. Or, on occasion, we feel relief and other emotional components when someone abusive in our lives leaves. Even though great relief often occurs, repetitive thoughts of those abusive events remain. The lack of closure, of explanation or redemption—forgiving or asking for forgiveness—never happens. The turmoil caused to one's sense of well-being may last a lifetime even when the threat is removed. Memories of such experiences and their negative repercussions are difficult to eradicate, leading to personally destructive emotional behavior. Rules of how to acceptably show emotion may tell us not to burden others with our sadness or discomfort. Such rules make managing emotional situations even more difficult. Sometimes, the shock of never really having noticed how much a life or a word or a condition affected us, leaves us unprepared to deal with a huge void left around us.

A person striving to act wisely understands that all behavior is lawful, including emotional behavior, learned through trial and error, rules, and consequences. Our emotional behavior patterns responding to various situations is neither the definition of who we are, nor of who we become. Those patterns lay a foundation that changes. Keep that in mind as you read this book. Nothing is carved in stone about who you are or how you behave, nor does how you feel at this moment determine how you will feel tomorrow. Choice and change, two first cousins of wise acting, are always alive and well. They are made richer by our histories of learning and how we generalize beyond the rules of conduct that governed us in the past.

Our Serious Response to Emotional Behavior

As suggested by Israel Goldiamond and T. V. Joe Layng, professors of psychology and experts in learning, words such as *fear, anger, happiness,* and *care* are used to indicate our reactions to changing environmental contingencies. Emotional behavior is learned, being recruited by operant contingencies. The word *operant*—operating on—refers to how our behavior changes in the face of various consequences, in easy and fun ways and in difficult and uneasy ways.

Understanding the effects of consequences over time on what you do in emotional situations helps you actively work to demonstrate emotional behavior that achieves better control as you define it for you. Learning from such patterns helps you arrange more skillful and more certain experiences going forward. Your response is less controlled by

PRACTICE 6.1:

Catch People When I Can, Doing Things Right

1. Track the number of times you tell people what you like about their words and/or actions, particularly when a situation could easily have ended up in angry words and/or actions.

2. You might want to track the number of times you saw someone stand up for a principle they thought was important. Even if you disagreed, describe what they said that was of value?

3. Note an event when you demonstrated recognizing someone for their actions; for example, when you complimented a mother on her parenting skills during a situation with her child that she handled without anger in the grocery store.

4. Be specific about what you liked about that event.

5. Find people doing things right and let them know you value their actions.

6. Notice yourself doing right as well.

the potential negative effects of people and processes around you. Gaining control means learning to recognize a situation as a threat and learning how to avoid or eliminate that threat. Thus, understanding these contingencies plays a major role in learning effective methods of understanding and managing emotional behavior. Sometimes, however, we don't recognize the signals that set off our emotional behavior.

Descriptions of emotions are important in our interactions with others. Emotional expression holds a sacred place in how we treat one another in our connections as humans. Much clinical work involves helping individuals establish congruence between expressed emotions and making sound-life choices. Equally important is becoming aware that we interpret others' emotional behavior based, at times, strictly on how we interpret our own emotional behavior.

Do we, on occasion, use "emotional tyranny" with our children, requiring that they understand they are to blame for our disappointments, sadness, anger, loneliness, or lack of fulfillment? Do we do this with our colleagues? Our students? Our partners? Do we blame them when they don't express themselves as we want? The harm that such suppressive, dismissive, and belittling strategies have on how we treat one another as individuals, across groups, and as a culture add up to a colossal failure of wisdom.

PRACTICE 6.2:

Using Emotions to Get My Way

A very personal practice of looking at you by you.

1. Describe when a close friend (partner/spouse) did things that led you to use threatening words in ways that ensured you got your way.

2. Did you feel justified in how you responded?

3. Use the Specific, Clear, Contextual method to describe more precisely the events leading to such a declaration.

4. Can you tell your friend specifically how you would rather they speak or act?

5. Can you ask them how you can act or speak differently to lead to greater satisfaction for you both?

6. Describe a time you used angry words and actions to get your way at work or at home. Did it feel good? How else could you have achieved the same outcome?

We cannot address our emotional behavior simply by talking about how we could have, should have behaved. Many of our current responses are based on patterns reinforced over time at high-and-steady rates. We often, unknowingly, interpret the emotional health of another based on biases that have nothing to do with that person's behavior. As discussed earlier, some of us believe we are great at reading people and knowing the meaning of their silence or when they appear unengaged. We are all learners and "labelers" as we go through life.

What would happen if you stopped labeling a person by an emotional characteristic and instead started describing their words and actions? Start considering the conditions that surround and shape how that person acts. Could you help that individual show up in more effective ways? Might you be more inclined to help if you walked in their contextual shoes a bit? We will continue to describe approaches that may help you do just that.

In our everyday life, at work or home, some people are known for behaving "emotionally" and see the controlling effect that certain kinds of emotional words and deeds have on others. As much as we may not like emotional outbursts, those who are overly emotional are treated, at times, with greater seriousness than others who have important perspectives. Often, emotional concerns are seen as reflecting greater honesty, rather than, by contrast, the never-ruffled, calm, and collected perspectives of people around them. As the saying goes, "The squeaky wheel gets the grease." As a result, time and effort are spent in dispute and other issues responding to the more emotionally expressive members of the group, often to the detriment of exploring solutions. Emotional words and deeds need to be addressed, but the way in which words are heard may shift attention from addressing real problems to working to calm the immediate emotional distress. Left behind are solutions that might avoid such distress in the future.

Emotional words and actions—tears, fighting, withdrawal—often disrupt events much more than calmer approaches do in resolving conflict. At times, emotional expressions by another are judged to be healthier than someone else's calmer expression. In those famous outtakes of crime drama, the very serious inspector says, "She is guilty. Just look at how she responded when the news of her husband's death reached her. She sighed and then, after looking around, could not suppress a laugh—you heard it! It sounded like a laugh. Only an unfeeling murderer could react like that!" In this very human area, a perfect storm of misinterpretation based on how people *should* react, leads us down terrible rabbit holes. The sigh may have been the beginning of loss, the laugh sound could be an overwhelming suppressed cry—a push of air that might sound like a laugh—a momentary hope that he was still there, remembering the joy or the utter despair in the loss of someone much beloved. Determining who is guilty or innocent is often much more difficult that we have been taught. Setting aside, if possible, our "great insight" into the meaning of such things as eye contact, folded hands, rigid posture, crying, sighing, a forced sound (unclear as to the message that sound really might convey). The subtle cues in behavior do tell us something. But making too much of your interpretation of that meaning, is dangerous, and often, fundamentally wrong.

Emotional expression sometimes is equated with truthfulness, the "real way" a person feels. And yet, those two words—*emotion* and *truth*—are not the same. Emotional words and actions may convey deep distress. At times, more cynically, they reflect absolutely no feelings being felt by the speaker. Emotional words and deeds have the power to quiet, threaten, or manage others' responses, leading at times to an individual getting one's way. Success when exhibiting large, controlling emotional behavior leads to the appearance of good results as in our partner acquiesces to our wishes, or our child stops crying, or we win an argument and get our way. Over time, or even in the short run, such controlling strategies are dangerous for many reasons. Success in using emotional behavior creates a high degree of certainty that such patterns may need to escalate if they are to continue to successfully control. Others avoid or dislike how we control them. Such actions lead to harmful reactions toward us by others. Particularly difficult is when people we value decide to exit our lives. Better to learn how to objectively examine the situation, use our behavior differently, and find success in calmer interactions.

To benefit from reaching the desired target, reduce emotionally controlling content that masks hearing, seeing, thinking, planning, acting, and evaluating. Admittedly, there is something about the drama of keeping people in perpetual uncertainty about whether tonight will be a calm or an explosive one. For 100 years, the Hatfields and Mccoys continued a bitter fight among family members. Terrorists in any city in the world encourage vile words with strong displays of emotion toward their enemies. Divorce often ends in huge disputes and hurtful words far removed from the original reasons for pairing or parting. Wisdom, as in wise acting, seldom shows up in such settings. Under such conditions, it is demonstrably hard for the people directly involved to hear, see, think, plan, act, and test methods that involve less anger, fighting, or bitterness. The emotional "buzz" itself often sustains and overpowers us.

A common belief is that others can't possibly understand who we are and where we have been if they haven't walked in our shoes. They will be unable to comprehend our sadness, exclusion, or anger. Perhaps not always a perfect match, but one of the beauties of being human is that we so often do relate to others' experiences. We might not repair others' hurt; nor have we necessarily personally experienced their experiences, but we understand a wide range of emotions.

Learning how to handle emotional behavior with clarity and calm helps us engage in helpful ways to those in need—a very important skill in learning to speak and act more wisely. We need to arrange conditions to compete with the reinforcement of being that out-of-control person located right in the center of attention. Again, not a flaw of character, but keep in mind how the conditions that surround a person keeps behavior going. To compete with such a reinforcing history, we may need a plan that differentially reinforces other behavior to get us much closer to wiser behavior. Just how do we learn to calmly handle emotional behavior?

A Culture where Emotions are Treated as Steps Toward Self-Control

Few cultures directly teach their youngsters how to respond to feelings, creating interpersonal problems, and for some, a sense of being controlled by the ways they respond to emotional events. In the early 1960s, Jean Briggs, an anthropologist, traveled to the Arctic Circle to live with an Inuit family for 17 months. Although living conditions were harsh, Briggs noticed adults in this community showed an amazing capacity for "self-control." They never reacted with anger or frustration. That was in sharp contrast to how Briggs reported responding regularly. Her emotional responses were seen by her Inuit family as childish and started to cause problems. "I wanted to know what had gone wrong in my relationships with my Inuit family, so that I could restore those relationships. The Inuit themselves conceptualized the problem in emotional terms: 'She's not happy here; she gets angry easily'" (Briggs, 2000).

Intrigued by this, Briggs turned to the study of how the Inuit learned to handle emotions. She observed that adults never raised their voice or used time-out as parenting strategies. They relied on role-play scenarios as a teaching strategy. Children learned how to respond to emotional situations through these dramatizations. Adults would ask them questions about possible ways to respond, then dramatize potential consequences through play. For example, a parent would wait to respond to his child until the child had calmed down after an emotional display. The two would then lightly role-play the scenario. Adults presented children with alternatives and asked them how they would respond. If the child repeated the undesired behavior, the parent would keep asking the child how else she could react. Over time, children generated alternative responses.

Teaching our children—and ourselves—alternative skills to handle emotional situations is one of the hallmarks of acting with wisdom. This practice among the Inuits allowed children to learn while they were calmer. They discovered that yelling and walking away are not effective ways to solve problems. They began to identify social cues that could guide them in how to respond.

"Teaching our children—and ourselves—alternative skills to handle emotional situations is one of the hallmarks of acting with wisdom."

The lesson here, and the lesson we see in our schools' teaching children how to handle emotional behavior today, is that alternative responses to angry or painful emotional expressions are necessary to live and work together successfully. Even in our current society, men and women frequently have been taught rules about how they should behave. Men, generally, should not express emotions like fear, pain, and loneliness. Too often, men are taught that asking for help is a weakness. Many would say we have moved far beyond this Neanderthal approach to masculinity, but in practice, not very far at all. This area needs attention regarding our use of words, often born of our biases. The language about "correct" and "true," so often does, if understood to be how each person should act, limit the potential of us all. They feed off our biases about the "correct" way for people to behave.

Failure at a task, the loss of status, the non-option to talk about how to act, and many other cultural constructs of masculinity make for the terrible trend of the isolated male. In a growing number of focus groups to address this issue, men are encouraged to express their feelings, but cultural expectations are rather deeply ingrained. Cultural givens or codes of conduct shape our view of "manliness." This vulnerability is not limited to men. They also shape our opinions of how a "real woman" should speak and act or how different races should speak and act—the many assumptions about how *other people* should act in this world.

Loss of Control

People describe events that led them to violate their moral code. The action taken was largely outside their definitions of "good" or "of value." When this happens, many emotional patterns are summarized by the word *shame*. Experiencing intense feelings of guilt is most destructive when the person does not have effective means of "counter-control." Complex skills that sum to resilience are often needed to get beyond this loss of self-esteem and confidence.

Counter-control is part of B. F. Skinner's analysis of social behavior. He describes needing to develop counter-control as managing behavior born of aversively controlling events. These control techniques exist in society's structures and processes—or our local social group—including rules of acceptable social interactions, the use of threat and fear, and institutionally codified suppression of diverse interests. When people experience aversive control, they often engage in various emotional responses including aggressive or avoidance behavior.

In his article, "Countercontrol in Behavior Analysis," Dennis J. Delprato stated that examining countercontrol techniques further defines cultural concepts like "freedom." These concepts inform the development of strategies for those with little political or economic control to manage the downpour of emotional distress they regularly experience. A network of friends and colleagues helps. Changes at the level of institutional structures and processes, opening new doors for those living under controlling systems, are of importance in making the kinds of changes that provide individuals a sense of real freedom and dignity in managing their daily lives. That tension between individuals and institutional processes and procedures that impose a required way to act, particularly as a member of a particular group, needs to be examined carefully. As B. F. Skinner (1956) wrote, something we may all agree with, "It is only through such counter-control that we have achieved what we call peace—a condition in which men are not permitted to control each other through force. In other words, control itself must be controlled." Social, legal, and procedural control over how one person acts, compared to how other persons act, is at the heart of many issues of society's "isms."

When individuals do right as they see it, that action bears repeating. But when individuals fail to do the right thing, a feeling of shame might remain. Those who are given tools to examine the flaws in their self-talk regarding their self-worth, and how to do things differently, stand a much better chance of moving on from shame. Sudden loss of reinforcement is often at the heart of our most difficult emotional moments—death, disappointment, abandonment, or isolation. But other events that change how we are perceived can lead to equally distressing behavior. Believing ourselves culpable or in some way blamed or shamed for something as simply acting as we always have or being who we have always perceived ourselves as being, leads to unrelenting emotional distress.

On the Use of Shame

Brené Brown, professor and researcher of social work at the University of Houston, describes such feelings of shame, among other things, as an intensely painful experience of believing that we are flawed and therefore unworthy of love and belonging. Her work addresses the profound loss experienced by those who are shamed by groups or across society. Shaming is very much alive and well in the USA, a quick way of letting others know they have violated some tenet held sacred by their group. Whether society disapproves, admonishments occur in the classroom, or a parent disciplines a child, shaming's lasting effects are not examined sufficiently. Shaming is easy. Substituting another behavior may be difficult, but the harm done to others by using shame often lasts a lifetime.

For example, when deeply shaming events occur publicly, the withdrawal of reinforcement in an environment surrounded by friends and colleagues whom we believed thought the best about us or we believe we have let down, leads to extreme reactions. We may feel as if we are unable to function. Sleeping is impossible. Moving around and engaging in daily tasks comes to a halt. Our self-talk becomes full of aggressive statements about others or ourselves. We may stop eating. Our life slows down, even to the point that it does not feel worthwhile to go on. To avoid such a loss of self-worth, learn how to anticipate and adapt to sudden changes that literally remove things we dearly love. It is not an easy task to anticipate and adapt to the potential loss of the elements in our life that give us meaning and security. The public part of how others might treat us—shaming or blaming—does not, however, have to stop us in our tracks. How might we respond with less destructive thoughts and actions when experiencing these kinds of hits in life?

Handling Emotionally Laden Words and Actions

It takes observation, objectivity, and preparation to gain control over circumstances in which you usually have aggressive thoughts or act in ways that would be described as aggressive. When someone yells in your face, are you able to say to yourself, "Hmm, an interesting way of maintaining control over me, yelling in such an aggressive manner"? or, do you think, "You will never talk to me that way!"? Are you able to step back to examine the other person's behavior and think about why they are behaving in such a manner? Can you imagine the possible consequences that are controlling his behavior? Learning to calm your initial reactions through stress management and anger-control techniques will give you time to calmly assess the threat, or lack thereof.

When we believe our emotions are causing us to behave in ways beyond our control, we have not adequately identified where the control lies. We have learned to attribute our actions to emotions driving us, but we act according to the conditions and history we bring to situations. We know that under a certain circumstance, we act in ways we might later call "stupid." Still, we open our mouths, and there we are. If emotional words and actions get in your way at times, a bit of initial advice is to gentle down. Yes, easier said than done.

When facing events that contain emotional content, the behaviors we exhibit are all learned—clenching our fists when angered, crying when seeing someone in distress, remaining decidedly quiet, or laughing at a good joke. In learning how to respond to highly charged events, getting physiological reactions under control is an important step.

"An important thing to do in learning how to respond to highly charged events is to deliberately learn how to get your physiological reactions under control."

A course in stress reduction helps. Deep-breathing techniques are often important in that breathing deeply is often just the opposite of what you feel like doing. Learning to calm the rapid rate of your heart when difficult physiological reactions are triggered helps. Stress over time is a very debilitating condition. If your level of stress as you see it is too high, or has gone on too long, seek help from qualified professionals. Many of us don't seek the help we need because we have been taught that needing this kind of help—help with our emotional life—is weak or shameful. Seeking help is a brave and good thing to do. You help yourself and you help those around you with every step you take to learn how to manage your emotional life better.

Responding in the Face of Emotional Triggers

Dr. Ray Novaco is a clinical psychologist and Professor of Psychological Sciences at University of California, Irvine. His body of work—research, clinical practice, and teaching—has focused on anger and tools to help manage it. Novaco has been writing about the effects of anger for 40 years. His research-derived application tools were drawn from those experiencing the full range of aggressive behavior—prisoners and others who dealt with anger issues their entire lives. He might advise us to become adept at handling certain emotional signals: anger before rage, love before obsession, sadness before despair. Dr. Novaco found those who reported anger-control issues were not particularly effective in addressing the concept of "self-control." As he puts it, "Anger dyscontrol involves a serious degradation in self-monitoring. One cannot regulate troublesome internal states without proficiency in self-monitoring" (Novaco, 2011). When any emotional event impedes our focus on what is urgent or most important, then that emotional expression (overtly or in our heads) becomes problematic.

Novaco suggests behaving in response to emotional cues when they

- become too frequent,
- become too intense,
- last too long,
- lead to physical actions labeled as "aggressive,"
- lead to doing and saying hurtful things to others, or
- disturb relationships with people or events that are part of our daily lives.

The risk for you, as well as others, is high if you simply ignore these signals. Patterns of self-management in addressing our own behavior arise directly from such criteria as to their frequency, intensity, duration, significance, and urgency. Begin noticing emotional signals and take notes on these dimensions to determine if it is something you need to focus on. This list applies to other behavior patterns as well.

These kinds of signals have been used in many settings to help determine when behavior needs attention in clinics, schools, the workplace, or in family life. Learning when to leave behavior alone and when to intervene or ask for help is important—with our own and other people's behavior. Along a continuum, behavior is almost always allowed to be expressed as individuals in our society desire, as long as it does no harm to self or others. That does not mean that changes might make you or someone else more content.

Start with assessing your behavior. Occasionally, you might feel angry and kick the trash can in your office. Do it more than once, and it may well be a problem. For some, once is too much. Learning how to handle actions and words without the kick may need a deliberate shaping strategy. That strategy may demand good observation by you to pinpoint *when, what, where,* and *how* events happen that are upsetting. Recognizing those conditions will allow you to be more aware of emotional behavior before it rages out of control.

PRACTICE 6.3:

First Steps Toward Emotional Control

Big triggers lie in facing aversive events or people.

1. Make a list of conditions that increase the likelihood of producing unpleasant or destructive behavior, whether observable to others or buried in your self-talk.

2. What is most difficult for you to manage during emotionally laden events?

3. What is helpful to maintaining emotional control?

What do you need to do to better manage your self-talk and actions? Remember the Inuit strategy: ask how else you could react. Again, there is nothing wrong with behaving emotionally except when it gets in the way of the action you want to take, or causes harm to you, to others, or to longer-term effects that are not good for society at large. Look at the Appendix to find links to various methods and tools that Novaco, Hayes, Layng, and Brown have developed in handling difficult emotional behavior and related content.

How do you remain objective when entering an "emotional setting" or with people who you really do not like? We act with greater precision if we navigate through the emotional complexity with the help of certain skills: 1) pinpointing precisely what is happening to us and to others—a part of the setting we rarely examine enough; 2) knowing that behavior is maintained by histories of reinforcement and how we respond to them; 3) developing skills in alternative ways to address core issues that produce emotional behavior; and 4) looking at the conditions, those sources of reinforcement, that promote behaving in one way or another. The timing, type, and certainty of consequences negatively or positively affecting your words and actions are also a big part of the equation.

Remember not to assign too much weight to the words you use in describing your emotional distress. Consider using fewer words. Listening instead of talking can help to clarify another's point of view. Even if you disagree, state the message you heard, seeking to ensure you understood, without adding emotion or evaluation to the conversation. Relate the words spoken back to the events. Remember to be objective, clear, calm, and immediate in identifying the message you understand and identifying areas still in need of addressing. Look at how others have a stake in the debate and see issues that you truthfully support—not to manipulate others to gain compliance, but because you truly believe their view has value. Does anything still make you angry or sad or anxious about being "misunderstood"? Is it the situation that is happening or the absence of something you expected? How do you reduce your anger?

As we said above: Look before you listen. Listen before you talk. Stay calm and carry on. Practice breathing. Exit, take a break, and return to the room if necessary. Get a drink of water. Be aware of your needs or wants and that of the other person or persons. Identify the "anger-producing" parts of the interaction and pinpoint the issues, not the feelings. The goal of someone behaving wisely is to hear and sort. In the end, even with less than perfect agreement, everyone might be ready to move forward.

Dr. Ken Silverman's work, which is discussed later, has demonstrated how difficult it is to exhibit high-and-steady rates of new behavior when reentering the exact same conditions in which you experienced threat, fear, or loss in the past. The same is true in conditions when you used threat and fear to control others. The old patterns, not only of yours but of others, return, sometimes with a vengeance. Dr. Eric Ericsson has much to offer about how we practice new patterns, and his work is described later as well.

Know that removing yourself altogether is necessary when the conditions that triggered emotional behavior remain dangerous to you and others, either directly through physical threat or psychological damage to self-esteem and well-being. Very little of our advice about your skills in learning to manage your emotions, to develop inoculation strategies, applies to those extreme kinds of conditions. Remove yourself from dangerous conditions. If you are feeling like you might harm yourself, seek help. No matter how bleak, every possibility exists for a new and better day, but you must be here to experience it!

How we arrange conditions to effectively deal with emotional reactions, sets up better or worse outcomes. As for acting wisely, emotional behavior may interfere with clear-headed objectivity. In Chapter 7, strategies to prepare for and address emotional content are explained in detail as recommended by Novaco. We also have reference materials for other outstanding strategies contained in Hayes' and Brown's work. Words are a large part of our emotional behavior. Our use of words sparks the potential emotional powder keg between us and others waiting to explode.

In attending to skills that sum to wisdom, it is helpful to have role models who are good at perceiving, evaluating, and handling emotions, particularly if you have a history that makes this topic difficult. We need role models in our lives—mature, empathetic, and genuine about their own strengths and needs—to help us evaluate events and deal with those conditions directly, with clarity and calmness. We may not have such wise actors readily available. Seek them out. Ask for help. Learning to reduce the control negative emotional events of the magnitude of anger or rage have on each of us is an important part of learning to act wisely. We continue with this topic in Chapter 7.

Chapter 7:

Anger Mismanaged:
Blowing Out the Lamplight of Reason

*"I have learned that people will forget what you said,
they will forget what you did, but they will never forget
how you made them feel."*

–Maya Angelou

*"Let us not look back in anger nor ahead in fear,
but around in awareness."*

–James Thurber

In writing about emotional behavior, we were aware that some who read this book may be in conditions where they experience, either through words or actions, the powerful and destructive motivational control captured in one word: *anger*. Learning more about the work by Dr. Novaco, mentioned earlier, may help. Several components of this chapter originated from a mimeographed manual provided to Dr. Darnell Lattal, co-author of this book, decades ago, with permission to use the manual in her clinical practice. She found the contents of the manual beautifully pragmatic, which is why the content is extracted and reused here, again with Dr. Novaco's permission.

You may be a victim of abuse, coercive strategies of change, or you may behave angrily to get your way. Using various angry behaviors effectively often leads to addictive behavior patterns, at times with terrible and occasionally unintentional outcomes. Because the use of threat and fear is so prevalent in our society, and so overwhelmingly destructive to wise acting, we added this specific chapter to provide a few tools that have proven effective by introducing methods of counter-control. Building and reinforcing new patterns of behavior across a range of abusive situations is key.

How does any of us inoculate ourselves to address, in the moment, emotional content with a calm, clear, and effective strategy? A simple-sounding solution is to learn to do things differently in the same settings that triggered our last outburst or produced bad effects based on how others responded. Working on new ways of responding helps us see volatile occurrences and our role in perpetuating such occurrences more objectively. This approach gives us the opportunity to handle emotional content differently in the future, beyond just the effective management of anger.

Self-control is when one remains calm and in control through difficult situations. That does not mean those demonstrating self-control don't experience strong feelings; but it does mean that they are sufficiently skilled to hear, engage, and work toward a better outcome than those who do not exhibit self-control.

You may know the sound ... words buzzing around in your head, which take on a life of their own; sometimes to the point you are talking out loud to yourself and making the most stellar arguments and confrontational speeches. If only you could deliver those exact words to your provocateur. The better side of valor helps you reframe. Yet, adrenaline pumps so hard, you often cannot think straight, let alone act in the best interest of yourself and others.

Real-life research is helpful when looking at actual consequences that led to the ways in which individuals handled things like embarrassment and hurt, and that special category, shame, that Brené Brown described so well, mentioned in Chapter 6. The meaning of words and how we interpret their specific meaning about us, whether intended or not, is important.

Emotional content leads to undesired outcomes—anger growing into rage, love unreciprocated growing into obsession, or sadness becoming despair. Related emotional cues become problematic when they lead to actions that are too frequent, too intense, or last too long. When such events lead to behavior labeled as "angry," self-control is often absent. The risk of continuing or escalating harmful outcomes is high in such situations, with reinforcement coming from dealing with those situations in ways that work for us, usually in the moment. When attempting to deal with the loudmouth in the room, a calm approach escalates quickly to expressing anger through verbal or even physical aggression. Such behavior sets up a cycle of loss of control and regret, with little opportunity to change real-time behavior, except to make a promise that next time, "I'll handle that better."

Novaco suggests that anger has many benefits as well as drawbacks. The following seven points summarize those benefits and drawbacks, based on his original work as mentioned above.

1. Anger is an emotional reaction to stressors, such as deliberate provocations or barriers to getting things done. Those provocations seem mild to some, yet very difficult to others. It all depends on their behavioral histories.

2. With anger, we may either fail to sort out issues and become quite impulsive, ready to act; or we address an issue that has bothered us and find that such an act helps to address the unproductive response of the past. From such actions come the satisfaction that lets us know how to better behave with a difficult person or event, leading to some progress. Once we realize how different elements exert control over us or others— words spoken attached to meaning played out in our imagination or played out in real life, and physiology that drives out everything else—we learn new intervening behaviors to guide us through such difficult times.

3. Anger has positive functions. It energizes us, mobilizes us toward self-defense, and provides the stamina we may need in difficult situations. The more we practice how to express ourselves when feeling anger, the better we get at describing the words/actions/conditions that are bothering us or, to address the words/actions/conditions that are bothering someone else. That adaptive skill is essential to constructively deal with anger.

4. Anger provides information about people and situations that bother us. Learning to recognize this is important. Feeling anger provides a needed cue that something is not working or is amiss. Often, we cannot extract the cues that distress us, but with practice we begin to identify the specific actions that preceded highly predictable and often ineffective actions on our part. Interrupting our interpretation of the meaning of words and actions changes how we respond.

5. Anger gives us enough energy to act. Sometimes we step up when the level of anger is too high, knowing it is time to diffuse or exit the situation.

6. On the other hand, anger disrupts our thoughts and feelings. It keeps us from being that wise actor in control, helping ourselves and others find good ways to deal with confusing and provoking situations. When we get hurt or embarrassed, we may engage in our ideas of solid, protective behavior. When our sacred beliefs are attacked, we may feel we need to defend them. Those actions drain energy from more productive ways of behaving.

7. We may use anger to intimidate or control others. If you find yourself demonstrating a lot of angry behavior, seek help. Controlling others and our world through aggression, threat, and fear, is powerful, often highly addictive, and a very dangerous pattern to our long-term well-being.

If we master the skills of introducing new behavior through deliberate practice, our behavior changes toward more appropriate patterns, step by careful step. Seeing mistakes or missteps as providing good information for improvement often helps individuals persist toward more productive ways of acting. Unfortunately, time is consumed dealing with people imposing their point of view without compromise. It is understandable that avoiding the aggressor, and the threat and fear in how that person might respond, may seem the only reasonable thing to do. Sadly, such compliance does nothing to teach the aggressor better ways to respond in the future. Rather, maintaining and strengthening such action, we are left feeling powerless, yet still angry.

Anger alerts you to danger, to situations in need of change, serving a useful function to get you moving if protection mode is required. Changes need to be made when you experience reductions in your freedom to choose your words and actions. Often people report exhaustion at having to respond to harsh words or actions just to keep things from escalating. Clearly, when anger is used, but not used wisely, the results are that it may lead to pain and suffering for many of us.

The intention that people assign to an action has a big impact on whether individuals respond with anger. For example, for some of us, people that make too much noise, unreasonable demands at a given point in time, or talk loudly when all you want is peace and quiet quickly being labeled as "rude," "inconsiderate," and "difficult" people, when they may be unaware or oblivious to their behavior. As soon as we ascribe our actions to the flaws of another, we add a reason to justify our own angry or aggressive acts. "He made me do it. Did you hear what he said?"

What if there is too much noise at the café where you work every morning? What if a friend's child breaks something you value? Of course, feeling angry might be appropriate in both situations. Each of these occurrences can be interpreted in many ways. Your response to a child who smears chocolate on your furniture when visiting may provoke a different reaction than a child who accidentally backs into your china cabinet breaking something. In both instances, the goal we suggest is to leave the child, and perhaps the parent, with information and actions that can make the future better, not worse. It might include wiser choices on your part about serving chocolate to small children in your living room … or to avoid the room with the china cabinet when small children are at your home.

If you are faced with a boss who yells, you may decide the wiser action is to exit the situation. At times you arrange to excuse yourself. Over time, yelling becomes a signal that you need to do something different. Be aware of how much such things affect you. Keep track of how soon, in small ways, you gain control over your breathing, thinking, or any other changes in how you respond. In almost all situations, you do not have to respond immediately. You take time to compose yourself in the presence of escalating words, and to mentally assess how you are directly adding to or lessening such escalation. Stepping back may be a very wise act, even if you do not get the outcome you want at the moment. Better, however, is to learn how to calmly handle the words of others, without undue emotion, and to know when it is time to leave.

You may feel angry by a perceived injustice or a lack of fairness. This can be in the immediate environment, a community, or a larger culture. Doing something about those issues requires activities that require good self-control in affecting positive change. You may have been abused and evidence of any kind of abuse may trigger deep and difficult emotional or physiological responses. It takes time to figure out when those triggers take over.

We are entitled to feel anger toward those who abuse others and ourselves. It is such a serious and deeply divisive issue. Laws do not always protect children from parents who are deeply abusive. The law often leans toward the rights of parents to determine how to raise their children. Clearly, in such circumstances, good people, teachers, neighbors, are stopped from intervening. Abuse can create psychological hurt, physical harm, even maim and kill. In the end, it is up to each of us to stop ignoring or tolerating behavior that harms. If a person appears to be out of control, ask for help. Do not assume help won't come. If you are on occasion abusive, remember that slapping, hitting, and yelling might get you want you want in the short-term, but it is not a wise strategy. Such approaches do not keep others safe from harm.

We often don't process words in context during emotionally charged events. We have no effective filter to see reality when strong emotional patterns of behavior are triggered. Those words occur in an internal dialogue not heard by others but magnified by a limited skill set as to how to respond. Your handling these kinds of signals depends on how successful you have been at navigating through troubling water in the past. Being limited in your perception of possible reaction choices can lead to high degrees of frustration (and anger). You may do something you believe will lead to a good outcome, yet it does not. Aversive outcomes may leave you overcome with roadblocks that keep you from getting things done, or, from being perceived as who you want to be.

Check the conditions that trigger physiological responding and "thick thoughts" that bunch up and stop you from being clear and calm. All too often, you may act quickly instead of taking the time to assess a situation to determine a workable solution. Sometimes we take things slow, and often, not at all. We learn to judge and label others. We judge harshly, or with humor. We learn to look at ourselves or not.

Learning to calm your initial reactions through stress management and anger-control techniques will give you time to consider and assess a threat. This is an important step as you learn to show greater wisdom in responding to highly emotional events in your life. Taking time to consider the situation allows you to get your physiological reactions and your private thoughts under control.

If you say, "I never get angry. I really don't. Nothing bothers me. I can handle anything," then we suggest you look into those statements as well. Being calm, cool, and collected is fine but responding appropriately to events that signal distress can be necessary at times, as in defending yourself in a physical attack. It is our reaction to these signals that matter. If you do not ever sense triggers of threat or aggression that could do harm to you or others, and all behavior looks rather flat to you, that may be a problem. Rules we are taught can make behaving with anger morally wrong as we see it. Work by Brown and Hayes may help you in dealing with what to do with that disconnect between who you wish you were and how you feel. Seeing behavior along an unemotional grid is not the same as being objective about behavior and its effects on you and others. If you find you are not fully in control and you want to gain control over angry behavior, the work by Novaco can help right now.

Novaco offers techniques to reduce the control that provocative situations have over physiological and behavioral responses. It would be nice if we all could behave in ways that make for a kinder, better, and more humane world. Start by examining your particular triggers that distort your skill in approaching situations with calm, clear, and effective strategies of self-management.

You may have a good repertoire of responses and ways of interpreting situations, reducing personal attributes while increasing objectivity. Most of us could use help. Begin by collecting data about the particular elements of when you feel anger (time, place, people)—and begin to understand the largest triggers stemming from your earlier learning or from repeat trials with a particular person. Continue to do something about it. Feeling angry is not a bad thing. It is, as Novaco says, a signal to act. It is the action we choose that matters.

PRACTICE 7.1:

Triggers to My Angry Behaviors

Record the triggers you experience the moment calm goes out the window, whether you demonstrate such reactions overtly or not. Here are a few examples:

- people who doubt what you say

- a rule of conduct violated

- someone disrespecting a value that you know is bigger than themselves

- the facts of a situation you know with certainty, yet you are told you got it wrong

- falsely accusing you of doing/not doing something

- seeing injustice done to others

- seeing a child pushed up against a grocery cart and being called an idiot by an adult (perhaps a parent) in the grocery store

- watching a homeless person being bullied

- hearing your partner complain one more time about all he must do for you, as if you are not doing enough to keep the family going

- spilling red wine on a new shirt when someone accidently bumps you

We encounter multiple kinds of triggers. Some are very understandable, but we could benefit from practicing how we handle our particular triggers. Make the list. Start watching your reactions.

Every Breath We Take

Muscle tension and agitation are often companions of anger. This is a good place to start. Tension is often reflected by a strained neck or tight shoulders. Take a moment. Step back and breathe. Count slowly to 10. Breathe deeply and slowly exhale. Slowly count again. Do this cycle four times and see how much you gain in terms of physical control. Our smartwatches remind us often to do just that. Learn to relax your muscles. Gain control over your breathing before you engage. Learning to reduce rapid breathing gains you some control in those traumatic situations when you feel your body taking over.

Introduce contrary behavior to the tone and tempo in the settings you find yourself—words and deed (speak quietly when yelled at during an argument, slow the pace of responding from rapid and quick to slow and steady). Focus on words that get to how we make this better. Stop using words of "wrongdoing" or insisting on making your point. Listen to understand. Start using words that seek a near-term solution. What can we do now to make this better? Stop trying to fix something that may have no right or wrong response.

The words we use

One of the most interesting aspects in gaining control over our emotional behavior, is self-statements. Work on your self-talk as you prepare for, then engage in, and finally evaluate your effects in given situations. The following four steps and content originated from Novaco's original framework (with some content elaborated on), to help people control themselves when entering, engaging in, and exiting provocative situations.

1. Prepare for provocation:

Understand, you will be entering into a situation where the pressure will be on you to act in ways that may not be in your best interest. If you do not engage in some degree of readiness, it will be hard to deal with words and actions until you are fluent in acting in ways that lead to better outcomes. One way to think of this is that you are entering into a temporary space where your goal is to stay focused on near-term, immediate outcomes. That initial outcome may have more to do with how you act and speak than in winning the argument. Look at the outcome you want at the end of this discussion, perhaps something quite modest.

You need not win a particular round. It is not about total victory, taking, or getting all or anything other than remaining in verbal and physical control. As often as needed, give yourself a verbal break—"I'll do the best I can. However, if I start to lose control, I will leave the situation, or I'll make a good effort to leave." Either action is okay. "I know I may slip. So, I'll try again."

2. Enter the confrontation:

Tell yourself to remain in control. Take time. Calm down for a few important seconds before responding. No rush. Use words carefully without blame or shame. Describe the situation as you see it. Take a bathroom break if needed. Look in the mirror. Breathe. Regroup. No need to prove anything. There is no benefit in having the better argument if it just leaves the other person angry. You do not have to indicate a shift in your position—unless you *have* shifted. Be ready to hear the wants of the other person. Tell yourself you are doing a good job of listening. A more-relaxed physical response can make this interaction easier. Keep your sense of humor. Stay focused on the near-term and your idea of success for this situation. Directly state your concerns with no punitive words and without raising your voice. Describe how this might work out for both of you, whatever it is you want to achieve. If you see there is no way to get to an agreement for next steps, or to end this dispute, acknowledge it, along with the actions you cannot take.

If the confrontation goes on too long, either end the debate or leave. No matter how right you are, winning right now simply means maintaining your calm and stating your needs in clear and non-accusatory ways—just the facts, so to speak. Your facts may of course not be the other person's facts. Don't dispute this. Your main goal is to remain calm.

Feel good that you planned in Step 1 and acted on that plan in Step 2 in the situation, letting go of needing to ensure the other person sees your point. Perhaps, you described the actions and outcomes you want. If not, feel good you are working to make this conflict better. Be kind to yourself in self-talk about your performance—from eye contact to humor to ease. Celebrate any improvement you made.

3. Coping with arousal of negative emotions:

You may be annoyed, deeply distressed, or afraid of failing, but there is no point in letting the other person get your goat. Breathe deeply. Pause in responding. Take time needed to collect yourself while in the situation. Take the issues point-by-point. "I don't want to get pushed around but I am not going to erupt either. I don't expect people to act the way I want them to. It is not about my wants and rules. It is how they have engaged with their world. That does not have to be my way of engagement." The engagement ends. Either you decided to end it, or it ended naturally on its own.

4. Evaluate your effect:

When the conflict is unresolved:

"It is time to think about other things. I cannot spend more time dwelling on the mistakes I made or the cheap wins the other person got." Just move on and remember, practice this until you get it right. Tell yourself you will get better over time. The conflict may not be as serious as you think. Try to find a bit of humor when you can. Consider the degree of respect, attention, or support the perspective you bring will offer to others. Different outcomes may happen if you consider their needs and wants. Often such disagreements are about holding onto views about how people *should*, *ought to*, or *must* act.

When either conflict is resolved or your own reactions are calm and in control:

Tell yourself that you handled things well. Acknowledge it was not as difficult as you thought. Celebrate steps forward and describe how you are getting better at this all the time. Pinpoint the parts of your behavior that you liked: eye contact, tone of voice, better listening than usual. Next time the other party may not have changed. Prepare again.

In PART II, be ready to look at your own entrenched biases and false beliefs that you have never addressed. Add new words to your vocabulary— one key trick to becoming wiser. This is best done by imagining while learning those new words how they might show up in action. How does a new word change the way you might see, feel, or think about something—or, ultimately, say or do something?

The Path to Wiser Acting

Chapter 8:

Old Dogs and New Tricks: A Lifetime of Learning

"With age comes wisdom, but sometimes age comes alone."

–Oscar Wilde

In the first part of this book, we talked about how we show up, how applying the science of learning and pragmatic tools increases the speed and strength of wiser choices. Do these individual behaviors we display sum to what we might call a *wisdom factor*? If wise in one setting, might we expect a person to be wise in another? Can we really develop wisdom according to society's judgement in navigating our choices?

Many of the topics in this book are pragmatic. Is acting wisely something innate or the product of experience? Can we really address our own deep-seated patterns of behavior? Do we get better just by staying alive? Many studies show a correlation between age and those characteristics associated with wiser action (Baltes & Smith, 2008; Vaillant, 2002; Webster, 2003). For example, Wink and Helson (1997) showed that practical wisdom, "good judgment and expertise in the pragmatics of life," significantly increased for participants as they grew older. Participants scored higher on practical wisdom in their 50s than in their 30s, for example. Certain events were also correlated with higher scores in practical wisdom, like occupation and life experiences.

A survey by Jeste and colleagues (2010) revealed that most psychological researchers on this topic agreed that wisdom is learned. They concluded,

"Wisdom is a uniquely human but rare personal quality, which can be learned and measured, and increases with age through advanced cognitive and emotional development that is experience-driven." From the perspective of behavior analysts, the world around us, along with our varied histories and sources of experience, either [may] advance or inhibit actions judged to be wise or unwise. Opportunities to practice expand across situations as people age and may lead to increased skills. However, many examples exist of young children acting with great wisdom and old people acting like the fools they were in their earlier years.

Wisdom conveys a unique understanding of relationships, core values, and effects. Certainly, an 11-year-old child most likely will not have the complex problem-solving skills of a 35-year-old adult. But let's not assume either that old dogs cannot learn new tricks or that the young cannot have greater insight than the rest of us, including the oldest among us. Age is not critical to acting wisely. Age is simply about experiences over time, organized into years, one continuous stream from birth to death—aging and behaving well, or not, across time. It is the knowledge we seek, the experiences we have, and our behavior across many situations as we age that help us make wiser decisions.

> *"It is the knowledge we seek, the experiences we have, and our behavior across many situations as we age that help us make wiser decisions."*

Experience at Any Age

Exposure to certain experiences provides opportunities to learn behavior associated with wisdom even at an early age. This type of expertise generally **increases** with age but can happen at any time in our lives. The more opportunity to practice behavior defined as *wise acting*, the bigger the behavioral repertoire we develop in responding to situations that demand a broader perspective.

Adora Svitak was 12 years old when invited to give a TED Talk. Since the age of seven, Adora had written extensively about many issues, including age and wisdom. She was offered a platform to express her idea of giving children opportunities to share their knowledge, not as exceptions but because of their words and actions that have echoed through the years as wise acting. In her talk,

What Adults Can Learn from Kids, Adora argued that children offer innovative solutions to complex problems in the situations in which they find themselves. They write extraordinary books fully relating the human condition and express optimism that provides a platform for others to find hope and to carry on. Her words were both funny and wise, extending how we look at each other, young or old, and how we accomplish positive effects on society's long-term good. She concluded, "Learning between grown-ups and kids should be reciprocal." Watch the video to hear Adora's insights about children and their potential to act with great wisdom (scan code to view the video on TED.com).

Adora's willingness to share her worldview at a very young age made her stand out to others as someone who was engaging in wise acting. She says:

> *... what have kids done? ... Anne Frank touched millions with her powerful account of the Holocaust. Ruby Bridges helped to end segregation in the United States. And, most recently, Charlie Simpson helped to raise 120,000 pounds for Haiti, on his little bike. So, as you can see evidenced by such examples, age has absolutely nothing to do with it. The traits the word* childish *addresses are seen so often in adults, that we should abolish this age-discriminatory word, when it comes to criticizing behavior associated with irresponsibility and irrational thinking.*

Adora has become a writer, prolific speaker, and ardent advocate for "feminism, youth empowerment, and literacy." *Pacific Standard Magazine* named her one of the "30 Top Thinkers Under 30." As Adora expressed in her TED Talk, "The world needs opportunities for new leaders and new ideas. Kids need opportunities to lead and succeed. Are you ready to make the match? Because the world's problems shouldn't be the human family's heirloom." Wisdom has been attributed to Adora, partly because she demands we understand that humankind's problems are not only for adults; those wise outcomes are not related to age but the impact of actions at any age. Having the tools to evaluate effects at various ages helps us all improve. Children, given a chance, help this world prosper wisely, advancing the human condition.

In her documentary, *I Am Eleven,* Genevieve Bailey filmed dozens of 11-year-old children in different countries and backgrounds. At an early age, they already demonstrated compassion toward others, resilience, humility, and were making a difference in the lives of their people. This is evidence that wise acting, bringing value for others' benefit, flourishes at any age under the right conditions.

The Bias Trap

We are often trapped not by our age or our experience but by our biases about age. Do you know the expression, "The child is the father of the man"? When it comes to wisdom, that can be so true. Here is an example. When Darnell's daughter, Rachel, was very young, her father fussed at her to put her toys away. She looked up at him, put her hands on her hips, and said, "Grown men don't talk to little girls that way." He stopped in his tracks, laughed out loud, hugged her, and said, "Oh, my gosh; you are so right." The child teaches the adult: this happens to all of us as parents. Unfortunately, we often fail to tell our children the incredible wisdom they show in such brief exchanges—signs of respect, care, and vulnerability. Parents who convey their appreciation, as Rachel's father did, teach their children valuable lessons.

Children need to hear that "tell me when I do it right" as much as adults. They need it just as much if not more than adults do in learning about the words and actions that add to a quality found in demonstrating wise behavior. It is an amazing learning experience to watch young children articulate to the adults the unfairness of our behavior. Laughter, hugs, and apologies are equally important. When children see adult behavior-models take accountability for their own mistakes, those actions will shape the wise adults that our children become. Such behavior is truly paying it forward. Many good lessons are available in the words that parents use with their children, words that teach the child universal truths about how all of us want and need to be treated.

That said, the developmental notion of decisions improving with age is also very real. Adults have a larger landscape to select from, more mistakes and successes to build into our future responses. Age can improve us all, but it is not, by itself, a condition that necessarily leads any of us to wiser outcomes.

Sorting the Wise from the Not So Wise

Becoming a wise-acting adult requires a review of how we come to behave. Avoiding charlatans, common fallacies, and faulty beliefs is a good place to start. Our prior histories are replete with oddball successes and struggles that enable us to make clear decisions in the future. If unaware that some of the "lessons" we learn lack validity, we are most likely doomed to repeat similar errors of analysis. Sometimes being "aware" of mistakes is very difficult. As Andy Lattal, professor of psychology, said, "Our errors are embedded in our history, a history that is there because such actions have been reinforced by the people and conditions that surround us—and by our measures of success, faulty as those may be. We use behavior established in another context and then see that it works with just a slight variation in a new context, even where it is less than optimal and maybe even counterproductive."

We then repeat our slightly modified, less than ideal, behavior, again and again. Our approaches to problem-solving are either punished by mistakes or reinforced by consequences. "Do it again … it worked the last time." Being alert that we may lack needed information, opens a wider world to gauge our actions—and become better at seeing the errors in our well-practiced ways.

It is not enough to say that awareness alone will get us out of mistaken patterns in using information. Indeed, one of our most significant reasons for seeing that old dog, the difficult or rigid adult, as unable to learn new tricks, is that he engaged in many annoying ways of behaving when a young pup. We may see him as having a lifetime of habits, misinformation, and unable to change.

We adults certainly may resist needed change, attend to the wrong information, and show the type of rigidity reinforced by our previous experiences (Arkes, H. R., & Blumer, C., 1985; Navarro, A. D., & Fantino, E., 2009). As we age, we are placed by those around us in a box of certainty. Older folks are sometimes characterized as rigid, unable to change. At other times, they are crowned with the halo of wisdom, as if living long enough makes it so. Most older people might well deny that they wear such a crown … *but sometimes— well, on occasion, sure, maybe.* By the time we have reached a certain age, we may well behave with greater wisdom than we did when we were 19. But don't count on it.

Children may lead us, but, in the end, the adult in the room—in the middle of a pandemic, for example—is the one who needs to pinpoint actions needed to achieve the greatest good of us all. Adults, after all, control the resources that support and influence choice. They are the ones who will invest in solar power, reduce the use of shame to gain obedience, teach our children to show concern for others, or make decisions that increase the possibility of world peace. For society's wisdom factor to grow, it bears repeating that it is, at a fundamental level, all about *you* and what you do along life's way. Keep your eyes wide open to evaluate your immediate and longer-term effects.

In summary, age alone does not strengthen wise acting; rather, experiences and their varied effects on us may help us make wiser choices throughout life. Older people who are considered wise get there through years of learning, modifying, and redoing. While society all too often equates wisdom and age, children are being taught to analyze an action to find the wisdom factor in the words they hear and say, and/or the actions they take. Sometimes children are the true wise voice in the room. How can we as adults become more alert? What problem-solving skills do we use that give us a guide to wise acting, perhaps learned at a very early age, but often coming back into focus later in life? Fundamentally, how do we make learning a lifelong process?

PRACTICE 8.1:

Showing Up Across My Lifespan

Childhood:

- Describe how you showed up in wise ways as a young child, an example that has stayed with you.

- Consider whether actions you took as a child had a good effect on someone else? Your mother? Your teacher? Your great pal?

- Note those, as good or simple as they may seem.

Teen and Early Adulthood:

- What did you do in your teen and early adult years that led to positive effects?

- What did you learn or are you learning to shape better outcomes in the future?

Experiences Beyond Young Adulthood:

- In the decades since, what has changed in how you arrive at decisions you make?

- Have you forgotten a few good things that you used to do to arrive at a better decision then than now?

Highlights and Lessons Learned (Hopefully):

- Are you proud of a few examples of your own wise acting? Are there behaviors in your earliest years or later, that you regret to this day? What lessons have you learned about how you now want to show up?

Chapter 9:

Knowing How to Know:
The 21ˢᵗ-Century Tool Kit

*"We now accept the fact that learning is a lifelong process
of keeping abreast of change. And the most pressing task
is to teach people how to learn."*

–Peter Drucker

Teaching Wise Acting in the 21ˢᵗ Century

As cultural practices change, the skills needed to demonstrate wise acting also change. Behavior needs to adapt to new environmental requirements. Therefore, new skills need to be prioritized over time. The 21ˢᵗ century is markedly different from previous centuries in two critical areas: the expansive global reach of knowledge electronically and the changing definitions of work and who the workers are—from human to robot, to artificial intelligence, for example. Learning how to adapt is essential to creating a place of meaning and importance for each of us, which is directly related to practical wisdom. Keep in mind the following:

> *"The more I live, the more I learn. The more I learn, the more I realize the less I know."*
>
> –Michel Legrand

These words are so true for the challenges we face in the fast-approaching future.

Finding meaning in the 21st century demands being alert to the changes that are redefining commonalities among cultures and practices, the worth of work, and core skills taught through the ages. The kind of world most people are well prepared for is changing, even as you read this. The march of automation is evolving into complex algorithms where mankind no longer operates the machines, and little is needed after designs are created, except to ensure the switch is flipped. Soon, even that will be managed by artificial intelligence devices of all sizes and shapes. However, knowing how to take advantage of the new reality will ideally free humankind to do other kinds of work valued by society and worthy of recognition.

Technology puts a wider world at our fingertips, making learning possible everywhere. A computer, a link, a cellular phone, a smartwatch—all provide access to an endless encyclopedia of information. Instantly, we access information about other people and cultures. This connection could make us all kindred spirits. This access to information makes it easier to see that humans have more in common than previous generations believed.

As the century progresses, more people in the farthest reaches of the world will gain greater access to this knowledge. Identifying how others come to believe as they do and assessing what they consider meaningful actions increases our understanding of how to coexist. New generative ideas, born in one setting but generalizing and expanding to other settings, are jumping across cultural barriers. Beginning to understand the currents that shape new ways of acting, breaking out of old rules of how to behave, strengthens the potential for deeper appreciation of how diverse environments establish practices that influence and enrich us all.

Learning to see commonalities and differences among us makes for a more inclusive understanding. At times, those differences have profound and immediate wise effects on how we behave. That spark of novelty in accepting new ways of acting offers the potential to behave in a more informed, relevant, and inclusive manner. The more exposure we have to one another, the more a firmly held set of values about our human condition might directly come into conflict with our experiences. From that exposure, many things about who we are, how special our group is, come into question. Finding behaviors that sustain the well-being of us all is a major challenge of the 21st century.

Seeing differences in how we behave is not about measures of one group's worth against another; but rather, how the conditions of learning affect how one group versus another has learned how to act. Testing our beliefs is a core skill of knowing. Knowing whether our beliefs and skills are necessary or sufficient for the situations we face, is measured by several factors, including our effects when we are required to act in novel ways. In other words, at the end of the day, wise acting is not just the accumulation of knowledge, but its application. The most comprehensive library in the world would be only decorative if not put to good use. Pragmatically speaking, that may be where the depth of our knowledge shows up most clearly.

> *"Testing our beliefs is a core skill of knowing."*

The global marketplace rewards organizations that innovate. Companies want workers who contribute to this environment. Innovation and creativity often require open access to diverse ways of thinking about particular issues, solving problems through the combined efforts of many. Careful assessment is needed about the influence on the culture where innovation is to be applied, aligned to clear goals and priorities (Mirabito & Layng, 2013).

Foundational communication skills are a priority in many countries as our world workforce comes in greater contact. Elementary through high school students are learning through social skills and self-reflection curriculums, about how they demonstrate qualities of inclusion, caring, and persistence, among other important things. Perspective-taking and effectively managing interpersonal differences is anticipated to be essential for all members of the global community.

How can we ever know with certainty that we are doing the right thing? Learning to navigate through complex, multifaceted choices that typically do not have one right answer is a necessary 21st-century skill. As Margaret Heffernan expressed in her TED Talk, *The Human Skills We Need in an Unpredictable World*, "Preparedness, coalition-building, imagination, experiments, bravery

... in an unpredictable age, these are tremendous sources of resilience and strength. They aren't efficient, but they give us limitless capacity for adaptation, variation, and invention. And the less we know about the future, the more we're going to need these tremendous sources of human, messy, unpredictable skills." Making complex decisions, even by young children, is critical in the years ahead. Identifying available options is key. Our value will not depend on how much information we have stored in our heads, but on how we use our knowledge to access the information we need to affect positive outcomes. Teachers, well skilled in decision-making models and in integrating conflicting data to arrive at useful outcomes, are of significant importance in teaching such skills to our children.

The table below lists concepts that some of our best educational researchers consider essential to navigate wisely through the expanding requirements of automation. Nothing on the list is necessarily revolutionary. Educators and futurists have outlined the requirements for an educated 21st-century adult

---

Knowledge for the 21st Century: Core Competencies Required of Students

- Mastering reading, mathematics, science—basic knowledge

- Appreciating arts and music—civilizing elements of knowing

- Thinking critically about information

- Solving complex, multidisciplinary, open-ended problems

- Applying "creative" skills to unconventional decision-making

- Communicating and collaborating with people across cultural, geographic, and language boundaries

- Making innovative use of knowledge, information, and opportunities to create new methods

- Taking charge of financial, health and civic responsibilities

- Working to create a culture that expresses the values you believe are central to your community/locality/business/company

to navigate through a changing, complex world. Such competencies shaped academies of learning from the early days of Greece, as an example, but with a world to influence beyond the Aegean Sea. Today, most of us have access to the endless streams of influence available through the Internet. The skill of sharing experiences in real time, even if halfway around the world, helps broaden understanding and reach agreements with people we would never have had the chance to meet in our daily life.

The table includes core elements needed to make this a better world. These are categories evaluated by well-educated graduates of the past as necessary to get through the challenges of daily life by those who are graduating now.

- Communicating and collaborating
- Thinking critically to clearly problem-solve
- Displaying flexibility and adaptability
- Navigating through differences
- Showing initiative and self-direction
- Acting in productive and accountable ways
- Taking part in new designs, new environments, applying creativity and innovation
- Appreciating aesthetics and the unexpected
- Showing emotional contiguity
- Assessing variation and similarities
- Integrating related and unrelated facts
- Practicing values-based behaviors that reflect the desired impact of certain actions on ethical, social, and moral imperatives

Teaching students to demonstrate the types of behavior that sum to wisdom, as in many centuries past, is still practiced by astute teachers today, achieving extraordinary effects. In these times, advances in learning technologies have changed the way in which teaching occurs, potentially expanding its impact and helping set up unique environments for learning.

PRACTICE 9.1:

Self-assessment

In this practice, assess yourself on a few aspects that are relevant to skills that are valuable in the 21st century. Check the box if you do the item routinely and well. If you need or want to work on this skill, circle it. Read, practice, and record how well you do in meeting the components of the skills below. Continue through other key skills of the 21st century.

21st-Century Skills

CRITICAL THINKING

- *Seek contrary evidence:*
  I consistently search for independent confirmation of "facts."

- *Link statements to validation:*
  I listen to the evidence provided by experts from various points of view.

- *Explore Alternatives:*
  I consider various explanations and how their validity can be assessed.

- *Envision the clearest path to get to end goals:*
  I seek to solve problems as simply as possible.

- *Explore alternative improvement options:*
  I continue considering other explanations as they emerge over time.

- *Showing up:*
  I commit to demonstrating these types of skills when engaged in critical thinking.

DECISION-MAKING SKILLS

- *Identify available options:*
  I identify alternative ways to achieve a particular goal.

- *Assesses effects of available options:*
  I identify (a) short-term pros and cons; (b) long-term pros and cons.

- *Requirements of available options:*
  I reflect on the (a) response effort and commitment required; (b) how long it will take to reach a desired outcome; (c) resources needed.

- *Showing up:*
  I commit to demonstrating these types of skills when making decisions.

PROBLEM-SOLVING SKILLS

- *Identify there is a problem:*
  I objectively determine (a) there is a problem, (b) who is affected by the problem, and (c) if the problem is worth addressing.

- *Define the type of problem:*
  I reliably determine if a problem is due to (a) information that is available or unavailable at the moment, (b) resources that are available or unavailable, (c) characteristics of performance—such as a new skill needs to be learned, behavior occurs too much, it occurs at the wrong time or place, incongruence between say and do, et cetera, and (d) consequences that might influence performance—immediate versus delayed, consistent versus inconsistent.

- *Generate possible solutions:*
  I reflect on whether (a) I have faced similar problems in the past, (b) others might have faced similar problems, (c) solutions that have been tried previously and worked, (d) whether a novel solution is needed, and (e) whether help or delegation is needed.

- *Evaluate the options:*
  I think of (a) short-term pros and cons, and (b) long-term pros and cons.

- *Evaluate outcomes:*
  I define (a) the optimal desired effects, (b) how those effects will be measured, and (c) alternative actions if the desired effects do not occur.

- *Showing up:*
  I commit to using these types of skills when problem-solving.

Knowing How to Know

No greater challenge to the future wellbeing of our country or the world exists, than the way citizens access and use information, and develop skill in using that information. Those who work in fields such as information science and library science see a part of their job is to help students recognize when information is needed and locate, evaluate, and use effectively the needed information. In this day of often distorted, even untrue, information, some would say attaining and applying valid information is one of the greatest challenges. Getting to wise acting requires an educated population who know how to access information.

Understanding how data are used on the web and the possibility of content mismanagement requires a different level of vigilance in keeping soothsayers and sorcerers from our door. Demonstrating measurable skills in how to obtain and evaluate core information is the basis for lifelong learning. It is also the basis for evaluating contemporary sources of information, such as the current misconception that any information is as good as any other information, with the added caveat that if the information supports my perspective, then it is better and more correct. These beliefs lead easily to a most dangerous distortion.

The Alexandria Proclamation, UNESCO, 2005 defined the term *information literacy* as a human rights issue: "Information literacy empowers people in all walks of life to seek, evaluate, use and create information effectively to achieve their personal, social, occupational, and educational goals. It is a basic human right in a digital world and promotes social inclusion in all nations." The United States National Forum on Information Literacy defined information literacy as "the ability to know when there is a need for information, to be able to identify, locate, evaluate, and effectively use that information for the issue or problem at hand." Presidential Committee on Information Literacy. 1989, p. 1.

Ways to Engage in Knowing

In this century, there are many ways to know and to learn how to know. Some schools and universities have started offering courses to teach these types of skills. An excellent example of a foundational course about the philosophy of knowing, and understanding such concepts as belief, truth, and verification is offered through the public school system in Ontario, Canada. The Ontario School System list includes the following:

- **Prior Knowledge**—knowledge or justification that is independent of experience

- **Deduction**—the inference of instances by reference to a general law or principle

- **Fatalism**—the belief that all events are predetermined and therefore inevitable

- **Groupthink**—the practice of approaching problems or issues as matters that are best dealt with by consensus of a group rather than by individuals acting independently

- **Hedonism**—the ethical theory that pleasure is the highest good and proper aim of human life

- **Intuition**—a thing that one knows or considers likely from instinctive feeling rather than conscious reasoning

- **Law of Nature**—a regularly occurring or apparently inevitable phenomenon observable in human society

- **Occam's Razor**—first seeking explanations of unknown phenomena in terms of known quantities

- **Probability Theory**—the extent to which an event is likely to occur

- **Scientific Method**—relevant data are gathered, a hypothesis is formulated from these data, and the hypothesis is empirically tested.

A student anywhere around the world can enroll, take this course, and engage in well-designed exercises about learning how to know. In it, a belief is said to be justified if there is at least one "justifier," such as an item of evidence that justifies it. Even when a claim is in doubt, justification can be used to support the claim and reduce or remove the doubt. However, knowing how to examine belief beyond that one justification, allows the learner to explore how well the content holds up to other ways of knowing. The more experienced in looking at a belief or a truth as you know it through various perspectives, the greater the opportunity to see things more clearly. We list similar ways of determining if information is true in Chapter 10.

Principles of Effective Teaching

Stellar teachers arrange conditions to ensure their students learn how to behave wisely. We will mention only a limited number of such teachers specifically by name in the next chapter. However, a few fundamental principles appear essential to being an effective teacher. The first Homo Erectus ancestors taught the up-and-coming generation to produce fire by rubbing life-changing sticks together. Passing down that skill had a values-based impact on future generations, particularly during harsh winters. This skill provided cooked food, warm shelter, and a weapon—if needed—to scare away the large animals that surrounded them, including other humans. Most likely it generated a feeling that arranging fire-stick practice is part of the curriculum of an excellent teacher.

What is it that a teacher needs to do to produce wise-acting students? A unique challenge lies in attributing wisdom to our words and actions. It is a label that can only be firmly attached after the act, *post hoc*, because such a label is verified by the *effects* of one's words and actions. Wisdom, as philosophers might describe it, is about a condition of becoming, a never-ending journey. Some important questions should be asked: Can we teach that wide-open concept, that condition of "becoming"? Can we teach that condition if it is not precisely defined? Can we teach behavior we judge to be "striving to be wise"? If we assess behavior's effects in the near term, we do, to some extent, check its effects over time—and begin to pinpoint who is likely to be affected by conditions that may enhance or compete with wise results.

Effective teaching includes

1. arranging conditions that provide students leeway to learn, to make choices, to learn from those choices, and to then make even better choices;

2. teaching students how to access what is known—and helping students discover how to access sources of information for what is as yet unknown;

3. understanding the science of learning—and how it affects the teacher as well as students;

4. sorting through content that the teacher may not know;

5. flexibility to know how to guide students to the knowledge desired, with skill in the use of tools to accelerate the learning process; and

6. foundational concepts and often advanced training but, fundamentally, steeping students in the *process* of learning.

It is in teaching the process of how to know that the teacher establishes tools for lifelong learning. Knowing how to help a student access new content beyond that in the textbook or in the teacher's lectures is a unique skill that a teacher brings to any engagement with a student.

To increase a teacher's educational impact on students, teachers themselves often report that learning occurs best when students are provided guidance to see progress along the way, moving at their own pace, with frequent measures of how well they have mastered information. Principles embedded in the learning curve, including the benefits of an unshakeable belief that anyone can learn, have created grand teachers for this 21st century. Jeremy, a teacher in Buffalo, New York, was exemplary in providing to his students the certainty that the students had just begun to reach their full potential. He stated that his job was to set the conditions and at some point, get out of the way of learning (classroom observations, Lattal, 2015). As he saw it, the basic measure of a good education was in the change produced by the learner. Students, mostly unsung and with little optimism surrounding them, were provided a spark of realistic optimism by Jeremy that lit up belief in their capacity to learn. His challenge was in entering a classroom where each student brought into that classroom individual histories of violence, poverty, and neglect. Entering as well were the glimmers of optimism, cooperation, and trust, that were there, ready to thrive.

Good advice about how to know if a teacher is skilled in the art and science of teaching is available, but none better than to look at how the student embraces and pursues learning as demonstrated by the student's actual behavior. The performance measures for a student are in the slope and rate of the learning curve, individual mastery, and fluency over baseline. That slope is an indication of how well they are mastering learning how to know—and, for Jeremy, how much he was setting up conditions absent of threat and fear. "As science itself has so abundantly demonstrated, the power of any technology depends upon an understanding of its basic processes. We cannot really improve teaching until we know what it is" (Skinner, 1968).

The Role of Teachers

"True teachers are those who use themselves as bridges over which they invite their students to cross; then, having facilitated their crossing, joyfully collapse, encouraging them to create their own."

–Nikos Kazantzakis

Teachers play two important roles. They provide: (1) the rules of learning how to know (for example, basics of reading, writing, arithmetic, advanced knowledge about such areas as the scientific method, decision-making criteria, and problem-solving); and (2) the conditions for the student to see, say and do, applying a growing knowledge about how to know actions. The teacher moves from "rule giver" to expand into the larger context in which knowledge will be applied, broadening a student's experience base. Many teachers shape independent learning in children who, through access to learning how to know, see the broader connections between situations, pointing to or focusing on critical elements, saying out loud their experience, and then knowing how to solve or better understand or prepare for future action. This kind of individualized focus requires well-trained teachers applying such knowledge to the content areas in which they direct student learning. They in turn shape the students into becoming their own teachers.

Teachers often serve as learning architects, finding, or preparing the actual materials students use to get to a clear understanding of the information they must know. In such settings, teachers prepare students by arranging a learning environment in which students have frequent opportunities to solve problems. Curriculum content is carefully designed to provide a seamless path to achieve learning objectives, moving from awareness to mastery to fluency. Janet S. Twyman and Adam Hockman (2021) describe this process:

Effectively teaching any concept requires thoughtful selection of positive and negative example stimuli (examples and nonexamples) based on an analysis of the concept's relevant and irrelevant features (critical and variable attributes). Equally indispensable to effective concept teaching is how, when, and what we say when presenting those stimuli to learners.

Fluent performance is characterized by longer retention, endurance, and application, which are important attributes to promote wise acting. Such depth of knowledge allows students to be better at handling barriers or emotional sand traps that might lie in their way as they go through life.

"Teachers often serve as learning architects, finding, or preparing the actual materials students use to get to a clear understanding of the information they must know."

Frequent practice opportunities and assessment, as well as talk-out-loud strategies of solving problems, are part of a well-designed learning environment. Students are guided on how to use available tools (books, pictures, precision teaching, videos, discussions, observation of others, sorting and making sound choices, talking out loud as they absorb what they know, and so on) to choose among many options. Students are encouraged to say out loud their thoughts and beliefs about possible next steps to take. The teacher asks clarifying questions or inquires as to why the student made a certain decision. Through a series of iterations, the student becomes his own teacher, using the teacher's powerhouse of knowledge to help direct him to new avenues, applying solutions to more and more complex problems. Ideally, this is how education works, with lots of knowledge and sources on *how to know* surrounding the student. The student, now better at knowing how to know, learns to use the tools available to make better choices.

The more students practice this, the broader and more inclusive their choices become. With positive support, such as meaningful comments from teachers about a student's actions, comes an acceleration in confidence and accomplishment. Hopefully, the child is asked to consider the near-term and longer-term effects of decisions she has made. Such consideration, practiced often and increasing in complexity as the child grows, increases thoughtful decisions.

In the workplace, we often expect the manager to have the knowledge, arrange the work conditions, pick the targets for change, instruct the workers, reinforce the correct effort, and correct off-target effort, either encouraging or stopping the worker from trying again. The broader opportunities that exist is to give the worker the tools and arrange conditions for individual success, providing periodic metrics on how well the individual is doing, indicating that business success is in the hands of those who do the work.

This more astute approach to management is also found in effective teaching. The student, the worker, our children, our life partner, a third-grade teacher in a K-5 school are all teachers and learners. Being a teacher or a student is to varying degrees, and at different times, shared. Keep in mind, the word *teacher* is not reserved only for someone who holds that job title. Rather, we are all at times teachers—and all learners.

Imagine if students were to learn at such a rapid rate that they were doing junior high work while in fifth grade! What if a teacher's performance was specifically measured by the pace of students' learning curves, mastering content at rapid rates? Well, chaos would occur, some would say. Mr. Jones, fifth-grade math teacher, may not meet his quota of students to fill his class if they are all allowed to advance beyond fifth-grade math in the fourth grade. If you find your school focusing on grade-level achievement and placing limits on advancing too fast, you may have a school where order is more important than learning. Order has been a very big measure of a school's success all too often— "Be quiet, be docile, be still" (Winett and Winkler, 1972)—but the more important measure, of course, you say, is the success of the student. Working to provide order (a safe school environment) is essential in too many of our schools. Orderly promotions for teachers and a clear path toward the knowledge that must be acquired, all contribute to definitions of *order*.

It is not orderliness *per se* that stifles learning but rather the cap placed on the students' rate of learning. With a number of factors affecting the school, there may be little reason to figure out how to address students inside classrooms all performing at varied grade levels, developing at their own rate. Mr.

Jones may be faced with the empty classroom and that does not mean he wants students to fit into boxes or grades. He too may want to advance his students at a good rate. How he is evaluated, and the resources schools have to help in such individualized student progress may be inadequate. This is a real-life example of how learning architecture, classroom management, orderly progression, and obtaining resources interact to limit learning. This is where the drama about funding, teacher employment, books that the school orders, and classroom quotas to be filled, all come into play.

Language-Enriched Environments

Words, words, words! Nothing is more important, as we discussed in Chapter 4. And yet, nothing is used with less precision and clarity as to their effects on learning curves and problem-solving. We adapt to and adopt knowledge accumulated by others through oral and written words that would be difficult, if not impossible, to learn through our experience alone. We also learn efficient ways of acting through words.

Our early experiences with words have an impact on the skills we develop, including critical thinking and problem-solving. This impact can make a noticeable difference on our future achievements. Children raised in families with little verbal interactions tend to exhibit limited repertoires. In contrast, children growing up in socially rich environments, demonstrated by words used frequently and with variation, show quicker acquisition of language and other skills (e.g., Moerk, 1990; Hart and Risley, 1992; Suskind, 2015). Betty Hart and Todd Risley carried out a longitudinal study of this relation. They followed 40 families for a period of 2½ years. Families were representative of most American households in size, race, and socioeconomic status. During that time, they recorded the frequency and quality of parent-child interactions. They observed that all families displayed the same frequency of "business talk." This type of interaction was defined as giving directives to the child; for example, "Come here," "Clean your room," "Get your backpack." The big difference was with the addition of "richer" verbal interactions in some families. Besides the simple, command type "business talk," some families asked children how their day went, questions about current events, and other topics. These types of interactions were more stimulating in generating varied words from children. Children in such settings use words to respond, expanding their language abilities. Children raised in this type of interactive family performed significantly better in language and IQ tests at the conclusion of the study than those who were rarely talked to or asked to engage in problem-solving. The more words the better!

PRACTICE 9.2:

Establish a Continuous Learning Environment by Using Word

The Hart and Risley findings are among the most profound studies in demonstrating how to advance learning by expanding the use of words. Its lessons are needed wherever you find yourself—with your colleagues, children, or friends.

1. Invite people to solve problems by using words to explore issues, not simply responding with a yes or no.

2. Remind yourself to use the "why" questions in suggesting the values they want to see immediately and over the longer-term.

3. Record times you are asked to consider your situation and solve problems in a manner that helps you assign the proper value for why you want to do something.

4. Consider times when you are not asked to engage in an exploration of activities; rather, you are simply told to follow orders. How does the "business talk" mentioned by Hart and Risley, (yes and no answers to requiring no answers at all) limit or expand your approach?

5. Strike a balance, but aim for establishing an environment rich in words, more than just following the rules or commands.

6. Consider the divide created by the simple use of words to enrich our exposure to ideas and values and understanding why, often in everyday life, such concepts matter.

Hart and Risley showed the significant impact parents have on the future success of their children in terms of advances in IQ through these simple activities—talking a lot, involving the child, asking questions. Imagine the impact we could have on the development of wise acting if we were to expose children to ideas and values early on and use our words and theirs to help them understand why such concepts matter.

"Imagine the impact we could have on the development of wise acting if we were to expose children to ideas and values early on and use our words and theirs to help them understand why such concepts matter."

The Teacher in Us All

Let's look at an example to illustrate the way in which children start learning skills in how to know at home from an early age. This is about exemplary learning, an alert parent/teacher, understanding that the sources of ideas and mastery lie in the very simple to the complex of everyday experience. A person who understands that children are, over time, our best teachers, as they explore the world in front of them with delight. Jen Maas is a parent of three children. Soon after their birth, she began talking, singing, and guiding them, treating them as the learners they are. Jen started with her small infant, eyes still unfocused, looking up and around as Jen put a storybook with pictures, or a bright object, in the infant's eyesight. She proceeded to describe the object, laughing, noticing her child looking back at her while attending to the object. Gurgles and scanning led to pointing and choosing, and finally, saying and/or doing together or by taking turns. Darnell watched this amazing person teach her three children how to know, broadening their vision when in larger settings, looking up at the clouds and down at the plants growing up around them, and grabbing, touching, tasting when appropriate. She responded to her children's laughter by smiling in return. And so, every day and every night, her children learned to see/say by their interactions with her. They then began telling their own stories of their day, sharing stories of their activities, the lessons they learned, and even their thoughts.

Jen accepted it all; occasionally shaping a gentler or different interpretation or helping them sort out how to get to good outcomes, but always reinforcing the child's sharing. She demonstrated that she understood that the children around her were independent beings, learning how to know about this world.

The world is fortunate to have many parents like Jen, persistently dedicated to her role of helping the child learn. Gently guiding their journey by their side through their early years and always on the ready throughout their lives, she has taught them how to know. Children become their own teachers as they continue to grow, practicing doing the right thing, surrounded by conditions that promote such actions, with candor about their curiosity and mistakes— children on the way to becoming outstanding learners, thinkers, and doers.

PRACTICE 9.3:

Evaluating What is True

For each of us we have ways to determine what is true. Seeking out informed sources; talking to trusted advisors; using the scientific method; the impact on what is called "truth" on others and ourselves; what we learned from our parents or those who raised us; our religious beliefs; and so on. List a few of the ways you evaluate what is true for you.

The environment that surrounds us—people, processes, and systems— matters significantly in learning how to behave wisely. Understanding behavior in context—its history and the effects of the immediate environment as well as the larger social conditions that surround our actions—is essential in creating a wiser behaving "us," and a wiser culture. Such understanding provides insight into the reciprocal conditions needed to promote learning. Teaching tools to promote thoughtful, inclusive, and effective decision-making is a good thing. Pinpointing, measuring, and evaluating effective practices about the immediate- and longer-term common good provides a guide to behaving in ways that lead to a wiser culture. Being taught how each of us as individuals, in groups, across communities, and as a culture, thrives while promoting the good of all, is at the heart of our hopes for an education that leads to a better tomorrow.

Chapter 10:

Designing Learning Environments: Unleashing Our Unlimited Potential

"The first aim of a good college is not to teach books, but the meaning and purpose of life. Hard study and the learning of books are only a means to this end. We develop power and courage and determination, and we go out to achieve Truth, Wisdom and Justice. If we do not come to this, the cost of schooling is wasted."

–John B. Watson

The success of learners largely depends on rules that give students guidance and contingencies arranged by their teachers and parents that reward effort. Effective classroom contingencies promote active engagement to develop fluent performance. Exposing students to many examples and non-examples of relevant concepts helps them to transfer skills to new situations. Students receive immediate and frequent feedback based on their responses. Ideally, teachers modify instruction based on the success of their students. Thus, success is influenced by the learning environment rather than solely by innate *talent*.

In his book, *Chasing Stars: The Myth of Talent and the Portability of Performance*, Boris Grossberg examined the careers of more than a thousand people identified as "star" analysts at investment banks. According to a review by *the Princeton Press Review of Books*, he concluded that those people judged to be "exceptionally talented" suffered a decline in performance after changing firms. He argued that earlier success does not exist in the "stars" or in those judged to be "talented." Rather, success depends in large part on workplace environments. Accessible resources, a positive organizational culture, useful networks, and supportive colleagues are all critical to a person's success. All help provide stability and the necessary settings in which to meet or exceed requirements.

Thomas Gilbert arrived at similar conclusions. In his book, *Human Competence: Engineering Human Performance*, Gilbert showed how to promote exemplary performance through a mathematical formulation about the conditions in the workplace. Sustaining success through performance excellence requires observing cultures of learning surrounding the performer. The average performer rises quickly to the top performance levels. Once again, internal attributions, like an incredible intellect or a set of skills the performer has, do not predict how fast and how far they go in achieving desired outcomes; instead, success is predicted by how behavior and the surrounding conditions interact.

"Success through excellence in performance is found in the observable cultures of learning surrounding the performer."

Anders Ericsson and Robert Pool summarized 30 years of research into conditions that make for excellent performance in their book, *Peak: Secrets from the New Science of Expertise*. They show how deliberate practice is key to mastering performance goals rather than internal states or biological limits. *Deliberate practice* reduces errors by practicing correct responses with structure, guidance, and positive support. While we understand much about how individual learning occurs, we still have much to learn.

From birth, there are great variations in how one individual interacts with the environment when compared to another. Some very young children respond to sound in ways different from siblings or peers, becoming extraordinary pianists at age five. A young child solves math and logic problems with greater accuracy than trained mathematicians. Occasional headlines announce chess masters at a very young age, and children passing SAT exams with perfect scores, heading to college before finishing elementary school.

We tend to explain away these differences by calling that capacity "genius," as if this label explains such remarkable performances. Anders Ericsson wrote of the role of *perfect practice* in the development of these types of skills. Genetics and immediate receptivity to various stimuli may each play a part, but based on research, genetics plays more of an important role in sports because of body type and height necessary for certain activities. Since Ericsson and his colleagues first worked in this area, they have more precisely refined the term *deliberate practice* to the fuller conditions that lead to excellence in mastering various skills. He and his colleagues now call this *structured practice,* emphasizing the role of active coaching and immediate feedback (Ericsson and Harwell, 2019).

Current research explores the environmental conditions that accelerate rapidly expanding capacity in mastering complex skills. Such examination includes different rates of adaptation to the environment and persistence in achieving desired results. Knowing more could illuminate the initiation and motivation that influences those extraordinary rates of learning described earlier. Do keep in mind that skill mastery at extraordinary rates does not tell us anything about who will demonstrate greater wisdom in their actions. A masterful chess player or a college freshman at age nine does not indicate that such amazing skill mastery alone makes the individual more likely to behave in ways that peers or society would label as wise.

One characteristic of excellent teachers we discussed in Chapter 9 is that they know how to arrange conditions for students to learn. If the student does not master content, such teachers pinpoint, shape, and reinforce practices that help the student. To quote Alexander Den Heijer, "When a flower doesn't bloom, you fix the environment in which it grows, not the flower." Teachers help the process of discovery and application. They know about learning methods that allow the student to reduce errors. Using each student's accomplishment over baseline performance is a valued measure these teachers apply to their measures of successful teaching.

The root cause of many teachers' failure to address every student's learning opportunity lies in the way administrators assess worthy teacher behavior—all too often punishing failures to reach certain scores, or rule-governed behavior based on classroom, hallway, and cafeteria comportment, and other measures of teacher success as they see it. It is a complex subject in our under-funded and overcrowded classrooms and schools. It rolls up to how our society sees learning and establishes conditions that are intended to reflect how a good school should look. When classrooms are designed so that the baseline and learning curve is the central measure of student, teacher, school, and district success, it changes the teaching approach, validating individual success and lending momentum to class success. To do that well, requires the following:

1. Determining the behaviors, both academic and social, needed at the student, teacher, administrator, and parental level to ensure schools are positive places of learning excellence.

2. Designing positive reinforcement in daily activities.

3. Accelerating and sustaining mastery in individual learners.

4. Designing instructional material to allow the student to get to new levels of learning and fluency with accuracy and speed.

5. Developing systems for tracking individual gains in visible ways, allowing students to keep data on their learning progress.

6. Providing new ways to recognize the success of teachers and schools across our nation based on tracking and celebrating the continuing success of students.

7. Celebrating the wisdom teachers demonstrate in helping students understand how to accelerate their own rate of learning (a much wiser way to design the experience of learning).

Schools as centers of excellence and community change thrive when de-signed so that students know they will be recognized and rewarded for behav-iors that are good for them and their communities. Bringing the community into the school can help. The late Nipsey Hussle and others were and are work-ing toward such goals. Beyond public marches for social and economic justice, public policies need to be designed that take a careful look at the consequences embedded in informal structures, processes, and systems that limit the founda-tional needs of students and their families.

Exemplary teachers and schools make student errors an opportunity to learn, not something wrong or something to be embarrassed about. Seeing errors as opportunities for improvement helps identify skills to practice and is one of the most effective ways to build competent performance. This idea is often talked about but very seldom put into practice. Errors show the teacher areas in which the child has mastered learning and areas that require more work—nothing else about the student's ability. Gene Stromberg and Marilyn Chappell (1990) describe how a particular teacher did this: "To encourage students to try problems they might not know, she called errors 'learning opportunities.' If a student errs, an opportunity presents itself to learn correctly."

PRACTICE 10.1:

My Most Excellent Teacher

- Describe your best teacher (or two if you were so lucky). How did they stand out?

- How did this teacher make you want to do more or better?

- What characteristics do you wish others might experience?

- Have you told that person how you feel?

- If the teacher is no longer alive, have you written to that person's family?

- It can be just as helpful to pass on to your family the lessons learned. Is there anything you remember about this teacher's methods that could be applied today in how you teach others such as family, friends, colleagues at work?

Competency-Based Objectives

Becoming a wiser acting person may not be easy, but it may not be as difficult as we might think. Almost all of us learn behavior patterns that are helpful in navigating through life. Those patterns are identifiable. While their specific forms may vary among us, we recognize their effects. A functional approach such as looking at progress toward performance outcomes to evaluate the learning environment, helps us see what is truly helpful.

Some educators champion using a competency-based curriculum. While they may not intend it, it can appear that they are suggesting that teaching to a list will make one well-educated, mastering many topics. There is some truth to that. However, Jude Collins, retired Ulster University Senior Lecturer and "unretired Irish writer" as he put it, said that "[t]he problem with competency-based curriculums is that learning becomes a matter of being able to perform certain tasks efficiently (and so does teaching). And the importance of looking at a wider horizon—the relationship between what's being taught and social matters, political matters, matters of value and worth—become not just beside the point, but not even thought about."

If taught early to look broadly at that wider horizon Collin writes about, our children not only begin to understand how they interact with the world around them, but they see the importance of learning. They tell us in no uncertain terms that seeking knowledge is a lifetime's journey. Knowing how important it is to show that they respect others through their actions, children demonstrate early-on kind and compassionate behavior. As examples in this book have shown, children, acting wisely, often put adults to shame. The teachers we highlight in this chapter do an amazing job of creating thoughtful, caring, and value-based decision makers as young as four or five years old.

> *"If taught early, our children not only begin to understand how they interact with the world around them, but they see the importance of learning."*

Many hopeful signs are happening around us. Children will often tell us what is of most concern to them about the future as they look at it. They are influenced by their parents and others, but they also develop clear concerns. The world is reportedly more dangerous and uncertain for children today. They have had to deal with great uncertainty in the time of COVID-19 about all the normal issues of growing up with parents who appeared at times, and for the first time, uncertain about what they really knew to be true. Parental uncertainty was often a surprise. The one absolute that many teens indicated they had always believed in was that their parents knew what to do to make the future better. They appear to be learning at an earlier age that parents are not only also uncertain but confused about what to do, how to ensure they enter a wiser, safer world as adults.

Lattal interviewed a group of teens individually about how they know what is true. While little can be made of such a survey, their responses were reassuring and at the same time indicative of the need for stability and certainty for our young on their learning journey. They report knowing what was true for them by 1) what their parents teach them; 2) how they are helped by using the scientific method to examine what they hear; 3) whether the actions they take has a good effect on themselves and others—if not, several indicated they would keep looking for answers that made them feel good about their effects, even if the facts alone were against them. COVID-19 had eroded the usual sources of trust and truth for some. One 18-year-old said, in relation to the turmoil of his last few years, "Without my own ... ability to evaluate, a sense of truth would not belong to me, but rather the most vocal, and sometimes unfortunately malicious, voices in society."

One area where children are finding a unique voice is to let adults know that planetary destruction is abhorrent and it's time for adults to step up. Greta Thunberg as a young climate activist fighting to stop climate change, addressed the United Nations. She implored, "You say you love your children above all else, and yet you're stealing their future in front of their very eyes." She and other activists believe that in fact both climate needs and energy needs can be linked. Horse-drawn carriages, after all, made way for gas-powered cars that are making way for electric to solar power. Vested interest in the current state may keep us from addressing these elements. But if wiser actors prevail, we may succeed at addressing climate and energy needs—and in other ways listen to the voices of our children.

Encouraging Lifelong Learners

In the 1960s, Ogden R. Lindsley, a behavioral psychologist, took his research out of the laboratory to the classroom. He wanted to empower teachers and increase their educational effectiveness. Lindsley promoted an inductive and pragmatic approach to education known as *Precision Teaching*. In this approach, students take an active role in their learning. Teachers encourage students to set learning goals for themselves and practice frequently successive steps to mastery of content. Students measure and graph their own performance to check whether they are on track to reach their goals. Fluent performance promotes new combinations of skills, which is a key element in problem-solving and flexibility (Lindsley, 1996; Binder, 1996, 2003, 2010; Robbins, 2011).

With the help of their teachers, students acquire skills to become lifelong learners. In the best examples of actively working to teach wiser choices, rather than remaining a vessel waiting to be filled, students take active control of their own learning. Group measures are important at times, but in the end, educational accomplishment, measured against a student's individual rate of acquisition, is the most important measure of teaching and learning success.

Classrooms designed to capture individual learning frequency, moment by moment, advance content mastery and teacher effectiveness much further than those that focus on group accomplishment as the most important measure of classroom learning. A very responsive method to chart individual progress revolutionized how to gauge the rate of learning at the level of the individual, not masked by the mean or median or modal scores of the whole. As behavioral science was advancing in its understanding of the unique meaning of individual learning curves, "… the standard visual display of the cumulative records showing changing frequency measures profoundly influenced how effective rates of learning were evaluated, starting with Lindsey in the 1960s. Having spent years using a cumulative record to record behavior change … The glory of science stood before him: a standard, absolute, universal measure of behavior (frequency) could appear on a standard visual display," called the *Standard Celeration Chart* (scan code for Standard Celeration Chart ebook from centralreach.com).

 No doubt every teacher and every learner would benefit from understanding the power of this simple tool as a direct way to demonstrate the effectiveness of student mastery and teaching effectiveness.

Charting the rate of content mastery on a *Standard Celeration Chart* defines how quickly, and accurately, new learning is occurring. Such clarity regarding the rate of learning provides the teacher with a very clear summary of how well the conditions that support student learning have been arranged, measured against the student's own baseline. This tool was made suddenly visible and popular by the way in which Johns Hopkins University tracked how fast COVID-19 was spreading across the United States and the world. This cumulative rate allows comparative analysis to occur about the spread and rate of the disease—a celeration chart, with great social impact. For the individual child, the graph makes clear how quickly mastery is occurring, providing the student and the teacher a clear view into the student's own learning curve.

Generative Learning

Since its foundation in 1980, Morningside Academy has developed effective teaching practices to promote *generative learning*. Generative learning combines existing repertoires to solve new problems in the absence of further instruction. The methods used by Morningside have outstanding data (from Lindsley, 1995 to Johnson, 2021) to back up the research these learning specialists have been documenting for over 40 years (Engelmann & Carnine, 1982; Lindsley, 1990; Johnson & Kevo, 1993; Sherman, Ruskin, & Semb, 1982; Whimbey & Lochhead, 1982). With generative learning, children master content at a very high rate, gaining advances in grade levels that are rarely matched. Often, they are labeled by their schools back home as "distracted" or "hard to manage" or "having a learning disability." Morningside Academy is active all year round and children from around the country attend summer school, making extraordinary gains in such subjects as math, reading, and writing. The mastery they take away from their experiences is reflected by their being placed in higher grades in their local schools or passing reading and math tests, on average, 2.5 grades higher than when they joined the program (Johnson, 1997; Binder and Watkins, 1990).

Morningside Academy uses five principles derived from the science of instruction: (1) students are grouped based on their skills, not based on their age or grade level; (2) complex skills were broken down into smaller teachable units; (3) content analysis occurred; (4) instructional protocols were designed; and (5) excellence in instructional design led to quicker mastery of core content. A new book called *Generativity* by Kent Johnson, Ph.D. (2021), has just been published. It is worth a read by every teacher, a standard for anyone who is committed to accelerating learning in a manner that ensures students' skills transfer into novel environments, creating the possibility of lifetimes of learning. It provides a roadmap for how to create conditions that support children— and adults—leaping over the familiar, the usual, linear, step-by-step model, to dealing with the unfamiliar, addressing elements of novel situations with ease. Novel situations become comfortable—still novel, but without a sense of dread that many of us have when encountering circumstances we have not experienced before. Currently, Kimberly Nix Berens, Nicholas Miller Berens, Kendra Brooks Newsome, and Donny Newsome are achieving similar results with the *Fit Learning* model.

Vicci Tucci's *Competent Learner Model (CLM)* produces startling results for both special needs and general education students. The intended outcome of the CLM is the development of *Competent Learner Repertoires (CLRs)*, which allow learning to occur in everyday circumstances within and across school, home, and community settings. The CLM utilizes best-practice recommendations supported by experimental, conceptual, and applied research from evidence-based practices. The CLM assists educators by providing them with the knowledge of the repertoires that need to be developed, the stimuli that serve as potential reinforcers, and the contingencies to effectively develop or weaken repertoires that work well or do not for the student. "The CLM curricula are designed to serve naïve learners, particularly those with special needs and learning histories that have made learning in typical learning environments very challenging. There are discrete applications of analytic skills applied to values and decision-making" (Tucci, V., Hursh, Daniel E., Laitinen, Richard E., 2004). Watching students in early childhood education apply these principles in group decision-making brings into focus the care built into the design of even simple discussions.

Students are introduced to problem-solving opportunities involving talking-out-loud strategies embedded in Tucci's model. The model helps to transfer verbal skills to the child, building at an early age, skill in accessing what could be called their *knowing how to know* repertoire. Watching their growing assertiveness and independence in finding new ways of operating on their world in such carefully designed classrooms provides the observer with a true lesson in humility. Discovering how wisely even very young children address problems is eye-opening. The curriculum is well worth examining if you want to know more. The students are provided competent learning repertoires to use in various situations until they become adaptive problem solvers. The teachers set up that opportunity, providing content to help students as they do more on their own. In the best sense, teachers get out of the way of the student's learning.

Thinking Skills:
Problem-Solving, Decision-Making, and Analytical Behavior

The benefits of word use are being added in exciting ways to early childhood education and throughout the learning experience, even expanding into adult areas where fluid knowledge acquisition is required. *Talk Aloud Problem-Solving (TAPS)* is one such strategy. Joanne K. Robbins has pioneered creating a culture of thinking and saying in the classroom to develop analytical skills. Such a culture is created by encouraging students to take active roles as both speakers and listeners in the problem-solving process. By hearing students vocalize their thinking, teachers can provide feedback and guidance. Students can also hear how other students vocalize their thoughts and learn from these examples. Once effective thinking strategies become fluent, it is no longer necessary to express such thoughts publicly. The strategies are maintained by the effects of the decisions made. Using words out loud and talking together about solving problems produces more ideas and better solutions. Children exposed to such opportunities show advanced skills in verbally expressed and values-based decision-making.

Francis Mechner, founder and director of the Queens Paideia School (QPS) in NYC, has created a learning academy that teaches its students thinking skills. They learn to use heuristics and decision trees to promote wise acting— sorting for themselves what is true or right for them in how to approach information and worthy outcomes. Teachers find opportunities to help students practice heuristics across a variety of common social situations—for example, how to deal with uncomfortable situations, such as when a friend asks you to do something that you don't want to do, or how to act in the face of differences or conflict. They prompt students to think through why others act the way they do. Decisions are evaluated by factors such as those that have shaped the actions in a story or lesson. What are the consequences that surround and maintain one action over another? They discuss how others might feel in specific situations—the old adage of "walking in the shoes of another" adds perspective. What are alternative ways of acting and the consequences of those actions? They encourage students to make connections across different domains. Mechner states, "I look at wisdom as a set of abilities that can be learned."

Following are some of the heuristics (potentially helpful self-talk) that Mechner cites:

- What is my goal in this situation?
- What are my alternatives?
- Let's give this some thought.
- Let's step back.
- Am I about to act emotionally?
- What other factors should I be considering?"
- What is the other's point of view?
- What is the likely consequence of doing this?
- Have I seen this situation before?
- Is this problem worth solving?

A repertoire of such heuristics can contribute to the set of potentialities and abilities we may refer to as *wisdom*. The goal is for students to create a habit of using these and other complex and overlapping patterns of behavior to develop critical thinking, reflection, and planning. Mechner's students learn how to look at situations contextually, not separate from the moment or events that came before, or separate from future possibilities, good or bad.

Flexibility and Adaptability

All too often, rules for their own sake dominate our expectations of children. "Good rule followers will always be good children." Those who deviate or find an innovative solution can all too often be punished or ignored and labeled "willful" or "spoiled" or "self-centered," among other names.

The value in teaching wisdom is understanding that variation and deviation can be the source of excellence. Outstanding teaching lies in knowing how to shape a child's enthusiasm into outcomes that can be shared. Encouraged to speak and develop many problem-solving strategies, particularly experiencing new ways of looking at a problem, is a critical part of how children (and adults) learn and generalize. Such an environment is not designed to catch anyone doing things wrong, but by not being overly concerned with errors, such an environment invites exploration. Such teachers often achieve excellent control of classroom "comportment" while they generate eager lifelong learners.

> *"The value in teaching wisdom is understanding that variation and deviation can be the source of excellence."*

Interpersonal Relationships and Empathy

In Denmark, every child from age 6 to 16, spends one hour a week in an *empathy enrichment* class where any issue—social, personal, work, or general—can be brought up, and the class works on qualities of listening, responding, offering alternatives, and valuing the solutions of the person bringing the issue forward. This is a two-part lesson. The first is about a person who has a problem and wants to learn how to use classmates and the socially supportive conditions to share, with confidence, any type of problem. The second part of this experience is to be on the listening end, hearing the person's concerns in a way that supports the person but also requires that the listener focuses on a useful solution. If no one in the group has an issue on a given hour of a given week, they simply talk about other subjects or "chill" together. The Danes won the happiness award for many years (and may still be receiving it), given out by the UN after an international survey of the participating countries' populations. They attribute their happiness, at least in part, to the engagement and general well-being of their children, gained through this focus in school on positive problem-solving and bullying reduction.

The Japanese place a great emphasis on school children learning to express positive regard for others and to act as part of a team, putting their needs second to the needs of the group. Placing other people first is considered a good thing, and by doing that, demonstrating a visible understanding of their commitment to the greater good. An individual's effort in this regard is a critical element when success is evaluated. In Japanese classrooms, striving to do the right thing is more important than the act of succeeding at any moment in time while the skills are being mastered. Each step forward is a part of that ultimate progress. While technically not called *shaping* as the word is used in behavior analysis, this approach is very much in line with the technical definition; that is, reinforcing positive effort without the use of deliberate threat or fear, *shaping* approximations toward desired ends. It is assumed that with the right effort, over time, success is possible by all, conveying a cultural belief in a child's capability to do better—at least around this critical issue of showing respect to others.

The values taught to Japanese children certainly help children become aware of the needs of others. The codes of conduct are clear. It appears that the structure of the response is practiced in these exercises. Clearly, striving to achieve good for the whole is important. And yet, anticipating how such training affects children's skill in evaluating when to follow the rule and when to deviate for the good of others or oneself can be difficult. A great amount of public conduct is designed to show how much one cares about the well-being of others, demonstrated actively by both children and adults.

Start with rules that get us going, keep us going, and then as the learning universe expands, add choice and opportunity to explore new ways to do things, to take the learner beyond the rule itself. Allow students to identify what is true and good for them, letting them add conditions to what they need to know as they experience the outcomes of what they say and do. Good teachers, such as individuals highlighted in this chapter, set up conditions for learners' success, without the need to use labels or biases about learning that limit the masterful way they promote their students' potential. They open doors to advance beyond an artificially imposed age requirement or preconceived notion of the limits of "this" young child from "that" background to improve.

The environment that surrounds us—people, processes, and systems—matters significantly in helping or hindering learning to act wisely. A love of learning often accelerates when anchored in principles that embrace the notion that there are many ways of solving problems, as well as for living life. Remember, at times, each of us is a student and a teacher. To set up conditions for children's success in school, Janet Twyman, Professor of Pediatrics, University of Massachusetts Medical School and Director of Innovation and Technology for the Center on Innovations in Learning, said in an interview for the Cambridge Center for Behavioral Studies in 2021 "Make sure the behavior is doable; ensure there's motivation and environmental support; reduce or eliminate coercion; always look to the contingencies." Again, the word *contingencies* in this case does not refer to making alternative plans in case something bad happens, a common use of the word. Rather, here it refers to arranging carefully the conditions that surround and support success, from the perspective of the learner.

Students often find reinforcement in seeing the good work they do along the way. If mistakes are made, remember, they contain information about where the student is, not where he should be. If mistakes are made, use them as good moments of learning. An error is an opportunity. Remember Ben Franklin's keen observation, *"Carve mistakes in sand and success in stone."* Arrange mistakes as steps to promote the positive outcomes you know are possible. Small or large steps toward goals should provide stories about success and how students did it. It can help them see how good they are. Surround them with positive goodwill from their peers and increase the trust factor in your support. Let them know you have confidence in them in the very behavior they exhibit. Effort, not perfection, is the goal. Celebrate their success, in ways they find meaningful.

Luckily, the children in the classrooms we observed have experienced the power of positive reinforcement in address issues in ways that advance their learning, reinforcing the belief that their curiosity is good. At times, they will have to address subjects they may not want to study, but the focus is on their capacity to do well. Good teaching arranges conditions to explore subjects without fear of failure. The measures in such exciting learning environments use the individual's own baseline—the starting point of their beginning performance. That means they are not compared to someone else but to their own wide-open potential. They can measure their own progress, and with the support around them, make gains in finding real solutions.

> *"Tell me and I forget, teach me and I may remember, involve me and I learn."*
>
> –Ben Franklin

PRACTICE 10.2:

What Made Learning Fun When I First Began to Learn?

- Think back to times when you were so delighted to learn something new; when you found adventures in stories, drawing pictures, or learning about numbers.

- What made you enthusiastically anticipate that event?

- What do you remember specifically about your teacher who brought you such cheer and confidence? Was your fondly remembered teacher your parent, a friend, or a traditional classroom teacher?

- What happened along the way and at the end of the learning experience? Does that experience still bring back good memories?

- If you did not experience such a memory, perhaps finding little support for you as a capable person, how do you wish your surroundings as a child differed? Many people do not have warm memories of their school days. Those memories are important, too. If school was aversive, what do you wish had happened to you? What can you take into settings where learning is occurring around you today? Do you manage, coach, teach? Situations that did not go so well can help you consider whether you are making any of those mistakes right now.

- Think of one or two things you see your child's teacher doing that adds good value to your child's days? Make sure the teacher hears that from you.

- Finally, if you are around children, ask them why they enjoy learning. Encourage them to pass on their *likes* to their teachers.

Chapter 11:

Bubble, Bubble, Toil, and Truth: Science and Sorcery

"How do I know that? How do you know that? How do they know that?"

–Edward Tufte

Objectivity in Evaluating Information

Confident people telling us the "right" information can be reassuring, helping to eliminate uncertainty about our actions. At times, we like certainty. Confident people provide a kind of safety net—if we follow them, they will ensure we get to the right outcome. "There is no harm in following my pal, Keith. He has never let me down." However, to the degree such certainty may shape our actions, being persuaded by certainty alone is not enough.

Seeing the World as It Is: Relying on Science, Not Sorcery

Two broad groups of people have gained a reputation for accomplishing outcomes very different from scientific predictions. They have learned how to fool our senses and distort our reality. One group consists of those called magicians; the others are called psychics. A major difference separates these groups. Magicians challenge their audience to figure out how they do the amazing sleight of hands they perform. The audience is aware the magicians are performing tricks for the audience's amusement. Yet, psychics want their audience to believe they have a special skill to predict the future or restore something lost. A deep desire to believe will, on occasion, suspend our skepticism.

Charlatans who claim great powers to predict the future or to do magical tricks that confound our senses are often compelling. They use strange acts that appear to violate the laws of physics. Or they might claim to hear from our dead loved ones, pulling words back from the other world exactly as we remember the tone or words of the people we loved. Indeed, they may appear to have special skills, granted by heaven above. Suspending disbelief and going along with the information contained in the palm of my hand may reveal just the information I need to hear, especially when the messages I am already telling myself are confirmed. Individuals spend large amounts of hard-earned money to have their futures predicted by such individuals and find comfort or dread in their predictions. Such soothsayers are easy to believe, especially if they meet the criteria for one's expectations at some level—be it terrible news or good news.

Randall James Hamilton Zwingeder operated under the stage name of "The Amazing Randi." He was a founding member of the *Committee for the Scientific Investigation of Claims of the Paranormal* (*CSICOP*). His lasting claim to fame was his insistence on using the scientific method to prove real phenomena. Randi was in a unique position as a magician and skeptic to reveal the tricks behind the claimed "paranormal" abilities of others. He set up experiments in which those individuals could try to prove their "special" abilities. But, when placed under controlled conditions, such abilities could not be performed. He revealed the tricks those people were using to perform seemingly amazing feats. He even set up a challenge in which any person who could prove their paranormal or psychic abilities would earn $1 million American dollars. No person was able to claim the prize in 51 years (for those of you wanting to take him up on this bet, unfortunately, the challenge was terminated in 2015).

Be entertained and educated by the work of this brilliant man. *The Skeptic Society* is another worthy organization to investigate. Use fact-checking websites to help you sort rumors from facts. Become more like Randy if you are not like him already. He was full of humor and insight about our great desire to be deceived!

In his book, *The Demon-Haunted World: Science as a Candle in the Dark*, Carl Sagan argued that science offers a "Baloney Detection Kit." To develop skeptical thinking, he recommended the following:

- Wherever possible there must be independent confirmation of the "facts."

- Encourage substantive debate on the evidence by knowledgeable proponents of all points of view.

- Arguments from authority carry little weight—"authorities" have made mistakes in the past. They will do so again in the future. Perhaps a better way to say it is that in science there are no authorities; at most, there are experts.

- Spin more than one hypothesis. If there's something to be explained, think of all the different ways in which it could be explained. Then think of tests by which you might systematically disprove each of the alternatives.

- Try not to get overly attached to a hypothesis just because it's yours. It's only a waystation in the pursuit of knowledge. Ask yourself why you like the idea. Compare it fairly with the alternatives. See if you can find reasons for rejecting it. If you don't, others will.

- If whatever it is that you're explaining has some measure, some numerical quantity attached to it; you'll be much better able to discriminate among competing hypotheses. What is vague and qualitative is open to many explanations.

- If there's a chain of argument, every link in the chain must work (including the premise)—not just most of them.

- *Occam's Razor.* This convenient rule of thumb urges us when faced with two hypotheses that explain the data equally well to choose the simpler. Always ask whether the hypothesis can be, at least in principle, falsified. You must be able to check assertions out. Inveterate skeptics must be given the chance to follow your reasoning, to duplicate your experiments and see if they get the same result.

The scientific method helps us be more objective in the way we assess information. It is a standardized way of making observations, gathering data, forming theories, testing predictions, and interpreting results. Critical thinking requires skills in (1) assessing information; (2) making judgments about what we hear and see; and (3) acting on those data. What happened? Was it as we expected?

Making "Sense" of Our World

As humans, we are constantly trying to make sense of our world, so it is only natural for us to look at ways to explain the actions we take. We have come up with many explanations over the years. Not surprisingly, most of these explanations are of little value. They rely on coincidences, anecdotes, and hypothetical constructs. They do little to account for our behavior in terms of behavior responding to the conditions that surround it.

To make sense of our world, look at the conditions that influence our actions. A common misconception involves the belief that behavior is caused by internal or private events. While we have said that belief comes from those events that shape our actions, it is still a very difficult concept for people to understand. It sounds as though we are saying people have no influence. They are shoved about by external circumstances. We are uniquely and independently ourselves—are we not? We are like snowflakes, no two of us are the same, but the cause to a very large extent is in our learning histories and experiences that are complex, full of twists and turns. Personality, the sum of many consistently used and fluently learned patterns of behavior, is often described as defining our unique selves—the "thing" that makes us who we are, the thing that makes us act as we do. Such a premise is more illusion than fact. Personality is defined by the behavior we do or do not do on a frequent enough basis to form a foundational summary about who we are. Most of us show consistency in terms of large patterns of behavior, tone, and physical presence.

The idea of how I show up based on personality theory means, for many, that the *"who I am"* is set and very difficult to change. Changing how we show up can be difficult in some settings; but the control is in the conditions. Think of yourself at work. You may appear quiet and behave as some might label an introvert. However, at home, surrounded by those you love, you are gregarious and lively. Some of the greatest performers and entertainers look confident and outgoing on stage, but they are reported to be reserved and quiet in their personal lives. That is a picture of you, twice over. There is much written about the difficulty in changing our behavior (often stated as the *intractable who we are*). Changing our patterns of behavior can be difficult in many circumstances. Given that change is influenced by the conditions that surround us, we may be changing often, sometimes in ways that seem "brand new," unique, or foreign to behavior that others expect of us.

Companies still use the much-discounted Myers-Briggs test to understand the potential of employees, including how to 1) relate, who to 2) promote, and what types to 3) assign to teams or tasks. Lattal found that in one company she worked in extensively, the results of where individuals showed up on the Meyers-Briggs were used for plush team assignments and leadership advancement, attributing "scientific certainty" to the test, zipping right past behavior of individuals that were varied and fine, behavior right before their eyes. The potential of employee advancement moved from the behaviors exhibited in great variation on a regular basis to a trait analysis based on a very flawed test. Bias of the senior leaders doing the reviewing, with no real knowledge of how behavior adapts quickly became the target to overcome, if one was to advance. Those senior leaders, persuaded by false data, were really the audience to impress. However, in many cases, the individuals climbing the corporate ladder had no idea how they got sidetracked, lost out on an upcoming promotion, or remained doing analytic work when they were hoping to join an innovations/new products team. Actual behavior was ignored, often accompanied by statements like "This result is so unexpected." "He seems so cooperative and innovative." "Behavior can be deceiving." No, in this case, sorcery can be deceiving in the hands of this very real Fortune 500 human resources leadership team discussing succession plans for candidates up for promotion, putting too much stock into the just-completed and invalid Myers-Briggs assessment of capability.

The power of personality tests in the hands of those who do not understand behavior, or the limits of such diagnostic tests in any case, can lead to a lifetime of pigeon-holed work assignments. Many such stories occur across corporate America. A fundamental challenge for all of us is to move beyond the belief that adult behavior cannot change in significant ways. Take one behavior at a time. Take your time. Reinforce small steps toward goals. Recognize and appreciate a quiet person for speaking up, however quietly. Compliment meaningful ideas or approximations toward more meaningful contributions. Shape. Take delight in people learning. Thank that person for the effort. Help build confidence one conversation at a time. See the effort, not as the result, not the final goal, but good movement toward the result. Changes made in a few visible ways in varied settings begin to shape a new narrative.

Most people take comfort in a congruent worldview of who they are and why they act as they do. They see themselves as the source of that uniqueness, no one or nothing else. An idea may define who they are—always fair, insightful, alert, uniquely capable when compared to others. Studies have shown the concept of a "unique me" is common around the world. Such studies show that the unique person I see myself as being is shaped by the same influences that shape similar behavior—thoughts, feelings, and actions—as those of my next-door neighbor, for example. For some people, learning how similar we are may seem troubling. In the end, no matter our desire to be unique, humans are more alike than different in some essential and fundamental ways (Lattal, K. A., & Lattal, A. D., 1967).

"In the end, no matter our desire to be unique, humans are more alike than different in some essential and fundamental ways."

Always think of the reciprocal relationship that exists between your actions and the conditions around you. These interactions might include thoughts, feelings, and sensations. Private events are a part of our "behavior stream." Private events, including how we talk to ourselves, can be triggered in the moment by the similarity to a prior experience. Prior experiences can certainly influence a sequence of actions. Behavior is reciprocal, always being affected by and influencing the interactions with the environment that surrounds us. However, our thoughts, feelings, and sensations don't take place in a vacuum. They occur in response to the changes in the consequence conditions of our learning histories and in the immediate conditions around us. If we see *wisdom* as descriptive of the way we want to act and believe that it can be learned, we can start arranging the conditions we need to solve the cultural challenges and social interactions that could use a little "wisdom."

Analyzing the Conditions Around Us

Behavior can be subtle (a slight facial twitch) or large (full body shaking); plain for all to see and hear; or obscure, difficult to understand, perhaps only sensed by ourselves. Behavior shows up in how we respond to the extraordinary events and transforming mysteries of great art or music to something as mundane as doing the dishes. Behavior is the totality of how we engage with our human condition.

Behavior is determined by the constellations of things happening around us, and to us, over the years—our learning histories. When we use the word *determined*, we mean that we make choices based on

> *"Behavior is the totality of how we engage with our human condition."*

experiences we are fortunate enough, or unfortunate enough, to have and the consequences of those experiences, rich with reinforcing or punishing effects on our behavior. We respond to those conditions that are part of our life path no matter our country of birth and regardless of the rules our culture's code of conduct might desire us to say and do.

The sources for learning are the same, no matter how we dress, talk, shave (or don't shave), dance, love, eat, bow in greeting or say "howdy"—everything about us sums to our human condition. We learn in the same way—*through sources of reinforcement that surround us*—a loving mother's touch, the priest or minister, the fond teacher who advises us, and the community that helps us do the right things. Fully understanding the similarities in learning about how we behave as human beings, provides us all a stronger link to one another as well as encourages us how to learn from one another. Such understanding may help reduce our fear of differences that are influenced by varied cultures and histories of learning. Knowing that we are all following the same principles about how to change behavior, embedded in the science of learning, can bring the people of the world closer. People behave, however, in many ways that we do not believe are right. We approach behavior through our own learning, our histories of behavior that we see as right or wrong.

To understand behavior, look at the conditions that surround any new or ongoing actions. The events that take place before behavior are called *antecedents*. The events that take place after behavior are called *consequences*. Antecedents set up the conditions for behavior to begin. Consequences help predict whether behavior will repeat in the future. For example, when presented with a problem (antecedent), we need to find a solution (behavior). The success or failure of the decision made (consequence) will determine whether we are more or less likely to repeat the same solution when facing similar problems in the future.

Looking at this sequence of events, antecedent-behavior-consequence (ABC), anchors behavior between two important contextual variables. It provides an objective and practical way that can be used to bring about the changes we want. Of course, we understand that this ABC concept is fluid and ever-changing. It is not linear but can at times be quite concurrent, with many Antecedents and Consequences and new Behaviors arising out of these intersecting conditions. Consequences become initiating Antecedents and behavior morphs and changes. Every day we improve or stand still, not a bad thing, depending on that ABC rolling ball of influence, including such variables as how we process information, feel connections, and integrate learning. Context wraps around us in a bigger ball of propelling us forward, and our experience with contingencies shape our future responses.

Without the brain's activity, we would be unable to operate in our environment, except in the most primitive ways. Behavioral science is helping provide answers for how we process information, learn in faster ways, or jump ahead to respond to new experiences. A robust life depends on our brains and our behavior. In the years ahead we will know much more, but we do know now that life, in the form of cells and synapses and behavior and experiences, are a part of an intricate learning architecture, extending capacity in reinforcing ways.

Consequence as Compass

Consequences from the earliest days of human experience are extremely important in learning to survive as well as we have as a species. Consequences are closely linked to our evolutionary survival. They taught us to run when large predators approached, to wear fur coverings in winter, to sharpen sticks to hunt for food, and all the other, more mundane things we do. Learning through consequences gives us the advantage of adapting to rapidly changing environments.

Consequences teach us how to behave in different and difficult situations and play a major role in changing our behavior. We are doing more and less of many different things at the same time. Consequences as we are affected by them are the motivating factor in our behavior. How much and for how long we do something is tied to the type of consequence, its timing, and the likelihood of its effects (as described in Chapter 2).

Understanding the use of consequences is important to promote change in a desired direction. Change is a process, not a static event. Changes in behavior don't always occur from one day to the next. In fact, changing highly reinforced patterns of behavior often takes time. Do not despair if you don't quickly see the changes you want. Moving in the desired direction is all that matters. Often, we gradually change behavior to get to a desired result, which is a process we have described earlier as *shaping*—and the steps to change are often described as *successive approximations to the goal.*

Shaping refers to behavior built strictly on the use of *positive reinforcement.* That means that shaping does not rely on the use of aversive conditions, such as threat or fear, to change behavior. The individual may still perceive the act of changing as aversive, but the change is managed through strategies that are designed to be *positive.* Build the behavior you want through the behavior that you see, reinforcing small steps toward the goal. Ask yourself, "What is the goal I am trying to achieve?" Are you getting closer to that goal each day? What are the next steps to that goal? Can you arrange consequences that support changes in the desired direction?

Reinforce approximations to the kind of behavior you want in your child, spouse, or self. Teaching behavior that reflects a positive problem-solving approach is a good place to start with your own children. For example, when you see your children engaging in two activities, one you don't want and one you do, attend to the one you want. Tell them why you don't want the other or ignore it, if not harmful. In any case, you want to create a positive path forward by encouraging the behavior of choice. When we point out good behavior we want, a person is much more aware of how to get to those outcomes. Building desirable behavior and expanding options decreases a constant focus on the elimination of problem behavior.

Coercion is defined as the practice of "persuading" someone to do something by using force or threats. Such strategies of control stop unwanted behavior almost immediately. Thus, the person using threat or fear is likely to continue using threat to stop other annoying behavior—for example, stopping a child from whining about homework by issuing a threat or telling someone their stated opinion is nonsense. Sometimes the threat is subtle. The boss asking, "We all like the culture here, don't we?" is heard as meaning that the employees better say they like it if they want to stay. The boss may not have meant to send an "or else" message. He may have wanted all to agree with him, however, and thought everyone should like the culture. He may have believed that if they did not, they could certainly leave, but he might never realize that he was using coercion to get his way.

When you use such words or actions, the undesired behavior of the child or the co-worker reduces or stops, sometimes gradually but at times, quite abruptly. By using this method of control, you may find yourself caught in something called "the reinforcement trap." You are reinforced by using coercion because it is highly effective (for you), increasing the likelihood of its future use. Behaviors you keep telling yourself to stop doing are maintained by the *reinforcement trap*. Look carefully at your behavior that you wish to stop. What is keeping that behavior going? The amount of reinforcement you get strengthens the likelihood of using threat or negative words again.

Individuals who experience positive consequences for themselves by using threat and fear are likely to use such strategies again and again. This strategy does not focus on building desired behavior. As a result, the punished behavior often comes back when the coercive elements of control are not present. For many reasons, learn how to *differentially reinforce* the behavior you want, rather than focusing on eliminating the behaviors you don't want. It might be helpful to read more about coercion and its effects, used too often in our society (Delprato, D. J., 2002; Sidman, M., 1993; Sidman, M., 2001).

People will engage in new behaviors if knowing that continuing to behave as they do will lead to punishing consequences. Children work quickly to change their behavior if told to do so by a parent who uses frequent doses of threat and fear. When told to start "answering in the right way," they try to do that as best they can. Young children often do not know the meaning of "the right way." Trying hard to please, they may end up in a continuous cycle of repeated errors. Failure to have the skills or know what to do or simply not do things fast enough often leads to increased threats that cause greater fear. Faulty reasoning about failing to follow orders by adults is at the sad center of many horrible tales of child abuse. Many times, adults are also in situations where they are told to do things differently under threat or fear conditions. Loss of a much-needed job may be one dreaded consequence. Failure to "do it right" can lead to lasting emotional turmoil or physical harm. Coercive conditions impact our behavior in very powerful ways. Nevertheless, people can act wisely in extremely punishing situations. Sometimes the wisest act is to leave the situation. However, for many caught in such excessively controlling situations, behaving other than as ordered is very difficult, often with few options.

Reinforcing the WRONG Thing

We know better and yet we do the wrong things. Ever said that? You knew better but you still did it? Take some comfort in the fact that our behavior is logical, even if it seems quite crazy. Behavior is lawful—it follows the laws of learning. Those actions that are reinforced are strengthened, increasing the likelihood we will do them again. All behavior can be reinforced, that is, strengthened, even problematic ones. White nationalists, for example, *reinforce* certain biases about how their members are to behave toward people of other races, religions, customs, or beliefs. They frequently *praise their members* who behave as they want, creating a sense of belonging, of *family*, mostly achieved through aversive control. However, using coercive methods to build commitment is unwise and does nothing for the long-term good of humanity. Gang members most likely also use aversive control within their group. Members of our larger society understand the incredible danger such behavior can initiate. Having the perceived right to use threats against certain people, if unchecked by the larger society, can spread. Threatening others is such an easy thing to do. Unintentionally failing to address harm done to others by looking down or looking away, endorses the right to do harm. Right now, you might look at the newspaper or TV and see harm being done to those who are different. Individuals who use such strategies often describe the intoxicating power of having people obey them. They may misinterpret their power as being a result of their excellent leadership, perfect parenting, or knowing how to manage people well.

There have been a host of psychological studies on obedience. Many people equate obedience with rules they have been taught about the need to obey those in authority. Many times, such obedience to following an order is essential to health and well-being. Other times, learning how to evaluate the events occurring around you vs. what you are told to do is important. Learning to assess the effects of actions you are asked to do in relation to the lives of others is also important.

Our histories of learning about following authority can overpower us when told to act in a way we know is wrong by a person in a particular role. Gaining confidence in saying no, even if not certain, is a skill we all need. Researchers are finding how to help people assess behavior that is requested of them and weigh it against other areas of knowledge or their own "gut reaction," alerting them that the orders or instructions are wrong. There are many examples of obedience studies and public instances of following orders over one's best judgment. For example, co-pilots have failed to override a pilot's decision, even if they knew it would bring down the plane. Nurses administered lethal procedures during surgery, knowing there was no justification for such acts, except that the doctor told them to do so. Engineers drove so fast they forced engines off tracks and oil rigs to exceed capacity to meet their bosses' desired production deadlines, leading to massive deaths and destruction. Soldiers are taught that their first rule, in times of war or under command, is to follow legal orders. Knowing that killing non-combatants is forbidden in the military code of conduct, they did so anyway in My Lai, Vietnam, because their captain told them to remove witnesses and protect their buddies—after a series of bad decisions led to great civilian destruction. Many things lead to such decisions: fear of discovery, fear of failure, fear of losing a well-paying job, fear of being banned through word of mouth from a particular industry, fear of retribution, even by your colleagues, as well as belief in authority. Many reasons exist to follow authority. Nurses are taught that challenging a surgeon's orders, someone more deeply trained, particularly during an operation, may lead to the death of the patient. If a co-pilot were to second-guess the pilot, the potential for chaos could be great.

If we are to create a wiser society, learning to say no, or to step back and seek more information, or to walk away are needed. Have you ever been told to do something you did not think was the right thing to do? Looking back, perhaps you decided to do it even as it made you feel bad because of the authority you perceived in the person who asked you. It could be much less of a life-and-death situation than the examples above.

PRACTICE 11.1:

Following Authority When the Direction is Wrong

- Do you remember why you followed directions of someone you knew was giving you wrong advice? A friend? A relative? A spouse? A trusted adviser? A boss?

- Do you know why specifically you followed bad advice?

- If you did not, what kept you from doing that? How do you pass on that kind of learning to others?

- What were the drivers for you to do a small or large thing you knew to be wrong, even if not originated from outside advisors?

- How did it affect you?

The skill in understanding the degree of control others exercise over us is a very good first step in getting out from under the control of false narratives or thinking we have no choice in situations when there are actually many choices.

Sometimes in our personal lives we do things we don't want to do, that we believe are wrong, but our best friend (as we define that person) wants us to. You may find that the person who asks you to act in ways that violate your fundamental values becomes less valuable to you, but you still listen and obey; sometimes out of fear and sometimes simply to maintain a calm homelife. Learn to say *no* or to identify another way. Learning when to leave if no change occurs is important as well.

Building Bully Behavior to Last a Lifetime

A parent may teach her child to be a bully to other children, yelling and kicking, and committing other destructive acts, to keep others from bullying her child first. She uses lots of *loving statements* about how tough and strong her child is. Voila! Little Baby Bully is created via the use of reinforcement for bad behavior. Baby Bully, however, isn't necessarily wise about when or how or why to bully; has not necessarily learned the art of distinguishing when and who and why. And, thus, *building* bullying behavior is not wise on the part of the parent. At times, such parental techniques might be done by a well-intended but desperate parent to give her child tools to manage conflict. Despite that heartfelt, genuine, nurturing intention, this kind of strategy is unwise. To keep one safe, it may seem the right thing to do. However, teaching a child how to use threat and fear is a strategy that affects their whole life. Little baby bullies grow into big-people bullies, which becomes a problem all along the way, potentially for a lifetime. In this symbolic *birthing of a little baby bully* example, let's say that the parent simply *shaped* the desired words and deeds she wanted her little baby to exhibit to keep the child a bit safer. She prided herself on not using coercion, such as the use of threat and fear, to get the bully behavior going, but only loving endorsement.

How many aggressive patterns are born that take on a righteous sense of good when born by such positive attention? At times, you may say, one must protect oneself, stand up for oneself. Just understand to the fullest degree possible, that many unintended consequences are also created. One can often deal with hostility in other ways that do not require reciprocating with hostility.

Parents take on big issues in teaching children how to survive in an often harsh world. Helping the child see that the bully has been carefully taught to get their way can help the child understand that it is the bully's behavior, not his basic worth, that needs to change. This may seem a small gain for those of us who have experienced a bully in our lives, but it is very important to help our children and ourselves see that how we respond to another person *shapes* us both.

The word *wise* is directed toward particular behavior that, when evaluated, leaves a person, the group, the community, or over time, the culture, better off. In the face of physical threat, some patterns of action are needed as alternatives. Unfortunately, many behavior-change strategies teach the "do this or else" approach. Many bullies learn bullying behavior because 1) by bullying they succeed, and want to succeed again, or 2) they are bullied at home. Therefore, they learn that if you want things sooner rather than later, "your way or the highway" bully behavior pays off. Much better ways are available to get desired behaviors going. Try telling that to an overworked, exhausted parent living in an abusive environment with not a lot of time or energy to teach a better way.

Rules about how people should behave may justify the use of these coercive techniques. However, some of the most dangerous behavior in the world is not at its root cause built through aversive strategies, but often built using *reinforcement*. Many gangs, racially motivated hate groups, various religious groups formed to exclude or eliminate other beliefs or patterns of behavior, end up keeping people together through their common, highly *reinforcing*, membership requirements, creeds, and expectations about how to act for the benefit of the group. This pattern is no different than the way other groups with positive agendas form. The group may offer a strong sense of recognition and support, a warm and *reinforcing* community, even if designed to do harm to individuals they dislike.

Remember, reinforcement in no way means that it is defined by adding to the "common good" or other values of society. It is simply describing the directionality and intensity of consequences. The argument is made by those on the fringe of society that teaching baby bullies to hate people of other religions or skin color has a good social value for humankind. That is not our perspective, and it has no moral standing. It is the source of so much that is scary in how diverse populations are identified and all too often terrorized. The bully has learned very effective ways to get the results he or she wants. Learning to change the acceptability of bullying behavior is as important as almost anything else we can do to create a wiser world.

Consider the individual's learning history. Most of a person's words and actions have worked for him or her in some form. In other words, their behavior has been useful for them in navigating through life. Sometimes that is called "useful working" but that is not enough to tell us that it is good for our common humanity. Getting something valuable or accomplishing something important strengthens those actions. This highlights a great responsibility when attempting to change someone else's behavior. It is not enough to look at behaviors that are problematic for us. We must explore why those behaviors occur in the first place, and how readily they generalize across conditions. We need to ask ourselves if the person needs to act differently for our benefit or for the individual? Do we have the tools to teach or model such alternatives? We must be alert to the values we are seeking to establish, looking further at a person's or group's "core beliefs." A more thorough analysis of this is needed to address the many "isms" held in various ways about how people *shoulda, oughta* behave. Changing what we say we value may offer us a boost toward changing our behavior. Changing our behavior may indeed change the way we express our wants, hopefully over time moving toward more inclusive values.

Growing up in an environment that provides limited opportunities for improvement can be a challenge even if you hope to do things differently. The Crenshaw neighborhood of South Los Angeles was one of those places in the 1980s. Gang culture and violence was common and permeated the streets. Threat and fear of acting differently or outside norms dictated by the social setting can end in disaster.

Ermias Asghedom was raised by his mother and grandmother in Crenshaw, surrounded by these types of conditions. Not surprisingly, Ermias joined a local gang as a youngster. A degree of safety in numbers came with this action, but also at great cost. Fortunately, he had the opportunity to visit his extended family in Eritrea, located in eastern Africa, in 2004. He was 19 years old at the time and stayed for three months, experiencing an altogether different culture; certainly, one contextually different than his neighborhood in South Los Angeles. For the first time in his life, he was in a place where people of color oversaw opportunities to achieve. He had a good number of role models that displayed new patterns of behavior. He saw firsthand the impact a different environment could have on members of a culture and how it affected him. He began to see that taking charge of his future shouldn't be through acts of violence, but instead to strive to do something positive for the future. He knew he had to set up consequences that would reinforce and build that kind of possibility in his neighborhood. He came back home thinking about ways in which contingencies could be created to promote success. Changing his name to Nipsey Hussle, he became a rapper and released his first mixed tape in 2005 to great success. He created his own record label and became a community activist.

Nipsey's vision was to create opportunities for the people in South Los Angeles. He acted inside and outside that community. His understanding of the rules within that community and the rules of the larger society enabled him to build a bridge in terms of contextual connection. The community embraced and celebrated his vision along with him. A reciprocal sense of opportunity grew among many young members of South L.A. and beyond. While investing in *The Marathon Agency*, bringing talent to venues where they could be heard, and in other ways providing entrepreneurial opportunities to local talent, people responded to Nipsey in ways that *reinforced* his efforts. He became the key driver to helping create positive, values-based behaviors promoted and *reinforced* by the local community. He spoke against violence, participated in prison reform and rehabilitation projects, and got involved in politics. He was mixing in a demonstrated pattern of positive respect for the lives of members of the community, building such values visually into the fabric through new ways of behaving. As he told *Mixtape Daily* during an interview in 2009, "I ain't really left yet ... I live somewhere else, but outta habit, outta convenience, how my foundation was structured, I'm still over here [South L. A.]. My loved ones are still over here. I feel like when I do come back [to the neighborhood], I bring opportunity. I'm not ballin' out of control, but I bring opportunity back. Not just 'cause it's cliché, but because I got loved ones that got potential to do other things than be in the street."

In Eritrea, Nipsey Hussle was exposed to conditions needed for a community to thrive. He brought back his experience and immediately established an environment to support his own, newly learned behavior to achieve the future he envisioned. The structures and systems he created for new ways to earn a living and bring values to life were attended to in detail. He saw changing the narrative of possibilities as key. He was determined to be a catalyst for positive change, using the resources and connections he had to create opportunities for the people in his community. He gave them an example of success and a vision of hope. He tried new methods of behaving and quickly reinforced the positive effects of aspirational values. He inspired people in his community, and, as well, Eritreans living far away. His actions were shaped largely by his experiences in Eritrea, however briefly, leading to powerful images of how to do things differently. He wanted to teach his neighbors to dream big and look out for one another. Changing the contextual landscape, Nipsey said that, through the power of words and actions, all of us, right here, can change our world for the better. His good work was interrupted in the very streets he sought to change. Sadly, Nipsey Hussle was shot and killed outside his business on March 31, 2019.

Everything Nipsey exemplified, especially when communities talk about role models and their value, adds to our collective sensitivities of the positive changes that wise acting can accomplish. Such unique human beings teach us quickly by example about how to escape the seduction of using threat and fear to get our way. While all too often such good lives end by very violent means, the effect of modeling new behavior served as a viable alternative for members of Nipsey's community. His words, full of expressed values and belief in the possibilities for everyone, and deeds in directing tangible economic and social change, set the stage for meaningful change. However, behavior drifts. Understanding the need to maintain a new culture through its early years takes commitment from the larger culture. Such persistence is one of the challenges in sustaining a wiser society.

Similarly, stories of context and change abound in how individuals move from positions of hate or distrust to very different and inclusive perspectives. A graduate student in behavior analysis, raised a Catholic, told her professor that she hated Irish Protestants for wrongs they had done to her distant family and their community. She then went to Belfast. Upon return, much to her professor's amazement at the depth of feeling expressed prior to the trip, she made a simple but obvious statement, "There are two sides to every issue." Her key learning was that in these kinds of conflicts, she needed to look beyond her engrained perspective to really see why people behaved as they did. It did not mean that she endorsed the actions of people on either side, but she had a very new awareness about how behavior can be colored, and how she could end up hating a group based only on their religious affiliation. Religious affiliation did not tell the full story of each side's desires to live lives of peace. Getting to know people on the other side, meeting them, seeing them, provided her the strong link to their common humanity.

We can only begin to see the reason for other people's choices by looking at the conditions that surround them and then to understand that they, like us, are striving to find a good life. Classifying a group by their religion, as if the religion itself was the cause of deeds that were brutal and unfair, and thus all members in that group classified as Protestant were guilty by association, was no longer of any real meaning to this young woman after her visit. Think of all the individuals we meet who are members of a group or simply associated by race or nationality or religion but not in a group that does harm. We should not reduce individuals to blanket labels regarding the group.

Those unique aspects of how we show up are part of the richness of this diverse world. Traveling to Columbia, Latin America, to Northern Ireland, or to the hills of West Virginia, USA, can help us better understand the conditions and the people we find there. We can read about unique customs as well. Nevertheless, bias is difficult to eliminate, perhaps impossible for some. Being aware of our own biases is a way to mitigate their influence. How do we begin to look objectively at others? How do others begin to see us, not a stereotype of who they think we are? How are you viewed? What is it that unfairly builds biases about you, perhaps in the same way you build biases about others?

PART III

A Vision for a Better World

Chapter 12:

Turning the Tides:
A Contextual Approach to Change

"Meaning is context-bound ... "

–Jonathan Culler

Context is found in the conditions that surround us and that shape our learning over time. Context is broader than immediate conditions. Context forms experiences we have brought to this moment and how the next steps we take will influence our actions or words in the next moment. Context provides meaning to our experiences. Established in the design of language, structures, systems, policies, and processes, context contains rules of conduct and consequences to support or suppress outcomes. Context creates freedom from fear to say and do the right words and actions. It strengthens punishing effects for behaviors that are off-limits, that cannot be said and done. Context supports many mythologies, belief systems, about the meaning of being a member of a particular race or nationality. It sets the stage through public policies and economic practices about those who live in poverty.

Context affects job availability, access to early education and higher education, incarceration for small offenses forgiven if done by others, higher rates of entry into military service among the poor or minorities, and where barriers are erected to ease in voting or obtaining financial aid. The context of where one lives often defines the availability of healthcare from early pregnancy to aging, or where overhead lights are placed on streets and crosswalks. Context is about the needed resources to feed oneself and find good food at a reasonable cost. It is found in the conditions that allow sleep instead of loud noise to surround you at night. Context is sustained by how well it has through rules, consequences, and histories of access, supported a variety of actions of people and financial support to sustain the same or similar access over time. The elements of context hold the answer to how to change behavior for the better.

Arrange the conditions that surround behavior and behavior will change. Well, not so fast. It depends. Behavior might increase, remain the same, or decrease. Conditions that affect you directly, regardless of how good others tell you they are for you, is like finding yourself in a gym surrounded by opportunity but not about to get on that bike or pick up a weight or run on the treadmill that may be very good for you. It is not enough to set conditions for success without considering the fuels for action. The larger context in which we find ourselves—political, social, environmental, cultural, the relationship to us and our behavior—our emotional life—sets the stage for a multitude of choices.

Since we view our culture as belonging to us—at the family, community, regional, and national levels—we tend to state the rules of that culture with certainty as to their correctness. Nevertheless, in every culture, people have different values about the "right thing to do." For example, in the United States, the current political climate highlights very diverse perspectives about the meaning of the word *America*. Individuals from all political positions may believe that they are defending the culture they have long come to believe is reflected by the word *America*. How does a person decide the right thing to do when a particular subculture's rules of conduct allow little to no deviation? How do people make reasoned decisions when their culture states that the truth is not found in some scientific notation or other objective criteria, but in their own *shoulds, oughts*, and *musts* belief systems? That kind of certainty can be applied across political parties, associations, and communities of all sizes.

In many cultures, little time is spent discussing how to evaluate whether an outcome is right or wrong. What needs to change in the conditions that surround us, the context that recognizes and rewards our behavior? Many groups have deeply held tenets about right or wrong. On the face of it, working to behave differently—wiser, you might say—can immediately lead to judgment and dissatisfaction with the actions you want to take because your actions don't conform to the group's rules.

Behaving wisely includes listening to conflicting advice, objectively examining the decisions of our community, discussing their intended meaning, and so forth. It means understanding that to act differently than the norm can lead to very uncertain outcomes. Culture is complex. People behave according to the rules as a means of acceptance, such as being a loyal gang member or a committed church member. Clearly, disagreement can lead to consequences that are not wanted. Threatening conditions can keep behavior going long after a person no longer wants to behave in the manner required to maintain membership. Exiting these conditions and the subculture of which one is a part can be difficult and even dangerous.

Access to a Better Life

Although humans have made great technological progress, the way we treat one another has not advanced at the same pace. High rates of crime, poverty, and illiteracy still exist around the world. We get into fights, engage in war, and inflict great harm on those with whom we disagree. We see people as either worthy or not, a part of us or one of them. We continue to warm the oceans and pollute the air we breathe. Changes in society are happening at such an accelerated pace that adaptation appears difficult. Many of us find much comfort, or *reinforcement*, in doing what we have learned is good for ourselves and for our community. Sometimes, we can predict the probable future if we do not change. Yet, we may have a persistent history and comfort with our behavior—particularly behaviors that fit our well-learned belief system.

The Multiple Layers of Context

Dwight Harshbarger, a behavioral psychologist, and expert in safety, reminded Darnell many years ago that context is so often at the absolute center of striving to do the right thing. He was writing about people in the workplace. Harshbarger's quote, with a few of our bracketed changes, can be applied to conditions that interact with behavior to increase the likelihood of individual and cultural well-being…

> *Imagine an input-throughput-output model that is embedded in a complex architecture [of our culture] that rises above and below the*

flow of behavior—architecture that structures and shapes that flow, creates, and limits possibilities and outcomes. And all this travelling forward in time with behavior always moving through. As historians, we can look back and retrospectively examine the three-dimensional architecture, structure, and behavioral flow [that led toward realizing a society's desired outcome].

–Harshbarger (personal communication, July 2012)

Context at a socio-cultural level allows us to examine the kind of values-based wisdom this book promotes. Applying science to conditions that surround behavior helps us see—*look before you listen*, as Thomas Gilbert would say. He meant that when we want to understand behavior, start first with what we see and hear. Observe. Behavior occurs in the setting in which we find it, responding to the conditions that support or impede it. If you want greater understanding between people, how might the conditions be arranged to get more of that? Take care to build the conditions that are more likely to lead to the outcomes you want. As long as you can, keep an objective eye on the conditions that surround the behavior you want to influence.

> *"...keep an objective eye on the conditions that surround the behavior you want to influence."*

Let's assume you are aware that bias, hate, and fear are present in some everyday events that surround you or a friend. On occasion, you may get to observe that *"boil, boil, toil, and trouble"* moment when words take on their own red-hot, explosive power, triggering more words and there you—and others go. You might not have participated in moments of extreme abuse but your wise acting stopped. Why was it? What did you see or hear that set you off? What were the socially expected rules? What happened to them? What did you do?

Was there a moment when outcomes could have shifted? Most of the time those moments are not open to observation, occurring only with the individuals who experience them, but if you are ever in such moments, try to consider some of the previous questions before you act. Wise behavior is so important in such moments and so difficult to come by. Using biased words or actions are often attributed to fundamental flaws of character—a lack of good judgment or too much hate. While such terms provide explanation to many, they do not help us change nor are they always accurate. The key to using different words lies in how we respond to the conditions that surround us. Each instance increases the likelihood of the next. The more we can assess and change our behavior, either as passive observer or contributor, the better for us all. We have, most of us, experienced those moments when we walked or looked away. This is not a morality play, as if we must be brave, but it is about expanding how we view the conditions that surround us. Try to identify how you can alter your future actions to affect better outcomes.

Working with extremes of disruptive behavior in prisons, criminally incarcerated psychiatric facilities, and with child and adult abuse, the authors have often observed extreme escalations in behavior occurring in an instant. Those involve very difficult behavior patterns often driven by years of abuse—perpetrators of violence often abuse others as they were once abused. Daily life is most often not about those extremes, but in everyday moments we can examine our behavior and see how we contributed to an outcome that was not good for someone else. If you understand the triggers that kept you from acting as you wanted to act, you begin to exercise control over your behavior to produce better outcomes. A trigger may be the way your friend speaks to you, and you know you need to discuss that with your friend. You may need to recognize and change your dismissive comments to your child's questions. Consider how quickly in everyday conversation, in the context of your work life, someone gets marked as worthy or unworthy, given access or denied access. Consider the biases and assumptions that people may have about you. Make it personal to change any behavior that sustains bias, threat, and fear. Sometimes we don't know how to act, so we do nothing, or our own history of reinforcement may shelter us from acknowledging certain circumstances. So, begin to observe as if you are looking at yourself from afar. We all have skin in how our immediate world is built, helping or impeding desired outcomes, and how that in turn might build a wiser world. Changing conditions of small-scale and large-scale oppression embedded in social structures often requires the actions of many, setting up new methods of reinforcing behaviors that lead to better results. Those events are more likely to build the change you seek into the fabric of the social condition, leading to better outcomes for all.

Individuals with an extended history of drug use and unemployment are often stigmatized in our society. They might be viewed as difficult to rehabilitate because they are perceived as lacking "self-control," "motivation," or "drive" to change their pattern of addiction. As a result, they often face limited opportunities, reverting frequently to heavy drug use after returning from rehab centers. Silverman, along with Holtyn, and Subramaniam (2018), researchers at Johns Hopkins University, shared the view of many that learned patterns of addictive behavior return quickly after rehabilitation unless new conditions surround these individuals upon their return, conditions arranged to promote new patterns of personal control and meaningful recognition. Silverman and colleagues studied the research about learning and sustainable behavior change, the conditions that surround and shape us. They set up an innovative approach to those reentering the community. They gave them meaningful and purposeful work and provided the opportunity to earn wages and receive, like other employees, feedback on their performance. Rather than using interventions focusing on health-related behavior—like drug abstinence—the Silverman team designed anti-poverty interventions to promote, hopefully, long-lasting, positive change. They did so by working with employers to ensure that these individuals did the same meaningful job-related work others did, that their work had purpose in adding value to the operation, and they could be evaluated as others were. They provided training in job-related skills and offered opportunities to work for wages based on meeting two requirements: 1) measurable job performance, and 2) providing drug-free samples to gain access to work.

A surprising discovery from these studies is that participants abstained from drug use if they were earning a wage at work and that wage was based on real job performance and documented abstinence. When they were offered stipends that were equivalent to the same amount of wages, without having to provide drug-free samples or demonstrate performance on the job, they were likely to drop out.

An environment that trains an individual to perform needed skills while demonstrating self-control (abstinence), and paying an earned wage (recognition and respect, as with any worker), led to drug-free, appropriate performance at work. These studies show that the interaction between behavior and the environment is critical to change troubling patterns, such as drug addiction. When the environment contains methods for recognizing effort tied to reasonable requirements, these individuals demonstrated an excellent degree of self-control. Positive behavior flourished when given a societally important task to do, a job, under the same conditions offered to other citizens. Adding a normalizing method to demonstrate control of their individual addiction while being appropriately productive on the job was a very visible demonstration of confidence in their abilities. These norms included

1. a real job,

2. a wage for doing that job, and

3. conduct defining expectations of a responsible (non-using) adult to do the job.

Much could be said about both dignity and managing a destructive history in new ways. When environmental conditions and opportunities are arranged, meaningful changes begin to occur. Such environmental engineering about the method of sustaining change and the normalizing of behavior demonstrates very wise outcomes for society.

These findings are so important for all of us when we look at the mechanisms required to change behavior. Consider yourself in a red-hot verbal event, as previously mentioned. How could you change the conditions that surround you and others to reduce the likelihood of engaging in the same patterns in the future?

Carlos, the co-author of this book, has a friend, Rubén, who lives in Medellín, Colombia. Rubén is a successful businessman, but what Carlos admires most about Rubén is his stated commitment to help every person he meets. If Rubén sees someone he could help, he approaches them, listens to them, and seeks to find out if there is something he can do to make a difference in the moment. Everywhere he goes, he treats people with dignity and respect. He always expresses appreciation and lets them know when he sees something he values in their actions.

Rubén helped create an organization, *Voz Solidaria*, to provide opportunities for poor people in his city. Through his work, he provides scholarships for people who need a way to get an education. As a father of two, Rubén talks to his daughters about the value of immaterial things and lives by example. He loves to travel and takes his family with him to expose them to different cultures and ways of looking at the world. Thanks to his influence, his daughters spent a semester in Tanzania helping build schools for children who lacked resources. In summary, Rubén has learned the importance of creating conditions that improve chances of success for the people around him. As Patrick Friman, Director at Boys Town, wrote, "Once we take a circumstantial view of things, everything changes. We soften our approach. We're more understanding, more compassionate, and frequently have a desire to help because we know we can do something about circumstances."

PRACTICE 12.1:

Events That Have Shaped Who I Am

Pat McArt and Jude Collins, journalists and educators in Ireland, have written a book called *What Shaped Me?* They interviewed well-known people describing events in their lives that had a large effect on who they are today. The events ranged from small moments never shared with others to well-known events. They described loss of loved ones. Repeated failures in school. A loving moment when in need of such support. Moments of deep shame and regret. Abuse by others and extremes of poverty. An unexpected hand reaching out. Think of events that stand out in defining who you are or who you wish to be, perhaps still shaping where you are headed. Describe two (or more) events, considering for yourself why your stories have a lasting effect on you. Reviewing those events and the conditions that surrounded you provides a method of examining lasting values and direction extracted from such significant moments. Take time to do this. It will serve you well in assessing how well you are doing in becoming the person you want to be.

Examining our behavior in context is only a part of understanding the effects we can have. Consider immediate as well as distant relationships between your desired outcomes and the behaviors and conditions that compete with those outcomes. Often, laws that convey new rules of conduct need to change for individual behavior to change. At times, large-scale changes are needed regarding education, health, and wealth. In the middle of war, individuals may have few resources to act beyond the immediate goal of staying alive. In an authoritarian government, acting according to your values can result in imprisonment or death. Even with laws on the books, wrong acts will not stop simply because they clearly violate the written law. The subculture that interacts with such laws may disagree and deliberately disobey them or not enforce them. How society responds determines how real espoused principles are in terms of governing the actions of the larger community. Even though it may seem at an insignificant level, that response starts with you.

Global Citizenship and Collaboration

Many people are committed to promoting long-term social policy based on a values-based belief about human potential and worthiness. Talk surrounds us all about the economic and social divides that keep one group from valuing the contributions of another group. Sometimes, those social divides lead to judgments about the worthiness of those who reside on the other side of a divide—the rich vs. the poor, one race over another, or customs or religious beliefs that allow one group to behave in superior ways over another. The rich are not in a position of privilege because of their "will" or "determination." They prosper because of conditions that surround, support, and reinforce their progress. The poor can be wise and compassionate, the same as the rich. Mark Twain so aptly reminded us of this truism in *The Prince and the Pauper*. Rich or poor, black or white, educated or illiterate: Is it possible to believe that we are all capable of having a positive impact on our world? Can we all learn greater wisdom in solving problems? Many do not believe those two questions can be answered with a *yes*.

Often people are taught to see their group as better at loving, caring, or acting wiser than another group. That blind spot can hinder the journey toward finding the wisdom factor. Dealing with our blind spots about others can lead us straight into a wall of our own making. Step back and consider that all of us master how we learn and believe in the same way—not in terms of individual "learning styles" but by individual consequences. Learning to hate people because of how they dress or talk or where they are from is based on the same conditions that act on us in learning anything. If we are to get to the next step of acting wisely, we will need to challenge our biases and hone the skill of looking at behavior objectively. Doing so provides a more inclusive way to see the potential in each of us.

"If we are to get to the next step of acting wisely, we will need to challenge our biases and hone the skill of looking at behavior objectively."

Steve Majors wrote an insightful editorial in the Washington Post on June 11, 2020, worth reading in full. He captures in a few paragraphs the ways in which our blindness shows up.

> *I walk a racial tightrope. It's one I've struggled to balance on for my entire life. But over the past several weeks, I've felt myself teetering. I'm black and outraged that racism continues ... I know the freedom of moving through a world that magically removes many barriers from my life and shields me from harm—all because of my ability to pass as white. My skin tone has given me white privilege. For more than five decades of the journey across my tightrope, I've had what feminist researcher Peggy McIntosh calls an "invisible weightless knapsack of special provisions, maps, passports, codebooks, visas, clothes, tools, and blank checks." These are the tools of white privilege, unwanted and conferred on me at birth by a white father who had a fleeting relationship with my divorced black mother ... I want to assure my white friends that white privilege is real, because I benefit from it every day. And I want to explain to my black family that even though this*

knapsack that whites carry is invisible, weightless, and present from birth, it's possible to teach yourself that it's there ... to explain why so many claim to be blind and unfeeling to something that has been present throughout the history of this country. Even as I continue to reap its benefits, I am ashamed of the white privilege I carry around because I know it comes at the expense of others who have every right to the same opportunities, advantages, and freedoms.

Jane Elliott is known for her "Blue eyes–Brown eyes" exercise. An amazingly astute teacher, Dr. Elliott introduced to her all-white class how it might feel to be judged by the color of our skins. She made it real for her students by labeling them by the color of their eyes, an important start to understanding how it may feel to be defined by a physical characteristic. She demonstrated how the condition of eyes (or skin color or right- vs. left-handedness) open opportunities for some and remove them from others, regardless of whether those so labeled had done anything wrong—or right. Because these students in her class were white, the hope was that the lessons of the three days would stay with many of them for a very long time, making them less blind to bias. She first conducted her famous exercise for her class on April 5, 1968, the day after Martin Luther King Jr. was assassinated. Elliott's classroom exercise was filmed with her 1970 third-graders to become *The Eye of the Storm*, the documentary film. This in turn inspired a retrospective that reunited the 1970 class members with their teacher fifteen years later in *A Class Divided*. You can experience through the films the life-changing exercise it was for the participants about who is a "worthy" individual. Immediately affecting the participants' sense of place in their world, it included growing unease, feeling unsafe, growing degrees of anger and humiliation, and a confusing sense of their own self-worth.

Seeing the future as full of promise, translated into a characteristic called *optimism*, helps us get to that promising future, as will adaptation and flexibility. Complex contingencies are constantly surrounding us. We need to understand the way actions extend humankind's best practices, leading to health, well-being, and survivability. These skills do not demand great knowledge or a lengthy resume. They enable us to quickly adapt to change, and to changes that are coming.

If we apply our knowledge wisely to advance the human condition, the future holds endless possibilities. That advance is not, however, the advance of one but of many. The focus in this book is on *practical wisdom*—those actions we take in the here and now at an individual level. However, for sustaining change, our actions must support values that influence change at the highest levels of society, with a significant number of others joining us. Again, a single act in difficult times can have an immediate and sustaining effect on the rapid acceptance of new practices for the benefit of many.

A Culture of Active Caring

Each of us can play a role in the promotion of wisdom in our cultures. It is part of the reciprocal nature of our interactions with others. E. Scott Geller is dedicated to fostering *active caring*—empathy to feel and compassion to act—at a cultural level. His work has inspired a movement known as *Actively Caring for People (AC4P)*™. When describing this model, Derek D. Reed (2014) writes:

> *(1) You observe an act of kindness (someone demonstrating caring for another person or for the environment) when going about your daily routine. (2) You personally thank the individual for caring, to reward this response. (3) You then give the person a special green AC4P wristband and ask the individual to pass it on when s/he sees someone else engaged in AC4P behavior. (4) You ask the person to share the story of this exchange on social media and tag the event with the code imprinted on the wristband ... Being part of this movement suggests that you are part of something special ... a network of humanistic behaviorists literally hoping to change the world.*

However, if we want to look hard at where the real lack of actively caring appears, no matter how well individuals treat one another or recognize individual acts, consider how practices arise, clearly benefiting one race over another in America, intentional or not. Read *The Sum of Us: What Racism Costs Everyone and How We Can Prosper Together,"* by *Heather McGhee.* In 2021, we continue to design public policies, daily practices, systems of community and political access into our environment to benefit whites while failing to examine publicly how the benefits designed by people of goodwill may exclude people of color. Read and consider how we use words to obscure, with polite, codified meanings, centuries of racism. No longer Jim Crow but still, promoting behaviors many have claimed to stand against—key lessons about behavior and its reciprocal effects. Look hard at noble intentions in what we do for "the good of all" and unintended consequences on individuals. Being alert to the need to examine and craft public policies that actually do what we want, in this case, actively care for people, can benefit us all.

"Each of us can play a role in the promotion of wisdom in our cultures. It is part of the reciprocal nature of our interactions with others."

Chapter 13:

Finding True North: Values-Based Principles

"What you do makes a difference, and you have to decide what kind of difference you want to make."

–Jane Goodall

"Never let your sense of morals prevent you from doing what is right."

–Isaac Asimov

"A people that values its privileges above its principles soon loses both."

–Dwight D. Eisenhower

This chapter asks you to consider both the immediate and the longer-term impact of your actions, identifying and applying a set of core principles that become "second nature to you." Such a values-based set of principles to guide decision-making provides critical criteria to guide actions designed to achieve wise acting.

Principles Defined

Let's start with an abbreviated version of *The Oxford Dictionary* definition of *principles*: "A fundamental truth or proposition that serves as the foundation for a system of belief or behavior or for a chain of reasoning. Many values are incorporated in a society's governing set of moral principles."

Principles describe standards of behavior defined by values a culture or country holds as essential to its citizens as individual beings, accompanied by a related document often described as a social contract that codifies such meaning. The Universal Declaration of Human Rights (UDHR) is the first universal declaration across countries of human rights. The Declaration was adopted by the United Nations General Assembly in Paris on the 10th of December 1948. It set out, for the first time, fundamental human rights to universal protection and it has been translated into over 500 languages. It provided inalienable rights of "all members of the human family," and borrowed language from The Napoleonic Code, which in turn greatly influenced the United States Declaration of Independence and later Bill of Rights. In 1803, The Napoleonic Code was the first to "formally recognize the principles of civil liberty, equality before the law—although not for women in the same sense as for men—and the secular character of the state." The UN Declaration put front and center the sacredness of every human life.

Principles containing rights about the fundamental dignity of human beings are designed to provide protections by the state to its citizens. Such principles demonstrate values extracted from how we as individuals treat one another. Concepts such as kindness and respect, truth telling, or other fundamental beliefs displayed in our daily conduct are included. They guide the development of such documents as constitutions and bills of human rights. These codes are often developed by the most inspiring of beliefs, intended for the good of all. Nevertheless, through the ages, groups that differ by origin, political orientation, language, religion, economic status, color, gender, or in other ways, have been excluded. While embraced, such codes are difficult to translate into protections that are demonstrated in the daily lives of people.

As the national motto of France declares, "Liberty, Equality, and Fraternity" are among the principles aspired to in overseeing the rights and protections of the French people. The U.S. Constitution sets out principles about the rights of all, the striving for equality and equity under law. The Bill of Rights further clarifies the protections extended to individuals. Those who are fully defined by their society as worthy, within the scope of a particular culture's code, come to expect treatment based on such principled beliefs, sustained, and shaped through life experiences. Practices, however, indicate to many that they are not perceived as worthy of full benefits, as judged by those who control access to the promises of society. Paraphrasing that famous line from George Orwell, *"All are equal. Some, however, are more equal than others."*

Early in life, children begin to understand just how much they—because of color, or poverty, or gender—are really entitled to (or not) the declared rights and justice afforded to others. These stratifications in society are wrong on their face when it comes to underlying principles of our common humanity. Unwise acting often equates to differential treatment in how a culture treats its citizens.

"Unwise acting often equates to differential treatment in how a culture treats its citizens."

These principles are useful guides about the degree of personal freedom a culture might strive to offer its citizens. They include the values determined by larger society, often over many generations. Many cultures make exclusion clear, based on such factors as ethnicity, gender, religion, and race. In the United States, our overarching principles are written to be inclusive, not exclusive. However, principles can conflict with actual behavior—that is, not our aspirations but our actions. Inclusion as a core principle has always gone through various definitions of exclusion, particularly by the groups that are included. Just as with wisdom, principles are not independent of behavior.

Sometimes we say we believe in equality, but we immediately act in ways that do not measure up to others' meaning of equality. Everything we are talking about is dependent on the conditions that surround us, that shape, reinforce, guide, build, punish, or eliminate behaviors that are or not representative of our stated principles. We may each, however, continue to say we demonstrate the principles we preach, blind in so many ways to the nuance of meaning a word like *equality* might imply. We repeat behavior (words and actions) for which we are reinforced. Keep that in mind, once again, as we discuss principles.

The corruption of the few, the ease with which bias, threat, and fear can rend a tear in a social fabric intended to expand equality, was made clear in the writings of such authors as Margaret Atwell and George Orwell. Orwell's famous political satire, *Animal Farm*, captures the dilemma of the good intentions of wanting to be free, rejecting a set of principles that held animals in bondage, leaving behind human masters, and allowing all animals to manage their own lives—until oversight and rules and decisions began to occur by chosen leaders about who that word *free* referred to among the "now equal" barnyard. The process of setting up governance made visible the seduction of power, the certainty of the perceived needs of others, and who was best at managing animals in all their diversity—and worth.

While initially, the animals were clear that it was good to exclude humans outright from this equality thing, it became apparent to the rule setters that various other animals were behaving as rather wretched creatures, no longer worthy of the highest degrees of freedom. President (*nee* Dictator) Pig Napoleon, said, in his most diplomatic way, "All animals are equal … but some are more equal than others" (Orwell, Animal Farm, 1945), perhaps the scariest line in 20th-century literature for its implications about the reality and possible future of humanity.

Concepts of equality and other principles about our human connection require tending, starting very early. Can our children talk about the meaning of living in a democracy? Why does it matter that they treat a funny looking person with kindness? Can they see a person from a very different culture as like themselves? How can they ensure that they treat their friends with dignity, free from bullying, or shaming, or jokes about looks, skills, or ethnicity? How our children learn to describe *good* can translate as they grow up into how they see good at larger levels across our society—and the awareness with which they handle the seduction of power. Remember the discussion about how perception—when our vision is clouded by our values or how we see ourselves—can be threatened at times. It is often difficult to know when or where we began to see some people as having more value than others. Identifying that moment can help alert us to behave with more wisdom.

Definitions of *good* at times move beyond individuals, groups, and particular cultures in finding universal standards. Philosophers and ethicists have long examined the meaning of words like *good*. Where does the idea of good come from and how should a culture demonstrate good in addressing the rights of people? Striving to match such superordinate notions of what is good for humankind, such as universal rights, when translated into practice, gets complicated. Like the animal farm, are we really talking about all of humanity? As we know, Americans say and do things valued by a subculture that are not beneficial for the whole, both within and beyond America's borders. You may find that some "morality markers" negate the possibility of acting wisely, as is the case of religious groups that may exclude people you value or approve actions you consider abhorrent. Do your actions advance or impede the rights and dignity of another? It is highly unlikely that any of us can always answer that with a *yes*.

Applying Principled Concepts about the Dignity of Humankind

Are there universal principles that societies have selected by which they hope to demonstrate their commitment to the commonality of humankind? Do they embody principles that are universally accepted? The answer is *yes* to the first question and *no* to the second. Use words to describe the intended, values-based effect you want. Learn to describe desired effects as you act to solve issues that may arise, issues that look different depending on the situations.

Striving to do the right thing for an individual, the local community, or yourself in the moment may outweigh how a decision may affect long-term benefits. In those instances, those striving to act wisely may be justified by urgency and impact in the here and now. Acting for the good of someone in the moment may be the wisest thing to do, even if it closes out the opportunity to keep a friendship going or includes a broader way to address an issue. This can happen for example when dealing with child abuse that you observe. You step up to stop it and you are greeted by anger and distrust. The parent may say you have no right to intervene in a private event. You are no longer welcome in their family.

We all may be able to think of a time when we let something happen that we did not think was right. So many things interfere with our actions, including the concern that we don't want to be judgmental, that we want to understand and respect boundaries, and so on. Knowing when we can do that in a way that allows for providing necessary help is good, but at times we act as we act, wise or not, with no link to some greater good.

"... at times we act as we act, wise or not, with no link to some greater good."

Those who sacrifice their safety for others in violent situations and live through it often report they could do nothing else. They do not report their act as being brave or as an act of self-sacrifice, but rather, the conditions that existed in the moment made it impossible not to act. They were not driven by inspiring thoughts or even by assessing the impact of one's action. An argument can be made that anything we do, whether perceived as for others or for self, is always acting in one's own self-interest.

The deeds of firefighters and soldiers are assessed against a code of conduct, a set of values bigger than themselves, and the danger they might experience. They often report doing what they had to do. If there is no chance of coming out of a building alive, the act itself is a demonstration of bravery and self-sacrifice for the greater good. Their "self," as they defined it, said, "Go!" We wish they hadn't had to take such a path, but we recognize it, with humility, for acting on the rules of conduct they learned, reinforcing an amazing commitment to the safety of us all. Those moments define many of our heroes.

Acting according to a principled set of rules in relation to others is about our learning history and the conditions that lead us to act or not. Historical context and contingencies—laws, policies, beliefs turned into rules, conditions of living, our definitions of *good*, those events surrounding us right now—shape our actions, as well as at times a sheer adrenaline rush when you step into dangerous verbal or physical territory. Everything we say and do reflects who we are. Behavior that has value in and of itself, done in the moment without much forethought, can provide a rich, learning environment from which to guide and sustain future actions.

Guiding Principles

Laws have been written in many democratic countries to protect the many and the few. Not all laws, written with religious fervor, or the fervor of a fascist political party, are necessarily about the good of all and the protection of the minority.

Much of what we do, day in and day out, has little to do with values. However, our behavior often has unanticipated effects on the values of others or ourselves, after the fact, values about our common humanity. Some of our greatest regrets are about failing to address an aspect of that humanity by a simple act, such as speaking up for a colleague who we know is being accused of something she did not do. As a child we remember failing to introduce someone we really liked because our other friends had just made fun of her. Doing these things do not measure our good, but rather highlight our reinforcers or how we are threatened. So, to envision a principled path, consider a few avenues to help make some choices easier as we go through life.

Describing a *Balance of Values Matrix*, Lattal and Clark designed a method to identify principle-based values that are common across many cultures. Such values might help individuals translate how they could demonstrate those values in their societies. You may find that it helps to describe principled effects even as you act to solve issues that may not sound as if they have much to do with high-minded principles. The principles below are by no means complete. They were selected to suggest how we treat one another in terms of values unique to each of us. The values selected were as follows:

1. *Common Good:* the benefit of the whole
2. *Equality:* the rights of the individual
3. *Equity:* the needs of the few
4. *Self-Interest:* the needs of the person

These principled-based values may show up as co-equal, or at various times, one or another may take priority in different situations. For example, in times of war, an individual may be asked to fight for the *common good* at the expense of *self-interest*. It may be that self-interest is preserved by joining a war to protect those the soldier cares about, including himself, and the country. Another example could be the decision to spend money on special elevators for those who are handicapped (*equity*—a need, not a right *per se*) vs investing in new desks for all (*equality*). A belief in the dignity of anyone, regardless of how that person looks or can navigate through life, protects such people through equal access. That protection did not exist, however, based solely on a personal belief or value reflected by one group action; not before society passed a law that was inclusive and identified physically handicapped individuals as entitled to equal access to work. We learned. We changed our investment strategy to accommodate a social good—to provide access. The concepts we espouse do not come out fully formed but are enriched through experiences.

Ramps do not exist in many countries, and not to the degree sometimes needed in our country. Ramps were built through collective actions to support several core beliefs—that everyone is entitled to access (the principle of *equality*), including the few (the principles of *equity*) who have special needs. No one can guarantee that our policies and practices will help everyone in need of access. However, in this case, Americans acknowledged a problem and made changes. This change happened thanks to many who saw the need first, before others turned it into law, and then further into practice. An additional principle, *common good*, is derived from the larger commitment of a society to benefit the majority. Closing one factory to be able to keep other factories operating may be an example of protecting the common good. You can add other values or principles you treasure. These four broad principles provide a way to examine how values and behavior interact with competing, variable, or concurrent needs of the group and the individual.

Understanding Our Effect

Part of the process of aligning behavior with values is to become more alert to the impact our actions have. This process demands an analysis of both short- and long-term effects. Behavior might have an immediate, positive effect but a disastrous long-term effect. We can save money by not paying our taxes but end up in trouble with the law in the long run, causing damage to both ourselves

PRACTICE 13.1:

A Balance of Values Analysis

When you look at your daily choices in relation to yourself and others, what broad values guide you when making decisions?

- *Common Good:* the benefit of the whole

- *Equality:* the rights of the individual

- *Equity:* the needs of the few

- *Self-interest:* the needs of the person

- Other:

Which one or several of the four broad values listed above that you think of readily when making a decision or in leading your life?

What value(s) do you rarely consider?

and to the larger social contract. Such actions can arise from a deeply held value by the individual. Conscientious objectors are often operating under a higher-order principle when they refuse to engage in combat—they will not kill, often arising from their religious beliefs that translate to principles of action by which to live a godly life. For some of us, we have, up to now, not considered our actions as being of real significance beyond a simple decision made in the moment. But, in the end, our actions are all there is—the single act of one person multiplied by effects, the never-ending infinity of humans doing one small thing that has ripple effects beyond its immediate consequence.

> *"... in the end, our actions are all there is—the single act of one person multiplied by effects, the never-ending infinity of humans doing one small thing that has ripple effects beyond its immediate consequence."*

Societal Definitions of Shared Values

Every culture employs stories to capture the larger meaning of human behavior. They are often seen as morality plays about good and bad values, good and bad people as well. Racial and ethical biases may seem self-evident when as an adult you read various fairy tales of old. Some of these stories may provide a moral ending to teach a rule about how to live a good life, while some stories are definitely not at all wise. Nevertheless, they often become a part of furthering a culture and its practices. Themes resound: the treatment of women, the worth of the aged, minorities, a particular group in time, deformity and poverty, beauty and the beast, the definitions of *barbarians*, and others judged outside a particular worldview.

Lessons about how to treat and trust one another are shaped by religion, economics, and political considerations, and those views shift. Time and experience change how we see the "truth" of the lessons in our cultural stories—and, as with all rules of how we need to behave, society's values shift as well. At times single acts by individuals have an undeniably strong effect on the pace of change, the embrace of values that have laid dormant. Rosa Parks demonstrated her certainty of belief about her value as a person by not moving to the back of the bus. Now, she reported that she did so because she was tired. She was not going to stand. No one had the right to tell her to stand, simply because of the color of her skin. The effect of this single act triggered a tidal wave of change, and to this day, illustrates in a very visible instance how we treat one another, with justice or injustice. Many things shape us and bring us to everlasting national or international visibility. We live our lives, and one day we do what we do, and it affects the lives of millions. Those who threw the tea into the Boston Harbor demonstrated by their individual actions, their belief in no taxation without representation. Recently the death of too many people of color is changing our narrative about who we are as a people and reshaping who we so badly hope to be, sometimes at extreme and opposite ends of that hope.

> *"We live our lives, and one day we do what we do, and it affects the lives of millions."*

Saying and Doing: Following Through

Behaving differently than what you say is often identified as a major source of distrust. In discussing overarching principles as a country, and personally learned values as individuals, a saying/doing correlation is very important. Determining when you can be depended on for many things can be difficult if you cannot be trusted to demonstrate that correlation. We do not examine carefully enough the match between what we say we will do and our behavior. Learning to understand why you say one thing and do another is important for *trust* and for acting wisely. Remember, for all of us, the match between "say/do" has many large cracks (Risley, T. R., & Hart, B., 1968; Israel, A. C., 1978; Huffman, R. W., Sainato, D. M., & Curiel, E. S. L., 2016). Those cracks also produce gaps at a societal level, leading to large-scale distrust. Grand principles of a country that espouses equal protection under law easily becomes a plaque on a wall—nice to read but don't count on it. In society, knowing that the citizens, as well as the larger governing society, will keep their promises is important. Without that, it is difficult to operate from a values perspective.

Plenty of people say one thing but do the opposite. This lack of consistency influences others and certainly influences practices in a society like ours. In such cases, values may remain unexamined, the place of wishes, best intentions, and our unrealized selves. Who decides what is considered "good" or "bad" in society? Who decides which actions are "right" or "wrong"? In a nutshell, we all do. We learn to label and recognize such concepts based on the effect actions have. Such labels help us recognize which actions are generally considered helpful to the group. This knowledge helps us coexist with one another. While we all might be able to point to certain things as good or bad, our breadth of vision and depth of knowledge given an immediate set of changing circumstances may limit how well we anticipate the outcomes of our actions and their ultimate effects, right and wrong.

"... our breadth of vision and depth of knowledge given an immediate set of changing circumstances may limit how well we anticipate the outcomes of our actions and their ultimate effects, right and wrong."

Uncertainty about which actions have social value—or for us personally, meaning—can have devastating effects on our health and well-being. According to the *World Health Organization*, 300 million people at any given time report feeling depressed. A lack of direction and disconnection from a "meaningful" life is a contributing factor. Many people report they are unclear about their values. How can we stand up for important values if we aren't clear about those values? Values represent behaviors that demonstrate our principles. Values are like an anchor or compass to direct our actions and bring purpose to our lives. We identify our values in part based on rules we have learned about the worthy actions for living a meaningful life. Over time, consistent actions represent values we believe our behavior demonstrates. This does not mean to simply align our words and actions with a predetermined list to demonstrate a particular value. A very wide gap may exist between how we believe we will behave and how we actually do behave. The conditions in the moment determine if the choices we make help or hinder a good outcome. After we act, wisdom is assessed against the effects of those choices we make.

"Values are like an anchor or compass to direct our actions and bring purpose to our lives."

In his book, *ACT Questions and Answers: A Practitioner's Guide to 150 Common Sticking Points in Acceptance and Commitment Therapy*, Russ Harris provides an example. A person could choose "influential" as the person's worthy contribution to others, a *value* used in that sense. As Harris indicates, the emphasis is on the words and deeds you use to influence others. That is where your values show up and are interpreted by others. Do you influence others through lying, deceit, manipulation, intimidation, coercion, cruelty, and bullying patterns of behavior? Or do you influence others in actions and words that are *measured against values* that are good for them and the larger social good?

Personal Values

In seeking to understand how you demonstrate your values, a good place to start is asking yourself, "What type of person do I aspire to be?" What impact do you want to have on the people and the world around you? How do you want to be perceived during your life, and how remembered? What qualities do you admire the most in the behavior of others? Even those characteristics of fictional characters could provide a guide (for example, Atticus Finch, Gandalf, Mary Poppins, Felícito, Count Rostov, Ismael, and Siddhartha). Moreover, think about some key life domains: (a) self; (b) family; (c) intimate relationships; (d) friendships; (e) education; (f) work; (g) recreation; (h) community. How would you like to participate in each of these domains? Being "caring," "assertive," "kind," "hopeful," and "just" are a few examples of values. Even a desire to be "wise" is a value. Think about actions that represent the values in each of these domains. For example, what can you do for your friends that show you "care"? How can you act at work that defines you as "just"? Some of the answers to these questions are how we reflect our personal qualities, and some reflect a higher-order, social criteria. For example, "just" as a value involves many aspects of an individual's and community's life.

Value statements are of different orders and types. Some are about how you will treat others as well as yourself. Some are about actions, the value or worth you demonstrate, such as "industriousness," while others are about being "calm" and "persistent." Such descriptions are valuable as they do reflect your individual behavioral attributes, described as aspects of your "personality"—the sum of change at an individual level, depending on experiences, and the circumstances that lead you to modify how you describe the characteristics you want to demonstrate reflective of a core value. You might consider wiser actions for yourself and others in given circumstances, those that translate into a social and moral code of conduct—a set of values for how you want to support outcomes you hope will be good for others and yourself. These values are often described as higher-order values, promoting the well-being of others as well as yourself.

PRACTICE 13.2:

Defining My Personal Code of Conduct

Do you have a set of well-defined rules of conduct that you believe are fundamental to how you want to show up? If you do, consider how they influence
you. Responding to a code of conduct is often not articulated but simply ex-
panded in your actions, as needed, to include new rules or guidance in behaving in ways you know to be right. Think of your family, your parents, or others
who helped to shape your choices of the behavior to strive for. Write down a
few of the values or principles you strive to do in how you conduct yourself.

It is easy to develop patterns of behavior in our daily routines that are
inconsistent with our stated values. Bringing awareness to such inconsistencies
could be an initial step in promoting values-congruent acting. A helpful exercise is to complete The Valued Living Questionnaire (Wilson & Groom, 2002).
If you choose to complete this exercise, you will (1) rate the importance of different life domains to help prioritize them; and (2) rate how consistently you
have been acting in accordance with your values in each area.

Scan to find an online version on Steven C. Hayes' website:

Assessing Our Effects

You can check the effects of your chosen values as you act upon your daily
world. Your values may, or may not, show up in actions or in ways you want.
However, our stated values arise from how we learn to describe our personal
life experiences. Those values feel truer to us, more integral to who we are as
a person. But they do not necessarily take on uniquely insightful moral truth.
Your history may lead you away from actions that truly benefit others.

In this journey to wise acting, the effects of your actions in the present
and over time matter more than statements about values you say you hold. In
striving to be wise, always look at the positive difference you are making—and
who, in some way, you may be hurting.

Value-Based Principles Versus Goals

Overarching principles are not the same as goals. Goals are concrete objectives you want to achieve. Goals exist in the future and have an end to them. You have to take certain steps before you can reach them. You can check whether a goal has been met. For example, you will graduate at a specific point, finish a book, take a dream vacation, or get married. At those moments, you can say with certainty, "I have achieved my goal." In contrast, values are ongoing and usually have no end in sight. It would be odd to say, "I have achieved my commitment to being a loving person, so, I am done with that now and ready for the next value challenge."

If goals are like a "destination on a map," values are like "True North," or an ever-present compass. They are your fixed point to help navigate through life. They are measured by your specific actions and words, that is, the way you conduct yourself. Therefore, they are observable by summing up your behaviors and/or characteristics that reflect values such as "trustworthy" or "forgiving." You will still face obstacles, but such analysis of actions against your stated values allows you to recalibrate or, even at times, find the path. Values do not exist as words alone when judging your effects on this world. They show up in their reported effects on the rights and dignity of others.

Congruence, or lack thereof, between stated wants and actions helps us understand the weave of our social fabric, how tightly woven or how loose it is. Until we understand the clashes of competing outcomes—for example, between saying we always tell the truth but lie to get a promotion over a colleague—we may not realize how large a gap exists between our words and actions, especially when immediate wants override the promise of longer-term good in our everyday lives. Of course, it's fine for you to want the job and to go for it, but not so fine to throw someone else under the bus when you approach the opportunity.

The Effects of Uncertainty

Conditions can arise that change everything we know about how the world will interact with us and all certainty is gone. How can we find meaning in life when faced with challenging and totally unexpected events? How do some people find purpose and keep going even in the most difficult of conditions?

Viktor E. Frankl was in a concentration camp during one of the most horrible moments in human history. He was a victim of Nazi Germany's view of who was valuable and who was not. Separated from his family, he lived under the most precarious conditions. Pain, abuse, hunger, and sickness were part of each minute of his waking hours. He describes three stages of adaptation in a concentration camp in his book *Man's Search for Meaning*. The first stage is characterized by "shock." The second stage is "apathy." And the third, and final stage, is "disillusionment." It was during the second stage of his imprisonment when he regained purpose and meaning in his life, as he reported it, regaining the will to survive.

While working outside in the snow, a fellow prisoner casually asked what their wives would think of them if they could see them in such a state. Frankl immediately thought of his wife. At that moment, he decided to find an honorable way to endure, inspired—as he reported later—by the love he felt for her. He saw in suffering, an opportunity to live by his values, and retaining the values inherent in human attributes such as "dignity" and "loving another." His stated goal was to remain as "human" as possible, living for the day that he believed he would reunite with his beloved wife.

While striving every day to act with dignity and love, he was offered the extraordinary opportunity to escape the concentration camp. However, for him at that moment, he felt a real sense of sadness, a sense of shame. At that instance, he thought about his fellow prisoners, the humanity around him. As a doctor, he could take care of them, helping with their pain. In his words, "Suddenly, I decided to take fate into my own hands for once. I ran out of the hut and told my friend that I could not go with him. As soon as I had told him with finality that I had made up my mind to stay with my patients, the unhappy feeling left me. I did not know what the following days would bring, but I gained an inward peace that I had never experienced before." Although facing uncertainty, horrible conditions, and potential death, he felt at peace in his decision to stay, guided by the value of being a "caring" doctor that could ease the suffering of others. He certainly applied his behavior in ways that affected the broad principles of the common good, the rights of the many to dignity and respect, even in suffering, and to attend to the needs of the neglected. He also considered his decision in terms of his own self-interest. While he could not anticipate the longer-term effects of his actions, uncertain there would be a longer-term life for him, this is one clear example of living a values-centered life. His exact thoughts or why he acted as he did is very difficult to unravel, but he left us with actions and his stated reasons. That is often all we have to go by.

Many actions do not necessarily arise from a moral *should*, but by a pragmatic *do*. Doing something is essential. Nothing can be assessed without something happening. Fortunately, so often, doing something is everything, shining a bright light on the possible ranges of morality as lessons for generations to come.

Chapter 14:

"In Spite of Everything, I Still Believe ...": Seeking Wisdom

"The saddest aspect of life right now is that science gathers knowledge faster than society gathers wisdom."

–Isaac Asimov

"Wisdom is the power to put our time and our knowledge to the proper use."

–Thomas J. Watson

During WWII in her attic home, shortly before discovery and her sad death, 14-year-old Anne Frank wrote words that give hope to millions, even today. Her earnest belief deserves earnest responses from those who can make a difference in the lives of individuals who are, today as then, surrounded by bias, threat, and fear:

> *In spite of everything I still believe that people are really good at heart. I simply can't build up my hopes on a foundation consisting of confusion, misery, and death. I see the world gradually being turned into a wilderness, I hear the ever-approaching thunder, which will destroy us too, I can feel the sufferings of millions and yet, if I look up into the heavens, I think that it will all come right, that this cruelty too will end, and that peace and tranquility will return again.*

And to keep us ever-humble, in her 14-year-old wisdom, she wanted us all to be action-oriented: "How wonderful it is that nobody need wait a single moment before starting to improve the world."

Wisdom is a very large concept long desired across humankind, embraced by cultures around the world, each working to define their versions of wisdom. We, the authors of this book, are not philosophers and cannot do much with philosophical definitions of the word *wisdom*. And yet, we know that behavior and its potential is unlimited, that we are not, by our nature, cruel and uncaring, but are fully capable of behavior that demonstrates Anne's words, "good at heart." In these last few years, how wise acting can benefit us all has been made clear.

In this chapter, we will revisit the larger concept as to words regarding wisdom through the ages. *Wisdom* is not a thing to possess, nor can it be defined in absolute terms. *Wisdom* is aspirational. It excites imagination and inspires people to strive to capture their beliefs and practice them inside their societies and in general practices. To demonstrate wisdom is often described in terms of principles that endorse the value of our common humanity or advance a cause related to families. In this book, we have adopted a pragmatic perspective about the importance of striving to behave wisely.

Factor—the third word in the book title—is the ingredient that makes for wise acting. It is found in our unique histories of learning and the environments in which we find ourselves. It requires behavior. The right "factor," or mix of history of learning, along with current conditions and our skills in addressing problem-solving and decision-making, primes the "wisdom potential" of each of us. The wisdom factor lies in understanding behavior in promoting outcomes desired across stakeholders and values demonstrated in the actions we take.

We hope this becomes your final takeaway in reading this book: Wisdom turns from an ideal state to a pragmatic approach to decision-making and problem-solving that reinforces behaving in principled ways. Remember, as unexciting as it may sound, our influence is felt in a single behavior, or a pattern repeated over time. It can consist of grand persistence over time; but one single, modest act can change the lives of many. A clear example is Rosa Parks. Acting with greater wisdom is an important goal to increase the well-being of us all.

"Wisdom turns from an ideal state to a pragmatic approach to decision-making and problem-solving that reinforces behaving in principled ways."

Toward a Definition of Wisdom

What exactly is wisdom? Many individuals have dedicated their lives to the study of wisdom. Philosophers, religious scholars, scientists, and others have approached this question and do not necessarily agree. Moreover, the concept of wisdom itself has evolved over time. Its definition is contextual. That is, *wisdom* might mean one thing for some people acting in one culture or at a period in time, but something else to others.

The Greeks are often considered the first interested in the serious study of wisdom. They identified two types: *practical wisdom (phronesis)* and *transcendental wisdom (sophia)*. This distinction has remained and continues to be debated by scholars. Simply put, *practical wisdom* involves understanding the best ways to act. It identifies the types of behaviors and decisions that will lead to a good quality of life. It includes learning to make the right decisions to achieve meaningful outcomes. This type of wisdom is acquired through experience. *Transcendental wisdom* is concerned with who we are and discerning reality. It is related to the acquisition of knowledge and skills to discern "truths." In his article, *Sophia and Phronesis: Past, Present, and Future*, Trevor Curnow distinguishes how these types of wisdom develop. He argues *practical wisdom* is acquired and can be lost. *Transcendental wisdom*, as he describes it, develops through transformation. Then, once a person becomes wise, wisdom will remain.

The premise that once a person is seen as wise, wisdom will remain is not true. This is a kind of explanatory fiction humans ascribe to the quality they see in others—perhaps out of hope that such a quality, once mastered, is always present. When it comes to our behavior, *transcendental wisdom* does not govern our actions, even for those we call wise. Behavior drifts and morphs—generalizing and changing, depending on its surroundings. There is no state of enlightenment that internally directs and releases wise action in all that a person does when wisdom is called for. A wise person, as society might define it, may behave in very thoughtful, mature, and reasoned ways on some occasions. However, that same person can be graceless, immature, and excessively emotional at other moments.

Wisdom does not reside inside the person. To paraphrase Aristotle, "… one season of wisdom does not lead to a lifetime of wisdom." This could mean that the person may have a well-developed set of problem-solving, decision-making, and complex-thinking skills in assessing the need in given moments to take actions that are later judged to be wise. The word *may* in this context is important. Wise acting can come from the uneducated, those who have few words, and even the individual who does many things unwisely, but occasionally gets it right.

"Wise acting can come from the uneducated, those who have few words, and even the individual who does many things unwisely, but occasionally gets it right."

Since the early 1980s, interest has renewed in the study of wisdom. As a world-renowned, lifespan-developmental psychologist, Paul Baltes' work, remains at the forefront. He led *The Berlin Wisdom Project*, providing one of the most frequently cited definitions: "[Wisdom is] an expert knowledge system concerning the fundamental pragmatics of life. These include knowledge and judgment about the meaning and conduct of life and the orchestration of human development toward excellence while attending conjointly to personal and collective well-being" (Baltes & Staudinger, 2000).

Baltes indicated that wisdom is observable. If that is the case, to objectively check words and actions would be possible, taking into consideration current consequences and prior experiences with similar events. Baltes suggested assessing wisdom benefits from an "if this/then that" analysis; challenging the rules, seeking better ways to get to the end goal; and, along the way, accepting "good enough" solutions versus "perfect" outcomes. Striving toward wise outcomes is an essential element of wise acting. Sometimes, speed and acting to thwart a bad outcome is wiser than reaching a more inclusive, yet difficult, outcome. Individuals who, at the moment, can balance conflicting interests and common ground are more likely to get to wiser outcomes for all involved. Checking the overriding noise of our emotional interpretations can help us obtain greater objectivity.

Baltes' research suggested that wiser-acting individuals work to ensure problems are solved for the greatest benefit of all those affected by their actions, reaching beyond the immediate issue. They exhibit practical problem-solving with an eye to the future. Values are a part of their analysis. Defining a *meaningful life* (values-based) and conduct that helps individuals achieve excellence in daily living (pragmatic acting), are both key elements in evaluating wise outcomes.

> "*Defining a* meaningful life *(values-based) and conduct, which helps individuals achieve excellence in daily living (pragmatic acting), are both key elements in evaluating wise outcomes.*"

In 2008, Carolyn M. Aldwin, a developmental psychologist proposed a definition of *wisdom* that integrates characteristics of both practical and transcendental wisdom. According to this definition, "*Wisdom* is a practice that reflects the developmental process by which individuals increase in self-knowledge, self-integration, non-attachment, self-transcendence, and compassion, as well as a deeper understanding of life. This practice involves better self-regulation and ethical choices, resulting in greater good for oneself and others." Aldwin states that these attributes result in the practice of wisdom. Yet, these attributes do not predict that we *will* behave wisely.

The table below lists some individual characteristics commonly associated with wisdom:

Sample of Charactaristics Associated with Wisdom			
Perceiving things in context	Synthesis	Insight	Good judgment
Self-knowledge	Transcendence	Skepticism	Effective communication
Detachment	Intelligence	Sagacity	Perspective-taking
Objectivity	Curiosity	Kindness	Empathy
Common sense	Justice	Understanding	

Table 1: Attributes Frequently Associated with Wisdom

More recently, The University of Chicago has established *The Center for Practical Wisdom*. Their goal, like ours, is to understand the conditions that promote wise decisions and how to arrange those conditions at the individual and cultural level. To quote Dr. Howard C. Nusbaum, their founder, "We think about practical wisdom as considering value commitments that are concerned with understanding the impact of decisions on others."

These are qualities often assigned to knowledge, character, and wisdom. They are attributional characteristics drawn from many types of behavior—words and actions that fit an interpretation of intelligent, insightful, and sagacious actions. They provide broad cues about how to approach this complex topic, including helpful information about striving to be wise. Once again, demonstrating any or all of these patterns that sum to qualities we call *wise* does not guarantee wise acting.

Because a *post hoc* definition is required to define *wise acting* based on its effects, such a requirement precludes us from following a list of attributes that, if demonstrated, predict that wisdom will occur. The list contains aspirational words. These lists cannot hurt, but they do not necessarily allow quick action often required to act with wisdom. They are important concepts in a civilized society—but they do not in themselves determine our behavior. If we want to create a wiser world, are there ways to increase the likelihood of wise acting? What do we as individuals need to do? Consider the following:

1. Develop skill in objectively analyzing specific words and deeds, their effects on the longer term as well as the immediate good, and how that all adds up to wisdom.

2. Understand wise acting in particular contexts.

3. Understand how institutional structures that govern social, legal, economic and workplace policies, procedures, and systems can limit or accelerate everyday practices.

4. Understand the motivations and impediments to behaving in a manner congruent with your values.

5. Develop models for yourself to increase behaving wisely in difficult situations—it is in the actions and the effect on values reflected in such actions that *wisdom* occurs.

All these things may help us become more aware but being aware does not cause us to act. What kind of learning history leads individuals from a wide variety of backgrounds to do things that society judges as wise, even at times jeopardizing their own social and physical safety? Working with the five items above cannot hurt, but they may do no more than provide a sense of readiness to act, wisely or not.

Does Wisdom Drive Action?

The previous sample of attributes associated with wisdom describe qualities a person is assumed to have learned, ingrained into their very being. This set of qualities is then assumed to lead them to act in certain ways, or motivation from the inside out. For example, a person is said to have "self-knowledge" to the degree she identifies the influences on her actions, predicting the outcomes of her own behavior, explaining the factors that control her behavior, and does something to change it. A person is considered to possess "kindness" if she says and does things that take into consideration the well-being of others—having an easily described set of behaviors that lead to kindness. Those qualities are most often described in our popular literature as a part of the person's nature, of who she is, not something that is driven by the external circumstances in which she finds herself. The idea of wise actions being driven by immediate consequences may appear to trivialize the very important and often too rare quality of acting wisely. Rising *above* circumstances resonates with many as a more significant way to describe wise acting. It is in the circumstances in which we find ourselves, however, that wiser behavior in our society must occur.

Curnow stated "Wise people can be identified by their doing wise things and saying wise things. In theory, their wise actions and words are often reported to emerge from their wisdom, but, in reality, we recognize their wisdom because of their wise actions and words." Curnow defines *wisdom* by wise acting, observable behavior, and the effects that sum to wisdom.

Even in doing wise things repeatedly, there is no guarantee that a person will always act wisely. A most annoying effect of a behavior pattern is that it drifts. An action is bound to repeat in ways that might miss a particular nuance. Behavior is subject to the conditions that surround it. Remember the river analogy. A behavior pattern is in motion, changing, learning in interesting ways how to speak and act. Behavior is fallible. It is human.

Keep in mind that "possessing wisdom" is only an illusion. Wisdom is not a possession internal to one's being. It is a label applied to the consistency with which problems are solved in ways that lead to wise outcomes. Wisdom is not a quality possessed. Many wise actions occur by individuals who are often not generally described as wise.

Functional and Structural Approaches to Wisdom

The current conditions, along with the short- and long-term effects of an action will determine whether behavior is wise. For example, the effects of either speaking out or remaining silent in difficult situations determine which action was the wiser thing to do. A functional approach, taking the necessary action in the moment to ensure the good of the person or immediate circumstances, is helpful in judging the outcomes of any action, but it is not always enough. Neither is a structural approach—one made of the rules of conduct that we follow "no matter what" in telling us if we are going to achieve a wise outcome—always the answer. Behavior is best evaluated against changing conditions whirling around it. Wise behavior on one occasion might be unwise on another.

Truth-telling is seen by some individuals as necessary to maintain a civilized society for many reasons beyond its immediate effect. For

"The current conditions, along with the short- and long-term effects of an action will determine whether behavior is wise."

some, honesty is described as necessary to their relationship with God. Any belief system that is governed by absolute rules may create challenges at times in determining wise acting for the greater good of others. It may represent salvation for the individual who holds such a belief. The problem with such a structural approach in examining ways to act wisely for the greater good is that telling the truth could be extremely unwise for even just one individual affected by the rule, depending on the context. The value of that individual then must be weighed against the value as determined by the truth-teller. However, the individual may still act as the religion he cherishes dictates, even if it means extremely bad things happen.

A classic case about not telling the truth was in the actions of Hermine "Miep" Gies, related in *The Diary of Anne Frank* and later told by Miep herself, who kept secret from her workers that a Jewish family was hiding above their workspace. It was both the absence of truth and the lying when she had to that must be considered a part of behavior that sums to wisdom in that case. Wise acting was not always promoted by the exact form of a particular value—for example, telling the truth. Miep's desire, her core value, was to act "as any person would act" to keep the stowaways safe. Lying to save lives seemed the correct thing to do in such circumstances, which is most likely understood by almost all of us. Yet, lying and justifying it in other cases could have nothing to do with larger principles associated with wisdom or wise acting at all.

And here comes one of the greatest difficulties with capturing wisdom in terms of prescriptive actions: Acting with wisdom is almost never absolute. The example about never lying because of core principles related to one's religion or moral code, when examined over time, may be a larger need of civilization. However, when actions are rule-bound, determined by absolute views about right and wrong, such approaches can lead to great difficulties as circumstances change.

"Acting with wisdom is almost never absolute."

Generational Shifts in Definitions of Actions Considered to be Wise

Take into consideration the environment (both time and place) in which behavior called "wise" occurs. Effects of behavior judged wise by a particular sub-culture may end up being measured in the harsh light of generational effects. Building monuments to uncles and cousins, brave soldiers of the South in the Civil War, clashes with a culture that is saying that honoring individuals who were maintaining racial injustice by their actions is wrong. Culture (the people who make up the culture) evolves and has a chance to make itself over.

Creating a More Tolerant Society

Principles of learning contain many pearls of wisdom, not the least of which is a 30,000-foot-high view of why racism, sexism, nationalism, all the "isms" exist and thrive. Making changes that matter is difficult when pushing against a tide of belief that works to maintain or return to a different social contract. The strength of conviction by which individuals' lives are governed, demonstrates how much rule governance persists despite competing contingencies designed to reinforce other beliefs. To a large extent, those rules of how we treat one another, about who we are and the values we stand for, learned at a point in time—those rules become the foundation of persistent honor codes.

The persistence of behavior in the face of great threat is at times a quality we need or want as a society: Gandhi, Martin Luther King, a soldier who runs into danger to save his buddy; a political protestor who stands in front of a tank, alone. Some of these people were not seeing themselves as bold or brave but of necessity doing the only things they could do—behavior we judge to be generous and helpful, wise in that these actions model how we can help one another in times of need and retain our human bond.

Persistence in doing the right thing is not easy when surrounded by the controlling effects of bias, threat and fear. No easy fix exists in moving individuals, any of us, from tenets we "know to be true." Telling the racist he is racist might do little good. He may be operating under a code of salvation for his people, or in fact, out of sheer hate for looks, behavior, words, religion, dress that represent destruction or invasion of his way of life. Or just as destructively, the targeted individuals are often easy to hurt. If raised in an environment of punishment, many individuals learn the joy in bullying others from having been abused themselves. Hurting a more vulnerable person can be all it takes to maintain such cyclical behavior. Neither appeals to reason or science easily alter those types of behavior patterns.

However, in many cases, a seismic shift happens when new learning is introduced, changing generational patterns that appeared fixed. We stop burning witches at the stake and begin to gladly embrace the colors of the rainbow in welcoming different people and beliefs. We might call it enlightenment or education, but deeply held patterns of right, the rules, have shifted the social landscape for thousands of years. Our beliefs today will shift again. Each generation is challenged with acting in ways that help to support an evolving social contract as they read it. Unfortunately, the shift is not always toward enlightenment.

Diversity in many forms reinforced in our educational, political, ethical, and legal policies and systems may change not only actions but our words. Women can vote as can people of color. Brown vs. The Board of Education changed fundamental rights of public-school access and thus began a reexamination of just who our fellow students are, finding our common humanity. Experiments in living in an integrated world, however, have not happened with any degree of consistency in where or how many of us live or how we experience our common humanity when going to schools that are not all that diverse. Principles of the science of learning alert us that changing the laws, instituting new policies and procedures that broaden our exposure to others, are often designed with goodwill but without including social or economic incentives.

New behavior, collaborating and developing friendships, the food and music of our various neighborhoods, how we do things here, can lead to new rules of conduct. People are free to choose where they want to live but only if they are truly "free" to make the decision. Actions that occur after new laws are passed often are assumed to take care of a new order of justice. Those same actions lead to new sources of consequences, reframing beliefs throughout levels of society.

Nevertheless, insidious changes can happen while implementing new laws, inadvertently supporting the long-held beliefs that the new law is supposed to replace. Many sides argue their "righteous" beliefs about justice in America. Again, learning tools can help us see the effects of consequences, closely held subculture rules of conduct, often unattended to, in lessening or changing our once solid beliefs. Creating equality in our school system or our housing system, are such examples. Getting to the day-to-day of how we treat one another requires more determined activity across economic, political, and social practices to build and reinforce the foundational structure of the culture we wish to embrace.

If this country desires to address sources by which to sustain wiser behavior for the benefit of all, all sustainable change comes down to arranging conditions to produce behavioral choice. These choices should benefit, accept, and expand options for those in need and for those who are hoping to begin or to continue to thrive.

Practicing Wise Acting

Using wise-sounding words is not the same as acting wisely. Talking in solemn tones with complex, lovely sounding words may have nothing to do with acting with wisdom. A person might appear wise if she takes our side on an issue, endorses our beliefs, and stands by our side against those who think differently. Such actions may be both wise and brave. But it may be that we are confusing wise acting with acting like a friend. Calling actions wise requires balancing many issues, including the values that govern the concept of good.

"A person might appear wise if she takes our side on an issue, endorses our beliefs, and stands by our side against those who think differently. Such actions may be both wise and brave. But it may be that we are confusing wise acting with acting like a friend."

Could we say a person is motivated to act wisely if specific actions address the urgent needs of a few, even if postponing the wants of the many? Absolutely! But, as with "kindness" or "good judgment," or any other labels we attach to behavior, we must check the effects of doing something we call wise on the few and the many, over time. It is not possible to provide a list of wise actions that will inevitably lead to wise outcomes. It is possible to describe skills—observable and measurable behaviors—that those who act wisely often demonstrate. While behaving in ways called wise are determined by effects in specific settings, general ways of approaching problem-solving and decision-making can guide us. Certainly, we can all develop greater skill in striving toward wiser outcomes.

Don't be fooled by the opinion that skill training is shallow, a stepwise thing to do, pragmatic and observable, and, thus, obviously not robust enough to address the ingredients that lead to wise acting. Skills are composed of complex behavior, responding to the conditions that surround the person in easy or difficult ways. *Learning to act in wiser ways* is about building a behavioral repertoire, a skill set. Implicit in the word *learning* is the concept of ongoing practice. It is based on our history of learning, including rules by which we conduct ourselves, and contingencies of the moment. Most likely, practice contains errors along the way, mistakes to change. Starting over may occur. It is also about how decisions, problem-solving, evaluation, and knowledge are applied at the moment. Success in solving problems helps to establish motivational "triggers" to act in similar ways. The easier it gets, the more we may make the mistake of describing ourselves, if only to ourselves, as wise. If you don't delude yourself, that can be a fine "atta boy."

Like Groundhog Day, the long shadow of varied circumstances indicates that wise behavior may start over, and then over again, taking on variation or unnoticed changes in behavior patterns to address the conditions in the present. Modesty and optimism, at times just plain pride, shape how much we credit conditions around us as to why we behave as we do—and how much we credit such fine behavior to ourselves. Again, our quiet, private voice vs. our out-loud voice may tell the tale differently. Since it may be hard to get reinforcement from others for acting wisely in certain circumstances, do pat yourself on the back when you do make wiser decisions. Note your actions that resulted in positive outcomes, if only to yourself. It is worth noting!

"Learning to act in wiser ways is about building a behavioral repertoire, a skill set. Implicit in the word learning is the concept of ongoing practice."

Wisdom Defined by Levels of Effect

Wisdom can occur at the individual, community, cultural, and even cross-cultural levels of analysis. An individual produces actions that benefit himself, the group, or the community. Communities promote practices that advance the well-being of their members, even if not all members benefit. Cultures promote practices and actions that serve the common good across communities, leading to values-based cultural sustainability. *Wisdom* is defined by behavior and its effects at an individual, group, and/or cultural level. Wisdom can fail to show up in outcomes as well at the individual, group, or cultural level of society.

Sometimes a decision made by a country may advance the human condition in other parts of the world. An example would be actions in one country to reduce global warming. Costa Rica's efforts to reduce plastic and other pollutants have inspired other countries to do the same. The use of solar energy in Japan is a step toward producing power while reducing pollutants and harnessing the power of the sun. There are peace treaties between neighboring countries such as the Marshall Plan at the end of WWII, and other cooperative agreements across people and cultures. Civil disobedience in India inspires others in their approach to the rights of citizens. Wisdom, through the ages, is about just that—generative effects across time and conditions, not requiring the originating person or entity, nor even the same conditions, to accomplish great deeds for humankind.

PRACTICE 14.1:

Butterfly Effects on My Behavior: Are They Wise?

Over your lifetime, major shifts in how people behave have occurred quickly. Take a journey down the last 100 years: Dance, song, technology, mobile devices, travel, changes in dress and speech; access to different rules of conduct. Instant access to other beliefs not at all like your local community through movies, streaming, advancing technology. How has these shifts affected you? List events and trends that are influencing you today. Look at changes in your own behavior not a part of how you were taught Highlight two changes in which you take delight and two or three that concern you. Are there changes that you do with ease that surprise you? Do you see new behaviors that you did not deliberately intend to do? How could becoming more alert to how easily these "butterfly effects" affect you, help you act more deliberately, with greater wisdom?

Where Does Wisdom Reside?

As mentioned in a previous chapter, the belief that wisdom is an internal trait leads to the erroneous assumption that wisdom is, like Jiminy Cricket, met-aphorically on our shoulder. All we have to do is listen to our conscience. Subsequently, one may conclude that people act wisely because they possess wisdom, or it possesses them. Therefore, by exclusion, others are not wise. This implies wisdom is a personal attribute: something the person has, something innate, possessed by those called "wise." Wisdom is not a quality forever present in our being, but rather, demonstrated in the effects we have.

Achieving outcomes defined as wise acting is difficult, impossible to pin-point before its occurrence. Wisdom is a unique accomplishment in life—a cul-tural or universal end-goal, a result that we might strive for. In other words, it is difficult to define *wise acting* before the fact. We can plan our actions in situations we are about to face with an eye on achieving our hopes for a wiser outcome for all. As we saw with Dr. Mechner's classrooms, setting up heuristics to talk through possible scenarios and solutions helps us know with greater certainty, how our actions may lead to the outcomes we want. Note the word *may*, meaning no guarantee but striving to get there is important.

> *"... setting up heuristics to talk through possible scenarios and solutions helps us know with greater certainty how our actions may lead to the outcomes we want."*

Chapter 15:

In Summary:
This Gift Called *Life*

"The world is before you and you need not take it or leave it as it was when you came in."

–James Baldwin

"Expert knowledge, however indispensable, is no substitute for a generous and comprehending outlook upon the human story, with all its sadness and with all its unquenchable hope."

–Winston Churchill

A Call to Action

This chapter is a summary of key points we hope you will take away, new ways of showing up. In Chapter 1, we identified two key elements critical to producing wiser results. The first is that conditions surrounding you, guide, to a large extent, your words and actions, and those conditions need to be arranged, on occasion, to produce a wiser world—and a wiser you. Do you see how conditions can be arranged to shape behavior in your everyday life that could produce wise actions, with immediate and longer-term benefits? At this point, we hope your answer is *yes*.

The second, the essential ingredient in striving to become wiser, is all about you and your involvement in changing the impact of your actions on the conditions around you. It is, as we wrote then, personal, a question for reflection: "Do your actions today have the effect you want them to have?" Only you know if this is the case. Without you at the center of this journey, the world will be less wise. We hope this book gives you a greater understanding of the factors that motivate and shape behavior, as well as a few practical ideas about how to increase your very specific, principle-based effects.

Finally, for the benefit of our larger society, a *call to action* for us all: Achieve a greater awareness of our own biases, and the uses of threat and fear, in developing strategies to change ourselves and others. Join in documenting your efforts to increase, where needed, positive strategies of change, working to produce outcomes that affect the betterment of us all, whoever we are, step by step, and day by day. Again, taking the lessons from Dr. Robbins, engage in talk-aloud, problem-solving strategies when you see conditions that may well promote uninformed bias, threat, and fear. Enlist others in seeking alternative solutions.

The Conditions Around Us

Our histories of learning and the conditions of the moment determine behavior, even when we are not alert to our own changing behavior patterns. Our histories strengthen (1) our thoughts and beliefs about right and wrong, (2) how we use words and respond to emotional events, and (3) when and where we act, building new patterns to add to our existing behavioral repertoires. That history of reinforcement helps us develop positive, or not-so-positive habits, as measured, not by whether we like our behavior, but by the effect it has on others.

Behavior analysis, arising out of psychology, is the science of learning that explores how behavior is shaped, maintained, or changed by a lifetime of conditions and experiences. Taking a scientific approach to accomplish desired effects opens a door to behaving wisely. Methods of bringing out the best in others, to paraphrase Aubrey Daniels, helps us become more like the person our culture needs us to be. All too often, new ways of acting are needed to produce the kinds of outcomes needed. Universal principles serve as a guide in evaluating how well we show up at the individual level.

Behavioral Effects

Look at the effects of behavior on others, including, the right to life and dignity. Remember, "ageless values" carved in stone or on a wall, while inspirational at times, are meaningless except as (1) they show up in how we behave, and (2) whether they enhance or harm others or serve a larger social good. Do these values, described as behaviors that sum to a good, add to the social contract, benefiting the way in which we live together in some way? Only when our behavior has effects that represent desired outcomes, do values derive meaning and potentially represent wiser characteristics. Values are not a thing—they are the sum of behaviors that equate to one's definition of a *value*. Remember that; for if we don't behave in ways that "show values" we have no way to access them. Values do not come off the plaque on the wall. Walking the "good" talk is the way a value comes to life.

Change as a Constant

Our behavior is in a reciprocal stream, and it is always changing, every moment of every day. Issues of equality, equity, economics, social structures, and ideology are often at odds, sometimes providing evolving awareness of their effects on different people, as we attain more knowledge. At times, we must confront our biases, upending our stable worldview.

As we gain knowledge, we learn how to make better decisions and address, if not fully solve, immediate problems. We also learn

Practice 15.1:

Living My Life Wisely

Sort through your most cherished beliefs about how to live. Take a moment to think about influences that guide your actions and when it is most difficult to act as you say you want to act. Be observant about the conditions that surround you. What do you do and say in one setting that you do not in another? Why? Test absolutes, the values you hold dear, against measurable effects accomplished, for others as well as yourself.

how problems of the moment relate to problems we have already experienced. As we encounter those problems in new settings, the consequences that established those earlier patterns of behavior continue to guide our choices in given moments. The choices we make are shaped by the effect of our decision-making along the way. Conditions that surround us in a given moment may be less important than our learning histories in terms of directing our actions. Experiences over our lifetime come together to shape, at times from something long ago, the choices we make in varied situations (Baum, 2003).

"Experiences over our lifetime come together to shape, at times from something long ago, the choices we make in varied situations."

How we solve problems may or may not be wise. If we evaluate the effects of a choice made against core values, we stand a better chance of moving in the right direction. We can increase consistent action to create a wiser world. Expanding our knowledge about people, cultures, and traditions can be beneficial. Evaluating our actions against our intended effects can help us better understand how well we solve problems in the moment for their immediacy of effect, as well as their potential to establish positive effects beyond the moment. Such self-assessment can help us become more alert to the kind of problem-solver we are.

Self-Management and Emotions

See emotional descriptions as signals to act. Emotional behavior reveals at times the principles, values, and beliefs that you care about. Excellent resources are available to help gain a new understanding of how to handle emotional behavior as we mentioned in the works of Ray Novaco, Brené Brown, and Steve Hayes.

Scan for resources from positivepsychology.com

Self-management strategies, including emotional behavior, help align values, goals, and behavior changes. They provide effective tools to increase committed action. Moreover, self-monitoring and graphing offer an objective way to assess whether you are moving in the desired direction. They play an important role in making environment-behavior relations clear, clarifying the behaviors that need to change.

Look at a Person's Behavior

Describing someone's behavior to them and telling them why you like that behavior can be an unexpected gift. This kind of personalized example-sharing allows others to better understand the value of their words and actions. Celebrating accomplishments might start very simply by asking, "How did you do that?" That kind of invitation is often all a person needs.

PRACTICE 15.2:

Use Talk-Out-Loud Strategies to Celebrate Progress

"Celebrating progress" is not really about gifts and thank you's but rather the gift of actively listening to people describe their behavior, their stories, about how they did what they did. Ask them to describe how they got to this good solution. Applaud them, even if they wished they had done more. Make stories by others a part of your life, helping others gain confidence. Words help people *see* what *they* did. For some, that is a new experience. Use your words to:

1. Recognize when others solve problems, particularly those that they (or you) might have thought unlikely.

2. Tell them about the *effects* of their actions on you.

3. Most importantly, ask them *how they did it*— mistakes, renewed actions, uncertainty. What they learned. People who are rarely asked to tell their stories do change how they see themselves. Ask loved ones to do the same. Pass it on (ref. Robbins, Daniels).

Telling stories aloud about how we did something helps visualize the actions, see the effects, and find clarity in talking about the specifics of how our actions did or did not work. Storytelling after the fact, while most likely not an exact match with our actions, provides us a way to examine and improve, and to receive feedback from others who hear the story how to improve next time. This kind of example-sharing allows people of any age to learn by listening how to act or not act when in similar situations.

The Power of Words

> *"Words, written and spoken …*
> *… are things, and a small drop of ink,*
> *Falling like dew, upon a thought, produces*
> *That which makes thousands, perhaps millions, think."*

–George Gordon, *Lord Byron*

If this generation is to pass on to the next generation tools to increase wise acting, much of it lies in using words to describe the events and conditions around us. Books open worlds well beyond our reach that, in turn, provide examples, good and bad, about how people influence their world. In our homes, schools, communities, and in our larger culture, words that surround us have huge effects on our own words and actions.

The more we talk out loud, share our thoughts and strategies about addressing the problems we face, the better off we will be in understanding, reconciling, and applying solutions to those problems. It is not only about this current moment in time that our acting on this world is felt; it may be that it is to that unknown future that our actions right now, today, through written words and recorded deeds, will be felt.

Not in Our Nature but in Our Nurture

George Floyd's terrible death ignited all races to see the injustices across countries and customs—a truly earth-changing moment of global awareness of the many things we have long known were wrong. Generations before us also knew these things were wrong. Protests in 2020, and beyond, march to drumbeats of

PRACTICE 15.3:

Starting with the Behavior You See, Learn How to Accelerate Positive Change

If you take one thing away from this book: use only positive strategies of change to help another person master more effective patterns of behavior. Leave harsh judgment at the door. Encourage small steps toward desired goals. Help others build new behavior from the skills they already have. Recognize effort and ignore, without deep sighs, false starts. Convey your belief in their capacity to succeed, even when making mistakes. Remember, significant change requires both consistency and persistence. Practice 15.3 by selecting someone you know who could use positive support in making desired change —e.g., a child, a spouse, a teammate. Be aware of your impatience. See what they say and do. Relax and support their progress. Become an amazing "shaper" of positive behavior. Experience the benefits that this approach has on your relationships with others.

---

varied voices seeking systemic fixes that are beyond symbolic change. Believing that humans will always be racist or violent is not a truism of the human condition; it seems as though it is, but it is not. Find the variance, and you find the range, the exemplar to strive toward. A popular video shows a very young black boy and a white boy toddling toward each other with glee at a very rapid, two-year-old pace, ending in an uninhibited hug. That is a learned response as real as fear and loathing is for equally young toddlers from different white and black families. Describe humankind as gentle as a flower or as violent as a volcano and you have not found our nature—we are our actions, actions not driven by some internal force.

> *"Believing that humans will always be racist or violent is not a truism of the human condition ... Find the variance, and you find the range, the exemplar to strive toward."*

Oscar Hammerstein II wrote the following lyrics that describe so well how biases about others are carefully taught:

You've got to be taught to hate and fear. You've got to be taught from year to year; it's got to be drummed in your dear little ear. You've got to be carefully taught; you've got to be taught to be afraid of people whose eyes are oddly made and people whose skin is a different shade. You've got to be carefully taught. You've got to be taught before it's too late. Before you are six or seven or eight to hate all the people your relatives hate. You've got to be carefully taught.

–Lyrics from "Carefully Taught," *South Pacific*

The peoples of the world get to where they are because of the same principles of learning shared by all humankind. We can get beyond hate, obliviousness, violence, and bias in the same way. More is needed beyond individual behavior change to redress the inequality of society. Still, behavior is needed to address poverty, biases that lead to hate, perspectives on who is good and bad, housing, clean water, education, healthcare, freedom from hunger, and actively working on reducing our institutionalized "isms."

Our greatest dilemma in seeking to act with wisdom resides in the incredible power that using threat and fear grants us. Sometimes, even the most well-intentioned of us have behaved in ways that brought pain and despair to others. We each may have memories of having done such things, and we may have behaved even today in a manner that we regret. Tomorrow is truly another day. Arrange the conditions for your success. Remember the subtext of this book is about using our behavior to reduce bias, threat, and fear. Actually, humankind *can* be kind.

"Actually, humankind can be kind."

Why do we so often describe our shared nature as related to that of warriors and aggressors? If you must keep these labels, can you as comfortably describe "human nature" as also containing the desire to be good to one another? No? Because that is not true? Really? Have you looked at the hundreds of humane acts of daily life multiplied by the millions, in the worst of war zones? Are you not aware of charitable actions every day across America and in other countries? Many people are much more likely to act generously than to act with aggression and suppression. What if we started talking about ourselves as, by nature, generous and inclusive? Powerful, negative examples might overwhelm us! We might be called, of all things, a Pollyanna—that totally unrealistic optimist. After all, look at all those tales in great literature, poetry, music, and art taking their meaning from man's inhumanity to man. That seems a more realistic view of the sad state of human affairs, right? Those same tales and tunes also take their majesty from love, sacrifice, and devotion.

Threat and fear are amazingly effective in controlling our behavior. Does the use of such strategies grow out of our nature, bubbling just under the surface? Can we do nothing else? We do know that in any way possible, we need to make such aggressive, suppressive behavior patterns untenable and inappropriate. Whenever such patterns are explained away as driven by forces beyond the person's control, by their very nature, terrible deeds are justified. Will there always be wars? Will abuse always happen, waiting to pour out through the door called our nature? If you remember nothing else from reading this book, remember that the use of threat and fear against our loved ones, our children, or strangers, in war or in industry, is learned, all shaped and often highly reinforced by their effects. At the most fundamental level, the use of threat and fear are destructive to this lovely human race of which we are a part.

> *"... the use of threat and fear against our loved ones, our children, or strangers, in war or in industry, is learned ..."*

The science of behavior helps us understand why we behave as we do. Conditions around us can redirect us to the reinforcing properties of behaving in ways designed to support another's positive skills and sense of calm or goodwill. We can do that! We can move beyond those who tell us to do all we can to protect ourselves from those who are not like us. Ask yourself as you observe events that surround you, "Could others, or could I make different choices that leave more of our common humanity intact?"

You may recall from an earlier chapter, Ben Franklin said that to optimize human potential, "Carve mistakes in sand and success in stone." This expression serves as a lifelong lesson in seeking to enhance another's well-being. It can, as well, enhance our own. Percy Bysshe Shelley, 18th-century British poet, stated that "A man, to be greatly good, must imagine intensely and comprehensively; he must put himself in the place of another and of many others; the pains and pleasures of his species must become his own." We are all part of the human species. The collective pain and pleasures of our species—our family, ourselves, those far distant from our shores—reflect our common humanity. Recognizing our common humanity takes us right back to shaping a better world. Remember, this book began with a question about how you want to show up. What can you do to increase value-driven outcomes in daily life, freeing yourself and others from conditions of threat and fear? Start first with yourself. See where that takes you.

"Hopefully what we are doing is protecting people from harm and helping improve lives. If that is what we are doing, then I am happy."

–José Martinez-Diaz

Appendix

Recommended Readings

Berens, K. N. (2020). *Blind Spots: Why Students Fail ... and the Science that Can Save Them*. The Collective Book Studio

Biglan, A. (2015). *The Nurture Effect: How the Science of Human Behavior Can Improve Our Lives & Our World*. New Harbinger Publications

Biglan, A. (2020). *Rebooting Capitalism: How We Can Forge a Society that Works for Everyone*. Values to Action

Daniels, A. C., & Lattal, A. D. (2020). *Live a Better Life: Using the Science of Behavior to Drive Personal and Social Change*. Aubrey Daniels International

Gladwell, M. (2000) The Tipping Point: How Little Things Can Make a Big Difference. Little, Brown in 2000.

Harris, R. (2008). *The Happiness Trap: How to Stop Struggling and Start Living: A Guide to ACT*. Trumpeter Books

Harless, J. (1998). *The Eden Conspiracy: Educating for Accomplished Citizenship*. Guild V Publications

Hayes, S. C. (2019). *A Liberated Mind: How to Pivot Toward What Matters*. Avery Publishing Group

Heath, C., & Heath, D. (2010). *Switch: How to Change Things When Change Is Hard*. Random House Canada

Latham, G. I. (1994). *The Power of Positive Parenting: A Wonderful Way to Raise Children*. P & T Ink

Lemov, D., Yezzi, K., & Woolway, E. (2012). *Practice Perfect: 42 Rules for Getting Better at Getting Better*. Jossey-Bass

Sagan, C. (1997). *The Demon-Haunted World: Science as a Candle in the Dark*. Ballantine Books

Schneider, S. M. (2012). *The Science of Consequences: How They Affect Genes, Change the Brain, and Impact Our World*. Prometheus Books

Skinner, B. F. (2005). *Walden Two*. Hackett Publishing Company, Inc.

References

Aldwin, C. M. (2008). Gender and Wisdom: A Brief Overview. *Research in Human Development, 6*, 1–8

Andersen, C. (1837). *Fairy Tales Told for Children.* C. A. Reitzel

Arkes, H. R., & Blumer, C. (1985). The Psychology of Sunk Cost. *Organizational Behavior and Human Decision Processes, 35*, 124–140

Aurelius, M. (2006). *Meditations.* Penguin Books

Baltes, P. B., & Staudinger, U. M. (2000). Wisdom: A metaheuristic (pragmatic) to orchestrate mind and virtue toward excellence. *American Psychologist, 55*(1), 122–136

Baltes, P. B., & Smith, J. (2008). The Fascination of Wisdom: Its Nature, Ontogeny, and Function. *Perspectives on Psychological Science 3*(1), 56–64

Baum, W. M. (2003). The Molar View of Behavior and Its Usefulness in Behavior Analysis. *The Behavior Analyst Today, 4*(1), 78–81

Binder C. (1996). Behavioral fluency: Evolution of a new paradigm. *The Behavior Analyst, 19*(2), 163–197

Binder, C. (2003). Doesn't Everyone Need Fluency? *Performance Improvement, 42*(3), 14–20

Binder, C. (2010). Building fluent performance: Measuring response rate and multiplying response opportunities. *The Behavior Analyst Today, 11*(4), 214–225

Briggs, J. (2000). Emotions Have Many Faces: Inuit Lessons. *Anthropologica, 42*(2), 157–164

Brown, B. (2007) I Thought It Was Just Me (but it isn't): Making the Journey from "What Will People Think?" to "I Am Enough" Penguin Books.

Collins, J. Personal communication to Lattal, November 27, 2021.

Curnow, T. (2011). Sophia and Phronesis: Past, Present, and Future. *Research in Human Development, 8*(2), 95–108

Daniels, A. C., & Daniels, J. E. (2007). *Measure of a Leader: The Legendary Leadership Formula for Producing Exceptional Performers and Outstanding Results.* McGraw-Hill Companies

Daniels, A. C. & Lattal, A. D. (2017). *Life's a PICNIC ... when you understand behavior.* Performance Management Publications

Daniels, A. C., & Lattal, A. D. (2020). *Live a Better Life: Using the Science of Behavior to Drive Personal and Social Change.* Performance Management Publications

Delprato, D. J. (2002). Countercontrol in Behavior Analysis, *The Behavior Analyst, 25,* 191–200

Epstein, R. (1999). Generativity Theory. In M. A. Runco, & S. Pritzker (Eds.), *Encyclopedia of Creativity*, 759–766

Ericsson, K. A., & Pool, R. (2016). *Peak: Secrets from the New Science of Expertise.* Eamon Dolan/Houghton Mifflin Harcourt

Ericsson and Harwell (2019). https://www.ncbi.nlm.nih.gov/pmc/articles/PMC6824411/

Fantino, E. (1998). Behavior analysis and decision-making. *Journal of the Experimental Analysis of Behavior,* 69 (3), 355–364

Frank, A. (1993). *Anne Frank: The Diary of a Young Girl.* Bantam

Frankl, V. E. (1984). *Man's Search for Meaning: An Introduction to Logotherapy.* Simon & Schuster.

Friman, P. C. (2021). There Is No Such Thing as a Bad Boy: The Circumstances View of Problem Behavior. *Journal of Applied Behavior Analysis, 54,* 636–653

Geller, E. S. (1991). If Only More Would Actively Care. *Journal of Applied Behavior Analysis,* 24, 607–612

Geller, E. S. (1995). Actively Caring for the Environment: An Integration of Behaviorism and Humanism. *Environment and Behavior,* 27, 184–195

Geller, E. S. (2014). Actively Caring for People: Cultivating a Culture of Compassion. Make-A-Difference, LLC

Gilbert, T. F. (1978). *Human Competence: Engineering Human Performance.* McGraw-Hill

Goldiamond, I. (1975). A Constructional Approach to Self-Control. In A. Schwartz & I. Goldiamond (Eds), Social Casework: A Behavioral Approach (pp. 67–130). New York: Columbia University

Goldiamond, I. (2002). Toward a Constructional Approach to Social Problems: Ethical and Constitutional Issues. *Behavior and Social Issues, 11,* 108–197

Goodman, N. (2014, December 22). The Science of Setting Goals. TED. https://ideas.ted.com/the-science-of-setting-goals/

Groysberg. B. (2010). *Chasing Stars: The Myth of Talent and the Portability of Performance.* Princeton University Press

Harris, R. (2018). *ACT Questions and Answers: A Practitioner's Guide to 150 Common Sticking Points in Acceptance and Commitment Therapy.* Context Press

Harris, R. (2008). *The Happiness Trap: How to Stop Struggling and Start Living: A Guide to ACT.* Trumpeter Books

Hake, D. F., & Schmid, T. L. (1981). Acquisition and Maintenance of Trusting Behavior. *Journal of the Experimental Analysis of Behavior, 35*(1), 109–124

Hart, B., & Risley, T. R. (1992). American Parenting of Language-Learning Children: Persisting Differences in Family-Child Interactions Observed in Natural Home Environments. *Developmental Psychology, 28*(6), 1096–1105

Hayes, S. C., Brownstein, A. J., Zettle, R. D., Rosenfarb, I., & Korn, Z. (1986). Rule-Governed Behavior and Sensitivity to Changing Consequences of Responding. *Journal of the Experimental Analysis of Behavior,* 45, 237–256

Hayes, S. C. (2019). *A Liberated Mind: How to Pivot Toward What Matters.* Avery Publishing Group

Hayes, S. C. (2005). *Get Out of Your Mind & Into Your Life: The New Acceptance & Commitment Therapy.* New Harbinger Publications

Hayes, S. C. (1993). Rule Governance: Basic Behavioral Research and Applied Applications. *Current Directions in Psychological Science, 2,* 193–197.

Hawthorne, N. Located in Brainy Quotes, https://www.goodreads.com/quotes/62241

Heffernan, M. (2019, July). *The human skills we need in an unpredictable world* [Video]. TED Conferences. https://www.ted.com/talks/margaret_heffernan_the_human_skills_we_need_in_an_unpredictable_world?utm_campaign=tedspread&utm_medium=referral&utm_source=tedcomshare

Hineline, P. N. (2018). Narrative: Why It's Important, and How It Works. *Perspectives on Behavior Science, 41*(2): 471–501

Huffman, R. W., Sainato, D. M., & Curiel, E. S. L. (2016). Correspondence Training Using Special Interests to Increase Compliance During Transitions: An Emerging Technology. *Behavior Analysis in Practice, 9*(1), 25–33

Israel, A. C. (1978). Some Thoughts on Correspondence Between Saying and Doing. *Journal of Applied Behavior Analysis, 11*(2), 271–276

Jeste, D. H., Ardelt, M., Blazer, D., Kraemer, H. C., Vaillant, G., & Meeks, T. W. (2010). Expert Consensus on Characteristics of Wisdom: A Delphi Method Study. *The Gerontologist, 50*, 668–680

Johnston, K. (1997). Morningside Academy. *Behavior and Social Issues, 1*(7), 31–35.

Johnston, K. (2021). Generativity. Sloan Publications

Kazantzakis, N. https://www.azquotes.com/quote/404642

Lattal, K. A., & Lattal, A. D. (1967). Student Gullibility: A Systematic Replication. *The Journal of Psychology, 67*, 319–322

Layng, T. V. J. (2017). Private Emotions as Contingency Descriptors: Emotions, Emotional Behavior, and Their Evolution. *European Journal of Behavior Analysis, 18*, 168–179

Legrand, M. https://quotefancy.com/quote/7964/Michel-Legrand

Lindsley, O. R. (1995). Ten Products of Fluency. *The Journal of Precision Teaching, 1*, 2–11

Lindsley, O. R. (1996). The Four Free-Operant Freedoms. *The Behavior Analyst, 19*(2), 199–210

Mattaini, M. A. (2013). *Strategic Nonviolent Power: The Science of Satyagraha.* Athabasca University Press

McArt, Pat & Jude Collins (2021). *What Shaped Me?* Multimedia Heritage Press.

McGhee, H. (2021). *The Sum of Us: What Racism Costs Everyone and How We Can Prosper Together.* One World

Mirabito, M. M., & Layng, T. V. J. (2013). Stimulating innovation (or making innovation meaningful again). In M. Murphy, S. Redding, & J. Twyman (Eds.), *Handbook on innovations in learning* (pp. 1N–3T). Philadelphia, PA: Center of Innovations in Learning, Temple University; Charlotte, NC: Information Age Publishing

Orwell, G. (1996). *Animal Farm: A Fairy Story*. Signet Classics.

Mechner, F., Fredrick, T., & Jenkins, T. (2013). How Can One Specify and Teach Thinking Skills? *European Journal of Behavior Analysis, 14*, 285–293

Majors, S. (2020, June 11). I'm a Black Man with White Privilege. I See How it Distorts America. *The Washington Post*

Mountjoy, P. T., & Sundberg, M. L. (1981). Ben Franklin The Proto Behaviorist 1: Self-Management of Behavior. *The Psychological Record, 31*, 13–24 https://link.springer.com/article/10.1007/BF03394715

Navarro, A. D., & Fantino, E., (2009). The Sunk-Time Effect: An Exploration. *Journal of Behavioral Decision-Making, 22*(3), 252–270.

Novaco, R. W. (1978). Anger and Coping with Stress. In: Foreyt J. P., Rathjen, D. P. (eds). Cognitive Behavior Therapy. Springer

Novaco, R. W. (2011). Perspectives on Anger Treatment: Discussion and Commentary. *Cognitive and Behavioral Practice*, 18(2), 251–255

Nusbaum, H. C. (n.d.). Center for Practical Wisdom. https://wisdomcenter.uchicago.edu/

Reed D. D. (2014). Actively Caring for People: Humanistic Behaviorism in Practice. *Behavior Analysis in Practice, 7*(2), 149–150

Risley, T. R., & Hart, B. (1968). Developing Correspondence Between the Non-Verbal and Verbal Behavior of Preschool Children. *Journal of Applied Behavior Analysis, 1*(4), 267–281

Robbins, J. K. (2011). Problem-solving, reasoning, and analytical thinking in a classroom environment. *The Behavior Analyst Today, 12*(1), 41–48

Schneider, S. M. (2012). *The Science of Consequences: How They Affect Genes, Change the Brain, and Impact Our World*. Prometheus Books

Sagan, C. (1997). *The Demon-Haunted World: Science as a Candle in the Dark.* Ballantine Books

Shelley, P. B. (2006). A Defense of Poetry and Other Essays. Hard Press

Sidman, M. (1993). Reflections on behavior analysis and coercion. *Behavior & Social Issues, 3,* 75–85

Sidman, M. (2001). *Coercion and its Fallout* (2 ed.). Authors Cooperative

Silverman, K., Holtyn, A. F., & Subramaniam, S. (2018). Behavior analysts in the war on poverty: Developing an operant antipoverty program. *Experimental and Clinical Psychopharmacology, 26*(6), 515–524

Silverman, K., Holtyn, A. F., & Toegel, F. (2019). The Utility of Operant Conditioning to Address Poverty and Drug Addiction. *Perspectives on Behavior Science, 42*(3), 525–546

Skinner, B. F. (1956). Freedom and the Control of Men. *The American Scholar, 25*(1), 47–65

Skinner, B. F. (1984). An Operant Analysis of Problem-solving. *Behavioral and Brain Sciences, 7*(4), 583–613

Skinner, B. F. (1968). Teaching Science in High School–What Is Wrong? *Science, 159*(3816H), 704–710

Smith, P., Leeming, E., Forman, M., & Hayes, S. C. (2019). From Form to Function: Values and Committed Action Strengthen Mindful Practices with Context and Direction. *Journal of Sports Psychology in Action, 10*(4), 227–234

Stromberg, G., & Chappell, M. (1990). Where Have All the Classrooms Gone? Journal of Precision Teaching, 7(1), 1–4

Svitak, A. (2010, February). *What adults can learn from kids* [Video]. TED Conferences. https://www.ted.com/talks/adora_svitak_what_adults_can_learn_from_kids?utm_campaign=tedspread&utm_medium=referral&utm_source=tedcomshare

Twain, Mark. (1881). *The Prince and the Pauper.* James R. Osgood & Co.

Tucci, V., Hursh, D. E., Laitinen, R., & Lambe, A. (2005). Competent Learner Model for Individuals with Autism/PDD. *Exceptionality, 13*(1), 55–63

Trowbridge, R. H. (2011). Waiting for Sophia: 30 Years of Conceptualizing Wisdom in Empirical Psychology. *Research in Human Development,* 8(2), 149–164

Twain, M. (2002). *The Prince and the Pauper.* Signet

United Nations. *United Nations Declaration of Human Rights.*

Vaillant, G. E. (2002). Aging Well: Surprising Guideposts to a Happier Life from the Landmark Harvard Study of Adult Development. Little, Brown and Company

Watson, J. B. https://www.azquotes.com/quote/690678

Watson, J. B. https://www.brainyquote.com/quotes/thomas_j_watson_147145

Whimbey, A., & Lochhead, J. (1982). *Problem-Solving and Comprehension.* The Franklin Press

Wilson, K. G. & Groom, J. (2002). The Valued Living Questionnaire. https://www.div12.org/wp-content/uploads/2015/06/Valued-Living-Questionnaire.pdf

Winett, R. A., & Winkler, R. C. (1972). Current behavior modification in the classroom: be still, be quiet, be docile. *Journal of Applied Behavior Analysis,* 5(4), 499–504

Wink, P., & Helson, R. (1997). Practical and Transcendent Wisdom: Their Nature and Some Longitudinal Findings. *Journal of Adult Development,* 4(1), 1–15

Index

About the Authors

Dr. Alice Darnell Lattal

Dr. Alice Darnell Lattal has spent a lifetime on issues of coercion and its fallout across educational, health, mental health, and workplace settings. A clinical psychologist by training, she spent her first two decades of professional life in special education, adult clinical, and community mental health while addressing the suppressive effects of poverty on infant development, child and spousal abuse, and literacy in rural America. She established her own consulting company, Context Management, Inc., in 1980. Joining several business-to-business consulting companies, she served as a coach for individual, group, and leader development. She served as President and CEO of Aubrey Daniels International. Inc. for 14 years, appointed as Board Chair for another two years before returning to her coaching and consulting work. Since March of 2020, she has served as CEO and President of ABA Technologies, Inc.; her wealth of experience spans more than 50 years and six continents. Her publications include Clark and Lattal, *Workplace Ethics: Winning the Integrity Revolution* (Rowman & Littlefield, 1993; University Press, 1998), *Ethics at Work* (Performance Management Publications, 2005); Lattal and Clark, *A Good Days Work* (2008), McGraw Hill; Ishida and Lattal, *Sustaining a Stress-Free Workplace using Positive Reinforcement* (English title translation) (2010), Toyo Keiza Press; Daniels and Lattal, *Life's a PIC/NIC® when you understand behavior* (Sloan Publishing, 2017), Daniels and Lattal, *Live a Good Life: Using the science of behavior to drive personal and social change* (Performance Management. Publications, 2020); and *The Wisdom Factor: Reducing the Control of Bias, Threat, and Fear while Building a Better World*, Lattal and Zuluaga, (KeyPress Publications, 2022). Among her positions, Dr. Lattal served as President of her state psychological association, a Board of Trustee's national board dedicated to reducing violence in America, and is currently a member of the Board of Directors of the Cambridge Center for Behavioral Studies. She lives with her husband, Andy, in Hilton Head Island, raising three children, benefiting today from the wit and wisdom of their seven grandchildren.

Carlos A. Zuluaga, M.S., BCBA

Carlos has been a Board Certified Behavior Analyst (BCBA) since 2007 and received his master's in applied behavior analysis from Florida Tech in 2006. Carlos' master's thesis was published in the *Journal of Applied Behavior Analysis*. As a member of the ABA Technologies team, Carlos has been a co-instructor for the ABA Online program since 2010.

He loves teaching online courses because it allows him to share his passion for behavior analysis with students and colleagues. Carlos has helped translate some of the courses into Spanish to bring ABA to new audiences. Prior to joining ABA Technologies, Inc., Carlos worked for seven years as a lead therapist at QuestKids, an early intervention agency. During that time, he learned to conduct various skill assessments such as the Verbal Behavior Milestones Assessment and Placement Program (VB-MAPP), develop verbal behavior programs, and teach various skills to children with developmental disabilities, train caregivers, and provide supervision.

Carlos enjoys reading, drawing, playing guitar, listening to music, and exercising during his free time. He is very excited to help disseminate behavior analysis around the world.

Register your book with KeyPress Publishing

Registered users receive exclusive reader benefits and stay connected with:

- **Special discounts** on books and ABA Tech Academy courses

- Opportunities to **preview new products**

- **Subscription** to ABA Technologies' monthly newsletter that delivers discounts, tools, tips, and articles focused on instructional design innovation, BACB® ACE CEs, and professional development courses.

www.KeyPressPublishing.com

KeyPress Publishing

We strive to provide individualized services and support to all our authors. Our team of experts is here to answer all your questions and produce your ideal products. We offer personal attention from the time you reach out, through the writing, submission, and review process, close partnerships with our design team to fulfill your visions, and our publishing expertise to help you publish, promote, and sell your book.

A Sample of KeyPress Publications:

"The book Key Press created for me is professional and beautiful, and we already have another book in process."

–Janis Allen, Owner of Performance Leadership Consulting

www.KeyPressPublishing.com